U.S. Labor Relations Law

U.S. LABOR RELATIONS LAW: HISTORICAL DEVELOPMENT

BENJAMIN J. TAYLOR
University of Oklahoma

FRED WITNEY
Indiana University

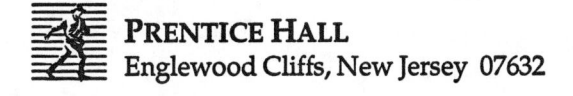

PRENTICE HALL
Englewood Cliffs, New Jersey 07632

Library of Congress Cataloging-in-Publication Data

Taylor, Benjamin J.
  U.S. labor relations law: historical development / Benjamin J.
Taylor, Fred Witney.
    p. cm.
  Includes bibliographical references and index.
  ISBN 0-13-928573-3
  1. Collective labor agreements—United States—History. 2. Trade
-unions—Law and legislation—United States—History. 3. Labor laws
and legislation—United States—History. 4. Industrial relations-
-United States—History. I. Witney, Fred, (date). II. Title.
KF3408.T38 1992
344.73'0189—dc20
[347.304189]   91-11507
                                                                               CIP

Production Editor: KERRY REARDON
Acquisitions Editor: ALISON REEVES
Copy Editor: KATHRYN BECK
Cover Designer: MIKE FENDER
Prepress Buyer: TRUDY PISCIOTTI
Manufacturing Buyer: ROBERT ANDERSON

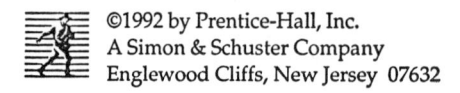

©1992 by Prentice-Hall, Inc.
A Simon & Schuster Company
Englewood Cliffs, New Jersey 07632

All rights reserved. No part of this book may be
reproduced, in any form or by any means,
without permission in writing from the publisher.

Portions of this book were previously published
in *U.S. Labor Relations Law, fifth edition.*

Printed in the United States of America

10 9 8 7 6 5 4 3 2 1

ISBN 0-13-928573-3

Prentice-Hall International (UK) Limited, *London*
Prentice-Hall of Australia Pty. Limited, *Sydney*
Prentice-Hall Canada Inc., *Toronto*
Prentice-Hall Hispanoamericana, S.A., *Mexico*
Prentice-Hall of India Private Limited, *New Delhi*
Prentice-Hall of Japan, Inc., *Tokyo*
Simon & Schuster Asia Pte. Ltd., *Singapore*
Editora Prentice-Hall do Brasil, Ltda., *Rio de Janeiro*

*This volume is dedicated to the memory of Ben Taylor,
my co-author, colleague, and friend.*

Fred Witney

Contents

PREFACE   xi

🍂 PART I: LEGAL SUPPRESSION OF LABOR UNIONS AND COLLECTIVE BARGAINING   1

1 LABOR UNIONS: UNLAWFUL COMBINATIONS   1
The Early Union Movement: Its Socioeconomic Content 1
Conspiracy Doctrine Applied to Unions 3
The Case against the Unions 5
Characteristics of the Conspiracy Trials 6
In Defense of Labor Unions 7
The State of Affairs before Commonwealth v. Hunt 8
Labor Unions Declared Lawful Organizations in 1842 9
Commonwealth v. Hunt: *Its Significance* 10
From the Conspiracy Doctrine to the Labor Injunction 11

2 UNION ACTIVITIES AND THE LABOR INJUNCTION   15
The Nature of Injunctions 16
Forms of Injunctions 18
The Injunction in Labor Disputes 19
The Concept of "Property" in Labor Injunction Cases 21

Abuses of Injunctions 22
The Yellow-Dog Contract and the Labor Injunction 28

3 UNIONS UNDER ANTITRUST STATUTES   35
Application of Sherman Act to Labor Unions 36
Economic Issues in Danbury Hatters *Doctrine* 40
Labor Movement and Political Action 42
Clayton Act: Labor's "Magna Charta" or Enigma? 44
Rule of Reason: Development of a Double Standard 48
The Bedford Stone *Decision: Effect on Union Tactics and Completion of the Double Standard* 58

❦ PART II: GOVERNMENT SUPPORT OF LABOR UNIONS AND COLLECTIVE BARGAINING   65

4 CONTROL OF THE LABOR INJUNCTION   65
The Changing Economic and Political Scene 65
Early Regulation of the Labor Injunction 67
Early Labor Injunction Legislation: Court Attitudes 70
One "Missionary" per Entrance 71
Labor Injunction Control Legislation Held Unconstitutional 72
"Holmes and Brandeis Dissenting" 74
Norris–La Guardia 76
Area of Industrial Freedom 79
Concept of "Labor Dispute" 82
The Passing of the Yellow-Dog Contract 83
Labor Injunction: Procedural Limitations 84
Judicial Construction of Norris–La Guardia 89
The Impact of Norris–La Guardia 94

5 ANTITRUST PROSECUTION UNDER NORRIS–LA GUARDIA   99
Norris–La Guardia and Labor Protection 99
Labor Dispute Defined Broadly in Norris–La Guardia 100
Judicial Reaction 101
The Apex *Doctrine Nullifies Effect of* Coronado *Decision* 104
Additional Application of Antitrust Violations 108
Consequences of Supreme Court Action 113

6 EMPLOYER ANTIUNION CONDUCT: NEED FOR GOVERNMENT PROTECTION   118
The Problem 118
Patterns of Antiunion Conduct: Industrial Espionage 120
Patterns of Antiunion Conduct: Attack on Union Leadership 123

Patterns of Antiunion Conduct: Strikebreaking Tactics 126
Patterns of Antiunion Conduct: Company Unions 129
Need for Public Control 131

7 PRECURSORS OF THE WAGNER ACT 137
The Beginnings of Legislative Support 137
The Early Laws: Yellow-Dog Contracts and Discrimination Unlawful 138
Attitude of the Judiciary 141
Events of World War I 144
National War Labor Board Abolished: Decline in Union Membership 147
Railroad Legislation 149
Railway Labor Act Amended in 1934 151
National Industrial Recovery Act 153
Section 7(a): Nature and Enforcement 154
Collapse of National Labor Board 156
Passage of the Wagner Act 161

8 THE WAGNER ACT 165
The Socioeconomic Rationale of the Wagner Act 165
Power to Regulate Interstate Commerce 166
Public Policy of the United States 168
State of Affairs Before Jones & Laughlin 170
Scope of Law 172
The Jones & Laughlin *Decision* 173
Application to Manufacturing 174
Due Process and Constitutionality of Act 175
Substantive Provisions: Unfair Labor Practices 176
Substantive Provisions: The Principle of Majority Rule 187
Unfair Labor Practice Procedure 189
Unfair Labor Practice Charge 190
The Wagner Act Record 192
Representation Procedure 193
Industrial Democracy 195
Wagner Act during World War II 196
Results of the Wagner Act 198

PART III: A FINAL WORD 205

9 GENERAL SUMMARY 205
Era of Legal Suppression 205
Era of Legal Encouragement 208

APPENDIX A: THE NORRIS–LA GUARDIA ACT	212
APPENDIX B: THE WAGNER ACT	218
BIBLIOGRAPHY	229
INDEX	233

PREFACE

This volume deals with labor relations law from the application of the conspiracy doctrine to union activities through the National Labor Relations (Wagner) Act. Covered are judicial and legislative policies until the advent of the 1947 Taft-Hartley Act. It provides the necessary background to understand and evaluate contemporary public policy regulating union and employer conduct in labor relations.

Of course, Norris–La Guardia, 1932, still plays a vital role regulating federal courts in labor disputes. Much of the Wagner Act as enacted by Congress in 1935 currently impacts the current legal conditions. Taft-Hartley did not repeal the substance of the Wagner Act. Its innovation was to impose legal controls on union conduct, not to repeal the legal protection of the right of employees to self-organization and collective bargaining free from employer interference.

Part I deals with the era of legal suppression of union activities by the judiciary. Chapters highlight union prosecution under the conspiracy doctrine; how the courts used the labor injunction to control union conduct; and the impact of the antitrust statutes on union activities.

Part II covers the era of government encouragement of unionization and collective bargaining. Chapters include the regulation of the labor injunction and antitrust application of union activities under Norris–La Guardia; need for government protection against employer antiunion conduct; federal and state efforts to establish unionization and collective bargaining as a matter of public policy prior to the National Labor

Relations Act; and development and operation of the Wagner Act for this purpose. A summary and discussion questions follow each chapter. The complete text of the Norris–La Guardia Act and the Wagner Act is contained in the appendices.

The volume does more than merely recite court decisions and legislation. Labor relations law has little meaning in the absence of an understanding of the economic and social environment in which it operates. Consequently, adequate attention is devoted to the institutional setting of the effort of government to define the legal rights, duties, and obligations of employees, employers, and unions in labor relations and collective bargaining. Within this context, landmark cases of the era are presented, including *Commonwealth* v. *Hunt, In re Debs, Hitchman Coal, Danbury Hatters, Duplex Printing Press, Bedford Cut Stone, Lauf* v. *Shinner, Texas and New Orleans Railroad, United States* v. *Hutcheson,* and *Jones & Laughlin.*

The volume is designed to serve several functions. For a one-semester course in labor relations law, it presents the material for the pre-Taft-Hartley Act period. For a two-semester course, it offers the reading requirement for the first semester. The volume should be useful in courses of labor history, American history, and public policy in economics and business. It should also serve the needs of law school courses concerned with the development and contemporary status of labor relations law.

Benjamin J. Taylor
Fred Witney

CHAPTER ONE

LABOR UNIONS: UNLAWFUL COMBINATIONS

THE EARLY UNION MOVEMENT: ITS SOCIOECONOMIC CONTENT

The United States ranked second only to Great Britain in industrial activity in the first half of the nineteenth century. The trend of the future was set during this period even though agriculture remained the nation's leading occupation. In 1820, of all workers gainfully employed, about 72 percent earned their livings on the nation's farms. Manufacturing and the mechanical arts accounted for only about 12 percent of U.S. workers. However, the trend was definite and unmistakable. By 1860, the number of workers gainfully employed in agriculture had decreased to about 60 percent, while manufacturing and the mechanical arts accounted for about 18 percent.[1] Indeed, the rapid rise of manufacturing after 1800 is one of the outstanding features in the development of the nation's economy. By 1860, the gross value of manufactured products was around $1,800 million.[2] This was ten times the estimated figure for 1810. In the nation's irresistible march to industrialism, household manufacturing became a casualty. By 1860, the factory had generally replaced the household as the locale for manufacturing. The factory turned out cheaper and better products than could be produced in the home. The machine required the factory environment for its effective utilization. Factory methods were first applied to metal and iron products, food, and furniture. The increase in cotton manufacturing was typical of what was to occur in other industries. In 1808, there were only 8,000 spindles in all the nation. In 1860, more than 5 million spindles were in operation. One writer reported that by 1850, "it had become possible for rich and poor alike to dress adequately and attractively in cloth of American manufacture."[3]

The rise of the factory system in this period did more than serve as a harbinger of American industrial greatness. It produced a distinct labor class and thereby created the basis for modern labor problems: the adjustment of workers to the economic and social problems of industrialism. In the colonial era, a male worker at least normally passed through the stages of apprentice and journeyman, and eventually became an independent master craftsman. In this role, the functions of laborer, employer, capitalist, merchant, and entrepreneur were performed. However, as the factory system arose, the economy took on its contemporary characteristic of specialization of function. This meant that an increasing number of workers were destined to remain "hired hands" throughout their lives.

As the market for the products of industry widened under the stimulus of an ever-improving transportation system, the economic position of the laboring class was changed. The products made in one locality competed with those turned out in other areas. When employers found that they were being undersold by rival producers, they frequently reduced wages to wipe out the price differential and still maintain profit margins. As a matter of fact, many of the strikes in the early 1800s were protests against wage-cutting. For example, in Manayunk, Pennsylvania, a textile manufacturing town, there was a strike in 1828 against a 25 percent reduction in pay. Commons, in this connection, declared, "Even at the old prices, it was said, a spinner could make only 'from $7.50 to $8.50 per week for himself by working the full period of twelve hours daily, and in doing this he actually earned for his employers from $40 to $50 per week.'"[4] Indeed, low wages were the lot for many of the newly created working class. This was particularly true in the New England textile factories which employed large numbers of women and children, groups notorious for their weak bargaining power. In some cases, whole families were employed in the factories, but their earnings were low. Thus, four members of a family worked a total of 93 days between April 25 and May 19, 1832, for a net return of $18.30.[5]

Other conditions of work in the early factories also reflected competitive pressures of product markets. Hours of work were long relative to current standards, frequently ranging from twelve to fourteen per day. The lack of protection for the prevention of accidents was not yet a public issue. Little attention was paid to the establishment of healthy working conditions. In short, in the race to create profitable enterprises, the early factory owners generally had little time to pay attention to the welfare of their employees. Thus, one historian, speaking on the lot of labor in the 1800–1850 period, concludes: "Although the factory system from the beginning brought to society in general increased leisure and many conveniences the value of which can scarcely be measured, the people whose sweat and toil made these changes possible profited little."[6]

The search for profits and the exploitation of new markets occupied the major proportion of the new factory owner's time. Riches stimulated the desire for still more riches. That the worker shared but little in the fruits of the newly created industrial system was of little concern to the predominantly agriculturally oriented public. Many publicly endorsed the philosophy of Alexander Hamilton, who once declared, "All communities divide themselves into the few and the many. The first are rich and well born and the other, the mass of people who seldom judge or determine right."[7] Social responsibility was not to become an important element of the American industrial system until industry grew to a more secure position in the economy. The precedent for labor unrest was set by the uncertainties of firm and industry survival due to fierce domestic and international competition. The framework for the labor-management strife of contemporary society was erected at the dawn of American industrialism.

👁 CONSPIRACY DOCTRINE APPLIED TO UNIONS

Stimulated by a more rapid rate of socioeconomic change, some workers formed labor unions to protect their interests. The American labor movement dates from the early part of the nineteenth century, though ephemeral organizations and sporadic worker protests occurred previously. In the early 1800s, organizations of a more permanent character were formed to provide workers with a shield of protection from the consequences of the new industrialism.

Efforts at organization of the early unions were confined largely to the skilled workers of the shoemaking, weaving, hatmaking, and printing trades rather than among the less-skilled factory workers. This feature of labor union development is easily explained. It is commonly accepted that the conditions of the factory workers were much worse than those of the skilled craft workers. But many factors operated to forestall the organization of the hired hands of the newly created factories. These workers, unlike the craft workers, were very easily replaced due to their surplus. Training for their jobs was practically unnecessary, as evidenced by the large number of children who successfully held down factory jobs. Moreover, a high proportion of factory workers were women and children, groups which for many reasons were not readily organizable at that time.

Many factory workers did not possess the necessary insight into the socioeconomic forces released by the growing industrial society. This is not surprising, for many of these workers were uprooted from the farms and had had little opportunity except for the most meager type of education. Although the evidence is not clear, one could say with a degree of certainty that a sizable proportion of the early factory workers was illiterate. The craft workers, of more worldly experience, quickly understood the necessity of effective organization of labor to meet the problems of the new structural arrangement of industry. This is not to say that the factory workers did not protest against working conditions. On the contrary, they participated in many strikes, most frequently carried out against wage-cutting. However, these strikes were poorly managed and generally unsuccessful. No union can maintain itself for long when it cannot strike successfully. Thus the early attempts at unionization by unskilled factory workers were usually unsuccessful. Indeed, it was not until the birth of the Congress of Industrial Organization (CIO) in 1935 that the nation's factory workers organized on a successful and permanent basis. Even then, their success was due to a more favorable government policy, which was not present in earlier years.

Of the early unions, the shoe and bootmakers' organizations were by far the most aggressive. Many of the other unions had a sporadic existence, the craft workers banding themselves together to carry out periodic strikes and then dissolving after the strikes were terminated. In contrast, the shoemakers' unions had a permanent existence during the early period. The Philadelphia shoemakers, for example, organized in 1792 and maintained their organization permanently for many years. So successful were these shoemakers' unions that shoemaker employers' associations were established, which had in part as their objective the neutralization of the craft workers unions. For a time, employers resorted to economic pressure tactics calculated to defeat the labor unions. Among their most effective weapons was the employment of replacements willing to work for wages below the scale demanded by unionists.

In 1806, some employers struck upon a new method to deal with the shoemakers' unions. They sought the aid of the courts. This procedure—the solicitation of government aid in labor disputes—remains to this day a persistent element in the industrial relations pattern. It is noteworthy that the precedent was established as early as 1806.

In that year, the Philadelphia shoemaker employers charged that unions were conspiracies. As conspiracies, they contended, labor unions were unlawful combinations. A conspiracy, generally defined, is the combination of two or more persons who band together to prejudice the rights of others or of society. Under the doctrine of conspiracy would fall, for example, the plot of a group of people who work together to bring about conviction of an innocent person. Likewise, the conspiracy doctrine

CHAPTER ONE

would apply to the action of a group that plotted to overthrow an established government. Before conspiracy can be charged, it must be shown that the group has caused or will cause an injustice to other people or to society. An interesting characteristic about the conspiracy doctrine is that conspirators can be indicted and found guilty before they commit any overt act. For example, it is a crime to plot the murder of a person even if the evil plan is not executed. Another feature of importance is that an action by one person, though legal, becomes illegal when carried out by a group. This characteristic of the conspiracy doctrine had particular significance in the labor union conspiracy cases.

How did the employers attempt to prove that labor unions were conspiracies and hence unlawful organizations? How did unions, according to this point of view, prejudice the rights of others or of society? How did employers support the contention that by regulating wages labor unions caused "great damage and prejudice of other artificers, and journeymen in the said act and occupation of a [shoemaker], to the evil example of others, and against the peace and dignity of the Commonwealth of Pennsylvania"?[8]

🍂 THE CASE AGAINST THE UNIONS

Employers based their case against the unions partly on the economic doctrines of the classical school of economics. It was to be expected that the people responsible for the prosecution of unionists would be influenced by the economic doctrines of their times.[9] However, the pure elements of classical theory were not realized in practice. This placed a greater burden on the labor factor than was commonly assumed. Resistance by labor to such philosophies resulted because full employment was not the norm of operations.

Control of wages by unions, it was argued, "is an unnatural, artificial means of raising the price of work beyond its standard, and taking an undue advantage of the public."[10] It was contended that the increase of wages by union pressure led to higher prices of commodities. This in turn was supposed to result in the reduction of demand for products, causing unemployment in the community. The net effect of the union, therefore, was to cause injury to the community, to damage commerce and trade, and to prejudice the rights of all workers. So ran the general argument of the prosecution.

In addition, it was argued that nonunion workers were injured by the refusal of unionists to work beside them. It was contended that "a master who employs fifteen or twenty hands is called upon to discharge that journeyman who is not a member of the body; if he refuses they all leave him whatever may be the situation of his business."[11]

In the early trials, much was made of the fact that labor unions had been declared unlawful in England by both common law and statutory legislation.[12] Prosecutors urged that English law had in fact established a precedent for American courts. In his charge to the jury, the presiding judge in one conspiracy case declared that "the common law of England ... must be deemed to be applicable....."[13] In other words, the American courts should be bound by the doctrines and laws prevailing in England. The prosecution conceded, however, that workers as individuals had the right to take action to increase their wages. Individual bargaining for higher wages, even individual quitting of work because of dissatisfaction with working conditions, was legal. The charge was that the combining of workers to force higher wages constituted illegal conduct. On many occasions, the principle of conspiracy law was cited, whereby "what may be lawful in an individual, may be criminal in a number of individuals combined, with a view to carrying it into effect."[14] In this connection, the prosecution in the first conspiracy case, in 1806, declared:

> Let it be well understood that the present action is not intended to introduce the doctrine that a man [sic] is not at liberty to fix any price whatsoever upon his own labor. Our position is that no man [sic] is at liberty to combine, conspire, confederate, and unlawfully agree to regulate the whole body of workmen in the city. The defendants are not indicted for regulating their own individual wages, but for undertaking by a combination to regulate the price of the labor of others as well as their own.[15]

In summary, the charges against unions were that (1) labor organizations are conspiracies because they injure society and prejudice the rights of individuals; and (2) unions were declared unlawful in England and English law is a compelling precedent for American courts. These factors led one of the judges in the very first conspiracy case to remark that "a combination of workmen to raise their wages may be considered in a twofold point of view: one is to benefit themselves ... the other is to injure those who do not join their society. The rule of law condemns both."[16]

❦ CHARACTERISTICS OF THE CONSPIRACY TRIALS

Between 1806 and 1842, there were seventeen trials in which labor unions were charged with conspiracy. Of these, shoemakers' unions were involved nine times. In all cases, the unionists were charged with engaging in a criminal conspiracy. This meant that if convicted, the defendants could have been imprisoned. However, the penalties that were assessed were in the form of small fines. In passing sentence, judges threatened a more serious penalty for second offenses. The effect of the judgments was to discourage union activities.

CHAPTER ONE 7

A Philadelphia court decided the first conspiracy case against a union in 1806. Later trials were held in Pittsburgh, Baltimore, Buffalo, Hudson, and New York. The doctrine established in the Philadelphia case spread to the other cities. Courts always pay close attention to decisions developed in other judicial jurisdictions. Had the Philadelphia court ruled labor unions to be lawful associations, it is likely that few, if any, prosecutions would have taken place in other cities.

The worker defendants in the conspiracy cases were tried by juries. An analysis of the composition of the juries reveals that the jurors were representative of the merchant and employer groups. For example, in the first conspiracy trial, three of the jurors were grocers, two made their living as innkeepers, one was a tavernkeeper, and the others respectively were designated as "merchant," "hatter," "tobacconist," "taylor," and "bottler." In the early days of our nation, property qualifications were generally a prerequisite for jury duty. Workers, who held little or no property, were generally excluded from jury service. This feature undoubtedly influenced the outcome in the conspiracy trials. In addition, the decisions were influenced, not only by the social and economic predilections of the jurors, but by the general background of the judges presiding at the trials. Some of the judges made little effort to conceal their antiunion feelings. For example, one judge, while making his charge to the jury, declared, "If these evils [organization of workers in labor unions] were unprovided for by the law now existing, it would be necessary that laws should be made to restrain them."

❦ IN DEFENSE OF LABOR UNIONS

Competent legal counsel defended the workers brought to trial in the conspiracy cases. Their preparation was such that they could make a thorough presentation of the workers' position. Arguments offered by the defense counsels reflected modern thinking on collective bargaining. The workers involved in the conspiracy cases had the benefit of learned and articulate counsel. Their conviction under the conspiracy doctrine was not attributable to lack of ability on the part of their defense lawyers. Workers, through their lawyers, argued that labor unions did not produce the evils so vividly portrayed by the prosecution. No empirical data or evidence was presented to bear out the prosecution's arguments, it was contended. It was also argued that collective action undertaken by workers to raise wages did not set in motion economic forces that resulted in hardship to the community. Defense counsels vigorously, but in vain, pointed to the positive contributions that labor unions could make to the economic and social life of the community. According to the defendants, English law did not apply to American courts, for by the Revolution, we divorced ourselves from British rule and "have shaken off the supremacy of English law."[17]

Furthermore, the defense objected to being tried under common law. It was argued that no statute or action by the legislative branch of government outlawed labor unions. Accordingly, why should a court outlaw this form of association when the legislature, the representative branch of government, had not seen fit to take this action? Freedom of action, it was further contended, applied not only to business people in the conduct of their economic activities, but applied equally to workers who sought to advance their position in the economy by collective action. The doctrine of liberty was not reserved for any particular economic group; instead, it equally embraced workers, farmers, and merchants. These arguments, presented in a most lucid and convincing manner, failed to sway the courts, for when the juries were polled, labor unions were indicted as unlawful associations. It seemed for a time that there was no place for unions in American economic life.

❦ THE STATE OF AFFAIRS BEFORE COMMONWEALTH V. HUNT

In spite of the conspiracy cases, workers continued to form labor organizations. Although the negative legal environment was "effective ... in checking the early trade societies," Selig Perlman, a foremost labor historian, reported that the early trade union movement was retarded even more by the industrial depression that set in after the conclusion of the Napoleonic Wars.[18] By 1836, there were several hundred local trade unions established in leading industrial cities of the East. The structure of the labor movement was taking on a more modern appearance. By 1842, city centrals had been formed in practically every eastern city in which local trade unions operated. National labor organizations also made their appearance during the years in which the courts applied the conspiracy doctrine to organized labor. In addition, the first federation of labor unions in the United States was established in this period. The National Trades' Union, as this federation was called, was organized in New York City in 1834. At its first convention, delegates appeared from many of the local unions and city centrals operating in New York, Philadelphia, Boston, Brooklyn, Poughkeepsie, and Newark. The federation sought to unite in one organization every local union, city central, and national labor union in the nation. The National Trades' Union had a striking resemblance to the present national federation, the AFL-CIO. Along with every other unit of the organized labor movement, it was swept away in the depression of 1837.

Thus, many workers organized labor unions even though the courts had declared their associations unlawful. Apparently, some workers felt

CHAPTER ONE

that they had too much to gain from their labor unions to disband them because of the declaration of unlawfulness. It may be that workers believed that collective action was the prerequisite for the satisfactory settlement of their employment grievances. As a matter of fact, employees in this period did protest against many economic and political conditions.[19] In addition, significant changes were taking place in political philosophy. The more liberal philosophy of Jackson and Jefferson was displacing the basically conservative doctrines of Alexander Hamilton. More attention was being given to the rights and liberties of individuals. Some writers in this period stressed that liberty and freedom in economic affairs were not the monopoly of any group, but rather the common heritage of all citizens regardless of occupational status. The poor as well as the wealthy could take action to implement their right "to life, liberty, and the pursuit of happiness." Many workers interpreted the emphasis on liberty "and the rights of man" as a philosophical justification for organization and collective bargaining. Moreover, employees probably felt that they were not violating a law by organizing labor unions. No legislative branch of government had embodied into statutory law the doctrines established by the courts in the conspiracy cases.

The totality of economic and political forces encouraged the formation of labor unions. Many workers believed that intolerable conditions of employment could be erased only through the process of organization and collective bargaining. They interpreted the liberal political writings of the period as the philosophical justification for collective bargaining. In such a context, the application of the conspiracy doctrine to labor unions appeared incongruous. So incensed were the workers against the courts that in 1836, in New York and Washington, mass protest demonstrations were held. During these demonstrations, two judges, who had previously convicted unionists as criminal conspirators, were burned in effigy.[20]

🐾 LABOR UNIONS DECLARED LAWFUL ORGANIZATIONS IN 1842

Such were the prevailing circumstances when Chief Justice Shaw of the Supreme Judicial Court of Massachusetts handed down his decision in the celebrated case, *Commonwealth* v. *Hunt*.[21] Before the case received Justice Shaw's attention, a lower court had found a group of shoemaker unionists guilty of conspiracy. The workers were convicted in the lower court because they refused to work for an employer who hired a shoemaker not a member of their union. The indictment was that the action of the unionists interfered with the right of the nonunion shoemaker to practice his trade. Shaw struck sharply and repeatedly at the conception that labor unions are evil organizations. He did state that, like any other organization, a labor union may exist for a "pernicious" and "dangerous" purpose. But he emphatically affirmed that labor unions may also exist for a "laudable" and "public-spirited" purpose. Rather than inflicting injury on society, he contended, a union may advance the general welfare of the community by raising the standard of life of the members of the union. In this connection, Shaw pointed out that labor organizations "might be used [by workers] to afford each other assistance in times of poverty, sickness, or distress; or to raise their intellectual, moral, and social conditions; or to make improvements in their art."

For a union to be indicted and convicted under the conspiracy doctrine, Shaw contended, it must be shown that the objectives of the union were unlawful, or that the means employed to gain a lawful end were unlawful. Unless this could be proved, a labor organization had to be considered a lawful association. In the case at hand, Shaw held that the prosecution did not prove that the conspiracy doctrine should have been applied to the labor union. In addition, the Chief Justice pointed out that not all union members were responsible if some of the body engaged in unlawful acts. In such a case, the law should only result in the conviction of the guilty party, not of the other members of the association. The fact that labor unions may adopt measures "that may have a tendency to impoverish another; that is, to diminish his gains and profits" did not constitute a reason for indictment of the organization. Accordingly, Shaw held that union members may agree not to work for an employer who hired workers not members of their association. By the same token, he implied that the action of workers to raise their wages by collective bargaining did not justify the application of the conspiracy doctrine. Though such action could reduce employer profits or even increase prices of commodities, the ultimate purpose of collective bargaining was to advance the welfare of members of the union, a purpose that Shaw implicity supported.

❦ COMMONWEALTH V. HUNT: *ITS SIGNIFICANCE*

Commonwealth v. *Hunt* was a landmark in the development of the law of industrial relations. Its effect was to dissolve the identity between the conspiracy doctrine and labor unions. Labor organizations taken by themselves were declared lawful, and unionists were no longer to be regarded as criminals in the eyes of the courts. In general, most other courts, though not bound by the Massachusetts decision, followed the doctrine established by Shaw. *Commonwealth* v. *Hunt* did not, however, mean that the courts were to withdraw from the area of industrial relations. Shaw did not advocate the complete removal of the conspiracy doctrine from the affairs of labor unions. In fact, after *Commonwealth v. Hunt*, the conspiracy doctrine was still utilized to proscribe particular labor union activities. The courts continued to scrutinize the affairs and operations of labor unions. Where the court in a particular labor case felt that a union was seeking an unlawful objective, or using unlawful means to gain a lawful objective, judicial action was undertaken to harass the labor organization. In 1806, the year in which the conspiracy doctrine was first applied to labor unions, the courts invaded the field of industrial relations. To this day they continue to influence profoundly the direction and character of labor relations.

❦ FROM THE CONSPIRACY DOCTRINE TO THE LABOR INJUNCTION

As noted, the courts continued to apply the conspiracy doctrine to labor unions even after Shaw handed down his decision in the celebrated Massachusetts case. Although the conspiracy cases after 1842 did not involve the legal status of labor unions per se, the courts made use of the doctrine to restrain a number of union activities. Professor E. E. Witte of the University of Wisconsin reported there were actually more labor conspiracy cases in the second half of the nineteenth century than in the first half.[22] During the period from 1863 to 1880 alone, labor unions were involved in eighteen conspiracy trials. In one of these cases, decided by the Supreme Court of New Jersey in 1867, the facts were essentially the same as those in *Commonwealth v. Hunt*.[23] A group of employees had formed a labor organization, a rule of which was that its members could not work alongside nonunion workers. The unionists took action against an employer to force him to dismiss two nonunion employees. The New Jersey court was not bound by Shaw's decision in *Commonwealth v. Hunt*. Nevertheless, the New Jersey court concurred "entirely ... with the principles embodied in the opinion" of the Massachusetts case, but still held that the New Jersey case was "clearly distinguishable."

After 1880, the courts made use of the conspiracy doctrine in labor disputes only infrequently. This development, however, did not result from a shift in the basic attitude of the courts toward collective bargaining. Subsequent years were to underscore the antipathy of the judiciary to the efforts of workers to better their economic position through collective action. Neither did this change in court policy result from a shift in employers' attitude. They still sought the aid of the judiciary in their conflicts with organized labor. Finally, the conspiracy doctrine did not fade away because of the slackening of the organizational efforts of workers. Organized labor in the second half of the nineteenth century made significant progress. The Knights of Labor,[24] a militant labor organization that sought to organize "men and women of every craft, creed, and color," was formed in 1869. By 1886, the Knights of Labor claimed a membership of 700,000, representing the high-water mark of union membership in the United States since the first labor organization was formed in 1794. The organization engaged in many successful strikes, particularly on the railroads controlled by that great financier of the period, Jay Gould. After 1886, the Knights of Labor declined rapidly, but in its place arose the American Federation of Labor. Even in the period of its infancy, the AFL gave promise of an organization well equipped to expand and implement the process of collective bargaining.

Some employers utilized economic pressure, which often erupted into open violence between the competitive groups. During and after strikes, organized employees were often confronted with serious obstacles in their collective bargaining activities. For example, in the famous Homestead strike of 1892, the Carnegie Steel Corporation hired 300 men from the Pinkerton Detective Agency to serve as strikebreakers.[25] Before the conflict was over, at least a dozen of the workers and detectives had been killed and scores were injured. In this framework of opposition to collective bargaining, it was to be expected that antiunion employers would seek the aid of the courts. The conspiracy doctrine, of course, could be utilized to discourage the spread of trade unionism. Prosecution of workers in conspiracy trials, however, was a rather cumbersome affair. Some of the trials lasted several days and during this time unionists could continue to damage the position of employers. It was increasingly more difficult to procure witnesses to offer testimony against worker defendants. Of even greater importance was the trend toward jury sympathy to worker organizations seeking to raise their economic standards through collective bargaining. Jury requirements were becoming liberalized, with the result that workers might be called upon to help decide labor conspiracy cases. In addition, some jurors, aware of the spread of industrialization and the growth of large corporations, were prone to side with unionists. It was necessary to seek a new legal weapon to discourage unionism. The technique had to meet the requirements of speed, simplicity, and definiteness. Above all, if employers were to resist organization of their firms, it was mandatory to remove the labor dispute from the jurisdiction of a potentially sympathetic jury. All these requirements were met by the labor injunction.

❦ SUMMARY

The application of the conspiracy doctrine to labor unions was an important factor in employers' resistance to the spread of the American labor union movement. Employers, concerned with the vitality of the early

CHAPTER ONE

union movement, enlisted the courts as an ally in their challenge to organized labor. The courts proved a vehicle for use by employers resisting organization of their employees. Juries convicted unionists as criminal conspirators who, unless restrained, would do evil to the community. This conclusion was reached by assuming that the economy would function best if it were free of organizations that placed unnatural restrictions upon it. Such an assumption was then, as now, open to debate.

Commonwealth v. Hunt was a landmark labor law case because it dissolved the identity between the conspiracy doctrine and labor unions. However, by 1842, the year in which the case was decided, employers and judges were casting around for a more effective legal device to contain unions than the cumbersome and uncertain conspiracy trial. Moreover, union activities were still subject to the conspiracy doctrine after *Commonwealth v. Hunt*, even though unions themselves were regarded as legal institutions.

❦ DISCUSSION QUESTIONS

1. Should employers be free to make any decision they might choose that involves issues over wages, hours, or other terms and conditions of employment?
2. Why did skilled craft workers organize earlier than did unskilled workers?
3. Explain the origin, nature, and use of the conspiracy doctrine. What impact did it have on union attempts to organize workers?
4. Was the conspiracy doctrine less important after 1842 than before? What factors influence your answer?

❦ NOTES

[1] Chester W. Wright, *Economic History of the United States* (New York: McGraw-Hill Book Company, 1949), p. 331.

[2] *Ibid.*, p. 319.

[3] James A. Barnes, *Wealth of the American People* (Englewood Cliffs, N.J.: Prentice-Hall, Inc., 1949), p. 224.

[4] John R. Commons and Associates, *History of Labour in the United States* (New York: The Macmillan Company, 1926), p. 418.

[5] Barnes, *op. cit.*, p. 288.

[6] *Ibid.*, p. 285.

[7] Charles A. Beard and Mary Beard, *The Rise of American Civilization* (New York: The Macmillan Company, 1927), p. 316.

[8] John R. Commons and Eugene A. Gilmore, *A Documentary History of American Industrial Society*, (Cleveland: The Arthur H. Clark Company, 1910), p. 64.

[9] *The Wealth of Nations* by Adam Smith, commonly recognized as the leading spirit of the classical school of economics, had just appeared in 1776.

[10] Commons and Gilmore, *op. cit.*, p. 228.

[11] *Ibid.*, III, p. 70.

[12] For a treatment of the application of English law to labor unions in this early period, see James M. Landis and Marcus Manoff, *Cases on Labor Law* (Chicago: The Foundation Press, 1942), pp. 1–28.

[13] Commons and Gilmore, *op. cit.*, p. 384.

[14] *Ibid.*, p. 69.

[15] *Ibid.*, p. 68.

[16] *Ibid.*, p. 233.

[17] *Ibid.*, p. 261.

[18] Selig Perlman, *A History of Trade Unionism in the United States* (New York: The Macmillan Company, 1929), p. 7.

[19] Grievances of workers in this period included the length of the working day, imprisonment for theft, the Pennsylvania compulsory military system under which rich people could avoid military duty, the failure of legislatures to enact machine lien laws to protect workers' wages in the event of employer bankruptcy, lack of free public education for the children of workers, and the general political and economic inequity between the workers and the rich.

[20] E.E. Witte, "Early American Labor Cases," *Yale Law Journal*, XXXV (1926), p. 827.

[21] *Commonwealth of Massachusetts* v. *Hunt*, Massachusetts, 4 Metcalf 3 (1842).

[22] "Early American Labor Cases," *supra*.

[23] *State of New Jersey* v. *Donaldson*, 32 NSL 151 (1867).

[24] For an interesting account of the Knights of Labor, see T. V. Powderly, *The Path I Trod* (New York: Columbia University Press, 1940). Powderly was the second "General Master Workman" of the Knights of Labor.

[25] Perlman, *op. cit.*, p. 134.

CHAPTER TWO

UNION ACTIVITIES AND THE LABOR INJUNCTION

The use of the labor injunction in labor disputes constitutes one of the most controversial issues in the area of industrial relations law. Representatives of management and organized labor sharply disagree on the use of the injunction in employer-employee conflicts. Parties not directly affiliated with either management or labor have added to the controversy by contributing divergent views on the subject. Jurists, scholars, legislators, and even lay people from time to time have condemned or praised the labor injunction. Fundamental to the controversy is that the labor injunction provides the basis for court entry into labor disputes. To some, court intervention in labor disputes is undesirable. They claim that the use of the injunction in labor disputes not only has interfered with the right of workers to collective bargaining, but has caused no end of disturbance in labor-management relations. Some contend that the state of industrial relations is improved to the degree that the court's power to issue the injunction is circumscribed. Opponents of the labor injunction further claim that the collective bargaining process is strengthened and promoted, and that management and labor representatives will be more prone to reach a rapid and peaceful settlement of their controversies when they become aware that the courts are powerless to determine the outcome of labor disputes.

On the other hand, there are those who argue that the use of the labor injunction is necessary to protect the employer from the "lawlessness of labor unions." They claim that its withdrawal from the field of labor-management relations would encourage the irresponsibility of organized labor. In addition, supporters of the labor injunction urge that it be retained to protect the public interest from unions, which, they argue, threaten the health and safety of the community.

Passage of the Norris–La Guardia Anti-Injunction Act did not eliminate controversy over the labor injunction.[1] The issue was tossed to the forefront by passage of the Taft-Hartley Act. Some people, mostly labor leaders, criticized this legislation on the ground that it once again stimulated the use of the injunction in labor disputes. The injunction controversy largely prevented any change in the law during the first session of the 81st Congress. When it became apparent that any revision of Taft-Hartley would nonetheless include the procedure, representatives of unions lost interest in attempts to change the law. Organized labor was not interested in legislation that would empower the courts to restrain union activities during labor disputes through the issuance of injunctions.

This chapter will trace the development of the use of injunctions in labor disputes. The objective is to gain a better understanding of the instrument to facilitate an appraisal of its worth as a technique of government control of labor relations.

❦ THE NATURE OF INJUNCTIONS

An injunction is a court order directing a person—and, if necessary, his or her associates—to refrain from pursuing a course of action. In a comparatively small number of cases, the court may order affirmative action on the part of the people affected by the decree. Injunctions are issued in nonlabor cases as well as under circumstances where employer-employee relations are involved. More recently, injunctions have been used to restrain the circulation of libelous, indecent, or seditious material. During the Prohibition era, the instrument was employed to enforce laws forbidding the sale of liquor. In the great majority of injunction cases, however, in labor and nonlabor cases alike, the protection of property rights is the issue. In labor cases, the issue of property rights is involved almost exclusively. Where the union seeks to obtain an injunction against employers, the property issue is not involved, of course. Experience shows that unions have made little use of the injunction. Up to 1931, employers obtained 1,845 injunctions against unions, while unions obtained only 43 against employers.[2] The National Labor Relations Board, however, has stepped up the use of injunctions against employers in recent years.

A special sort of court issues injunctions. In general, we think of a court in terms of a judge, jury, witnesses, cross-examination, and the like. This type of court is the familiar court of law, or trial court. In contrast, the court that issues injunctions is termed an "equity court." The distinguishing feature of an equity court is that the judge alone decides the case under controversy. There are no juries in equity courts. In cases involving injunctions, the judge alone decides whether or not one shall be issued. This is true in both labor and nonlabor cases.

In injunction cases, the judge alone decides all issues of fact and law. No jury influences the outcome of the proceedings. A person who violates an injunction is held in "contempt of court." It is essential to note that the judge who issues the injunction determines whether the injunction has been violated. Severe penalties can be inflicted on violators of injunctions, including the payment of heavy fines and imprisonment. One may question the entire injunction procedure. Is not the power of the judge of sweeping character? May not the judge abuse his or her power? Is it proper for the same person to act as judge, jury, and executioner of justice? As a matter of fact, the injunction is a valuable part of our judicial system. An equity court can protect property before any injury to that property occurs. A trial court may award money damages to owners of property only after the damage to the property takes place. The equity court is preventive, whereas the trial court is remedial. Of course, where the judgment of one person is the sole standard of reference, there is always a possibility of abuse. Even while admitting this feature, however, one would hesitate to condemn the entire injunction procedure.

Suppose two owners of adjoining coal mines disagree on the property line separating their respective mines. One owner proceeds to mine the coal in the disputed area. If later proceedings reveal that the person who mined the coal did not in fact own the area in dispute, serious, if not irreparable, damage has been caused to the other person's property. The injured party may, of course, sue for damages. But the person would be greatly grieved if events proved that the wrongdoer had no funds to pay the damages awarded by a jury. The injunction procedure would have prevented these unhappy circumstances. The injured party could have applied for an injunction, and the court probably would have ordered that no coal mining take place until the dispute over the property line had been settled. A court of law could not have served the cause of justice in this illustration. The injunction gives swift and definite protection to property. In its absence, the property in the illustration would suffer damage that even money obtained in a subsequent lawsuit could probably not remedy. Injunctions are issued when in their absence irreparable damage to property would occur, leaving the property owner with no adequate remedy in a law court to compensate for threatened injury.

❦ FORMS OF INJUNCTIONS

A person who seeks an injunction will support his or her case at the outset with a series of sworn statements or affidavits. A court will be petitioned to issue an immediate order to prevent injury to property. The plaintiff will contend that the matter is of such urgency that time does not permit a thorough investigation of the circumstances. There is no time for a full hearing, the questioning of witnesses, or other time-consuming judicial procedures. Frequently, the courts will heed the request of the plaintiff and issue what is termed a *temporary restraining order*. The purpose of this decree is to preserve the status quo until a full investigation is made of the circumstances. Temporary restraining orders are, in effect, injunctions. They prevent a person or persons from pursuing some contemplated course of action. Penalties for violating a temporary restraining order could be just as severe as those imposed for disobedience of a more permanent type of injunction. In addition, it should be noted that the temporary restraining order is issued before the merits of the case are determined. The defendant or defendants are not provided with an opportunity to present their side.

In issuing the temporary restraining order, a judge does not claim that the plaintiff is right and the defendant wrong. Rather, the order is issued to preserve the status quo in order that property might not be irreparably damaged before the merits of the case can be determined. The justification for the temporary restraining order is that the relative position of the parties will not be injured by the maintenance of the status quo. For example, in the coal illustration, the position of the parties would not have been affected materially by the issuance of a temporary restraining order. After the merits of the case were fully determined, the coal would still have been intact for the use of the victor in the injunction proceedings.

When a temporary restraining order is issued, the judge at the same time sets a date for a hearing. Under some circumstances, courts will not issue a temporary restraining order. Instead, upon plaintiff's application for equity relief, a judge may set a date for a hearing. In either case, the court will direct that a hearing be held shortly after the temporary restraining order is issued or application for injunctive relief filed. The court is aware that the interests of the defendant may be injured by the temporary restraining order. Consequently, justice demands that the defendant be given an opportunity to present his or her case soon after the court issues the temporary restraining order. Defendants, of course, have a better opportunity to be treated fairly if the court refuses to issue a temporary restraining order and instead orders a hearing to determine the facts of the case. However, courts frequently do issue a temporary restraining order, particularly under circumstances where irreparable damage to property appears imminent.

On the basis of the hearing, the court may dissolve or modify the temporary restraining order if one has been issued previously. If it is dissolved, this action ends the matter. The defendant may then carry out the line of conduct that the temporary restraining order prohibited. On the other hand, as a result of this hearing, the court may issue a second form of injunctive relief—the *temporary injunction*. The temporary injunction is a more permanent form of injunction than the temporary restraining order. However, the full merits of the case are still not determined when this form of injunction goes into effect.

The reason for this involves the nature of the hearing prior to the issuance of the temporary injunction. It is true that the defendant may present affidavits and offer objections to the arguments of the plaintiff. Still, the full judicial procedure is not in operation. Witnesses are ordinarily not called, and no elaborate investigation of the case is made. There may be little opportunity for cross-examination, most important for testing the credibility of evidence. Both sides may be represented by counsel, but the judge still must determine "where the truth lies amid the contradictions of the affidavits presented by the contending parties, without opportunity to see or question any of the witnesses."[3] Despite these considerations, the temporary injunction demands the full obedience of the parties affected by the decree. Violators will be punished. Even if future investigation proves the defendant right and the plaintiff wrong, the defendant may still be punished if the temporary injunction is violated.

The final form of injunction is the *permanent injunction*. This form is issued after a full hearing on the merits of the case is held. Witnesses are called, questioned, and cross-examined. At this point the defendant has the opportunity to present a full case. The judge has had the opportunity to study carefully all documents and testimony in the proceeding. The hearing on the permanent injunction may result in the termination of the temporary injunction, or in the issuance of a permanent injunction. If a permanent injunction is issued, the defendants are permanently enjoined from engaging in certain action. The defendant may appeal the decision of the judge if there is a higher court available. However, the terms of the lower court's permanent injunction must be obeyed during the appeal proceedings.

❦ THE INJUNCTION IN LABOR DISPUTES

This brief description of the general injunction procedure provides a basis for discussion of the use of injunctions in labor disputes. Labor injunctions in the United States were frequently employed after 1895. The chief reason for this was that the Supreme Court in that year decided the celebrated *Debs* case,[4] upholding the constitutionality of the labor injunction. One might speculate on the course of industrial relations had the high court held the use of the instrument to be unconstitutional. Such a circumstance would have had a most profound influence on the whole process of collective bargaining, industrial relations, and the development of labor unions.

The *Debs* case was indeed a landmark in the field of labor law. The case grew out of a dispute between the Pullman Car Company and the American Railway Union. In 1894, the workers of the Pullman Car Company struck in protest against a cut in wages and the discriminatory discharge of a number of union leaders. When it became apparent that the union could not win its strike by direct action, the workers through their union officers requested the railroads to boycott the use of Pullman sleeping cars. This the railroads refused to do. As a result, the union induced a series of strikes against the railroads.

Such strikes immediately involved the government of the United States. The railroads are used in interstate commerce,[5] carry the mails of the United States, and from time to time haul personnel and equipment of the armed forces of the United States. As a result, officers of the United States government requested and obtained an injunction ordering the union, including its officers, to cease striking against the railroads. Eugene V. Debs, president of the union, and a number of other officers of the union were subsequently imprisoned for violating the terms of the injunction. The case was eventually appealed to the Supreme Court of the United States. In affirming the use of injunctions in labor disputes, the Supreme Court brushed aside the contention that the proper arm of government to suppress or control the action of the strikers was the executive branch, stating: "Is the army the only instrument by which rights of the public can be enforced and the peace of the nation preserved?" And the Court continued in this vein when it declared that "the right to use force does not exclude the right of appeal to the courts for judicial determination and the exercise of all their powers of prevention." Not only may labor disturbances or union activities be restrained by local police officers, state militia, federal troops, and the like, but the high court of the United States held that the injunction process may likewise be properly employed.

With the constitutionality of the labor injunction affirmed, the instrument became a potent factor in labor-management controversies. Professor Witte reported that prior to 1931, state and federal courts issued a total of 1,845 labor injunctions.[6] Data on the number of injunctions issued after that year are largely unavailable until 1947. As will be pointed out, Congress and some states enacted legislation in 1932 regulating the use of injunctions in labor disputes. In light of this development, the number of injunctions issued in labor disputes from 1932 to 1947 decreased sharply. However, the injunction sections of the Taft-Hartley Act, along with Landrum-Griffin in 1959, stimulated the increased use of the instrument. From August 23, 1947, the date on which the Taft-Hartley Act became effective, until June 30, 1949, there were 69 instances in which injunctions were sought against labor unions under the terms of the law. From 1950 through 1966, the National Labor Relations Board petitioned for 2,405 injunctions involving labor disputes. Not all of these were directed against unions, but union actions accounted for a majority.[7]

❦ THE CONCEPT OF "PROPERTY" IN LABOR INJUNCTION CASES

As noted, injunctions are issued in labor disputes for the purpose of protecting property from "irreparable damage." It is therefore of considerable importance to determine the meaning of "property" for labor injunction purposes. If the term is defined narrowly, the opportunity for employing the labor injunction will be reduced. Conversely, if property is construed broadly, the possibilities for its use will be increased proportionately. The courts have attached a meaning to property that broadens the concept significantly. For purposes of court proceedings, the term includes much more than tangible items, such as machinery, land, buildings, physical goods, and the like. Courts in the United States have consistently held that the concept includes intangible items as well. The right to do business falls squarely within the meaning of the property concept. Likewise, the liberty to hire workers and sell goods to customers is included within the definition. In short, the freedom to run a business in a profitable manner falls within the boundaries of the concept.

The courts did not develop this definition of property merely to provide the basis for the labor injunction. This wide interpretation of the property doctrine was an integral part of American law long before the first labor injunction was issued. It was to be expected, therefore, that the courts would apply this concept of property to labor disputes. It is not difficult to see how the broad definition of the property concept would affect labor disputes. If a labor union interferes with the free access of an employer to labor and commodity markets, it is considered that there is damage to property. Should a strike, picketing, or a boycott decrease the opportunities for profitable operation of the business, an injury to property is deemed to arise. "Irreparable damage" to property can be inflicted, not only by violent destruction of physical items, but also by union activities calculated to interfere with the carrying out of business.

Some people contended that the courts were in error in applying the broad concept of property to labor disputes.[8] To support their views, they pointed to the practice in England. For injunction purposes, courts in England generally limited property to include only physical items. But the point of importance is that the restricted meaning of property applies to labor and nonlabor cases alike.[9]

The argument has been raised that a more restricted definition of the term *property* would make the injunction in labor disputes appear more just. This argument holds that only property in its tangible form should be used as the basis for labor injunctions. This contention rests on impracticable grounds. The broad concept of property is ingrained in the very marrow of judicial thought. It is extremely doubtful that legislation aimed in a contrary direction could stand the test of constitutionality. In the *Debs* case, for example, the Supreme Court failed to distinguish between the authority of the judiciary to protect physical property and property in its tangible form. The implication is that the courts may extend protection to property under both circumstances. With more significance than the constitutional question, this viewpoint fails to recognize the basic objections to the labor injunction. The mere limitation of the property concept to include only physical objects would not result in the disappearance of these objections. The broad concept of property provides for the wider application of the labor injunction, but the wide concept in itself did not stimulate the historical abuses growing out of the use of the injunction in labor disputes. What has been the accusation against the labor injunction? Why do these objections proceed from a more fundamental basis than that of how the mere concept of property has been as applied to labor cases?

❦ ABUSES OF INJUNCTIONS

Several abuses of the injunction process were common before the passage of the Norris–La Guardia Act. Some were more the result of the circumstances of the times than of any conscious attempt to usurp power on the part of the judiciary.

JUDGES AS LEGISLATORS

One abuse of the injunction was the legislative character of court action. Through its power to issue injunctions, the judiciary literally enacted legislation. Before a law is passed by Congress or a state legislature, there is ordinarily much debate on the measure. Public hearings are held on the more important of the proposed laws wherein any citizen has the right to be heard. Some citizens may object to a particular law enacted by a legislative body, but one can be assured that the legislation was passed by the collective judgment of the people elected to represent their interests.

When judges issued labor injunctions, their only standard of reference was their own social and economic predilections. No jury acted in injunction proceedings. In labor disputes, the judge alone decided whether an objective or activity of a labor union was lawful or unlawful.

Judges outlawed many union activities. Strikes engaged in for certain purposes were stamped out by the labor injunction. Some judges forbade the calling of strikes when they deemed their purposes unlawful. The "fairness" or "justice" of the strike's purpose is not the issue here. The point of importance is that the injunction procedure provided the courts with the power to determine the legal and illegal boundaries of union activities. In the absence of legislation, the courts acted in labor disputes as the legislative branch of government. Clearly, the economic and social attitudes of judges influenced their decisions. Every labor dispute had its social and economic ramifications. The manner in which judges interpreted their environment had an important bearing on whether or not an injunction would be issued. In equity cases, the judge alone, motivated by his own beliefs, attitudes, and prejudices, decided the issues. The decisions did not indicate dishonesty or unfairness of the judiciary, but rather reflected their legal training, their social environment, and their lack of knowledge of industrial relations. Whatever the reason, the result was to favor the interests of the property-owning group at the expense of labor groups.

THE BLANKET INJUNCTION

In the past, labor injunctions frequently made illegal acts that, standing alone, were lawful. Such injunctions were also applied to persons other than those immediately involved in a dispute. Even at the present time, anti-injunction laws notwithstanding, some injunctions have this effect. Labor injunctions in many cases have been directed against "all other persons whomsoever" who might have aided workers in a labor dispute.[10] This meant that an injunction was applied to persons other than those immediately involved in the controversy. People not directly concerned with the dispute, but nevertheless sympathetic to workers engaged in union activities, could not undertake action to support them. For example, such persons could have been enjoined from contributing money for strike relief when a court had previously declared a strike illegal. In addition, the labor injunction frequently outlawed activities which in themselves were legal. Thus the decrees often made it unlawful for workers and their sympathizers to "interfere in any way whatsoever" to further a labor dispute. Such language failed to make a distinction between activities commonly regarded as unlawful, such as violent destruction of property, and patterns of conduct commonly regarded as lawful, such as the exercise of the right to free speech. In 1911, the Supreme Court upheld an injunction that forbade anyone from speaking or writing to further a labor union activity.[11]

Sweeping or "blanket" terms such as "all other persons whomsoever" and "interfering in any way whatsoever" produced serious consequences.

Lawful acts were made illegal. Both participants and nonparticipants in the dispute were affected. Injunctions containing such all-inclusive terms could violate basic civil liberties guaranteed in the Constitution of the United States. Moreover, those terms were fundamentally devoid of definite meaning. One rule which could have been followed in injunction cases was that the terms of the injunction should be clear. There was very little clarity in terms such as "whatsoever" and "whomsoever." The average person would scarcely have known under what circumstances he or she could have violated a court order. For example, did a church violate the terms of a *blanket injunction* because it provided free meals to workers who participated in a strike ruled unlawful by the courts? The matter grew more serious because of the enforcement procedure of injunctions. When the judge who issued the injunction subsequently interpreted and enforced it, the problem reached a magnitude disproportionate to its importance.

THE STATUS QUO IN LABOR DISPUTES

A temporary restraining order and temporary injunction are issued for the purpose of maintaining the status quo between the parties to the injunction proceedings. Their effect is to stop at once action by the defendant, until a hearing and investigation can be conducted to determine fully the merits of the dispute. Justification of the procedure rests on the premise that the relative position of the parties will not be affected by the temporary injunction proceedings. If subsequent court investigations prove that the conduct of the defendant is not unlawful, the injunction is supposed to be terminated. The defendant should then be free to carry out the action she or he was pursuing, or had intended to pursue, before the court interfered. On the other hand, if the temporary restraining order or the temporary injunction had not been issued, the defendant might have caused "irreparable damage" to the property of the plaintiff.

This line of reasoning, though generally valid in nonlabor injunction proceedings, did not apply to labor disputes. Temporary injunction proceedings, regardless of the outcome of subsequent court action, had the effect of discriminating against the labor union. Events in labor disputes move swiftly. The ultimate outcome of strikes, then as now, could be determined in a few days. Interference with strike activities through the injunction process made it difficult for the union to carry the strike to a successful termination.

Temporary injunction proceedings had a far-reaching effect on the general public. Public opinion tended to turn against the strikers once the court order was issued. Regardless of the merits of the cases and notwithstanding the eventual outcome of the full injunction proceedings, the court orders branded the workers as lawbreakers. Newspapers unfriendly to organized labor exploited the legal proceedings. Editorial and news commentators could use the court order as a basis for condemning the purpose of the strike and the conduct of the workers. Labor unions had a difficult task in winning a strike when general public opinion condemned the undertaking.

Injunction proceedings also lessened the chance of winning a strike by directing the energies of union leadership to the courtroom. In some cases the proceedings were conducted far from the locality of the strike. The strategy was to strip the rank and file of its leadership. Time spent in court proceedings endangered the success of strikes. In addition, the expense of combating injunctions was often considerable. Money paid out for lawyers' fees was not available for publicity, strike relief, or the purchase of food for strikers and their families.

Perhaps the greatest effect of the labor injunction was to dampen the enthusiasm of workers for the strike. They became fearful and confused by the court's intervention in the dispute. This was particularly so when the workers were engaged in their first strike or when they were relatively new to the labor union movement. The injunction procedure in labor disputes was a rather complex affair. Usually, workers did not understand such legal action and as a consequence, the strike effort deteriorated.

These observations repudiate the contention that the status of the parties remained the same during the period in which the temporary restraining order or the temporary injunction was in effect. If an order stimulated fear and confusion among the workers, resulted in the dissipation of union funds, directed the energies of union leadership from the strike to the courtroom, and tended to turn public opinion against the strike, one can scarcely argue that the status quo between the parties had been maintained. Instead of protecting the employer's property against irreparable damage, temporary injunction proceedings could result in irreparable damage to the union's position. This was the usual result of injunctions, regardless of the outcome of later court proceedings.

TIME LAGS IN INJUNCTION PROCEEDINGS

Studies indicate that the courts made frequent use of the temporary restraining order. Frankfurter and Greene[12] reported that the temporary restraining order was involved in more than one-half of all federal labor injunction cases during 1901–1928.[13] Of the 118 officially reported federal labor injunction proceedings in this period, 70 involved the temporary restraining order. In 49 of the 118 cases, the courts actually issued the temporary restraining order.[14] In 45 labor injunction cases in the clothing trades in New York City between 1910 and 1927, the courts issued 26 temporary restraining orders.[15] Professor Witte, however, reported that in Massachusetts, in 234 applications for injunctions from 1898 to 1916, temporary restraining orders were issued in only 29 cases.[16] The defendant had no opportunity to present a case in temporary restraining order proceedings. The order was issued on the application of the plaintiff. Thus, in labor cases in which temporary restraining orders were issued, the union had no opportunity to answer the charges of the employer.

As noted, courts normally order a hearing concurrent with the issuance of the temporary restraining order. At this hearing, the defendant has an opportunity to present a case. However, from the date the temporary restraining order is issued until the hearing is held, the order is in force and has to be obeyed by the defendants in the dispute. Obviously, the interests of labor unions would be protected by a speedy hearing after the temporary restraining order was issued. A long delay would cause irreparable damage to the labor union. If a court enjoined a strike for any prolonged length of time, the strike was likely to be permanently broken regardless of further injunction proceedings. In nonlabor injunction cases, the lapse of time between the issuance of the temporary restraining order and the hearing ordinarily took from five to ten days. In the absence of injunction control legislation, the time lag in labor injunction cases was much longer. One study showed that out of 42 cases in which temporary restraining orders were issued, the intervening period was less than a month in only 16 cases. In one unusual case, the period was one year.[17] Recognizing the inherent unfairness of such a long delay, subsequent labor injunction legislation limited the time between the issuance of temporary restraining orders and the hearings.

A hearing on a temporary restraining order could result in the order's modification, continuance, or termination. If a court felt that activities of a labor union should continue to be restrained, a temporary injunction would be issued. Actually, the hearing on the temporary restraining order did not offer a great amount of protection to the labor union. The union could offer counteraffidavits to challenge the allegations of the employer. But in general at these hearings, "the usual safeguards for sifting fact from distortion or imaginings—personal appearance of witnesses and cross-examinations by opposing counsel—[were] lacking."[18] Thus, the hearing was of dubious value to labor organizations, and equally so when a court denied the application for a temporary restraining order and would instead direct a hearing to determine whether a temporary injunction should be issued.

Even today, the full injunction procedure is rarely exhausted in labor cases. Labor unions generally contest a temporary restraining order. But the bulk of labor cases terminate with the issuance of the temporary injunction. Unions rarely continue injunction proceedings to the point where the court decides whether to issue a permanent injunction, or to dissolve or modify the temporary injunction. The reason for this is that frequently the strike is broken or some other settlement of the dispute is made before the full injunction procedure is exhausted.

It is only at the final stage of the injunction proceedings that the merits of the case are fully determined. At this level, witnesses appear, and there is the opportunity for cross-examination. But these safeguards are worthless in labor injunction cases, for labor unions find little practicable value in exhausting the injunction procedure. These considerations moved Frankfurter and Greene to remark that

> in theory the final injunctive decree alone is an adjudication on the merits, temporary restraining orders and temporary injunctions are nominally provisional. In fact, however, the restraining order and temporary injunction usually register the ultimate disposition of a labor litigation, which seldom persists to a final decree. Lack of resources may frustrate pursuit on the litigation, or as is often the case, the strike has ended before the final stage is reached and ended not infrequently as a result of the injunction.[19]

QUALITY OF EVIDENCE IN INJUNCTION PROCEEDINGS

Judges issue injunctions only after considering evidence. This is equally true in labor and nonlabor cases. The character of the evidence presented is the real issue in the issuance of the labor injunction. "Character" does not mean the *amount* of evidence. Employers and unions alike support their positions with a considerable quantity of evidence. The challenge relates to the quality of the evidence. Affidavits constitute the chief—if not the exclusive—form of evidence that courts consider before ruling whether or not temporary restraining orders or temporary injunctions are to be issued.

Experience with the labor injunction has demonstrated that the affidavits submitted in labor cases are in large measure unreliable. One judge reflected this point of view when he stressed the "utter untrustworthiness of affidavits" and further asserted: "Such documents are packed with falsehoods, or with half-truths which in such a matter are more deceptive than deliberate falsehoods."[20] In some early cases, courts decided injunction proceedings on the basis of affidavits sworn to by private detectives hired by employers to break strikes and unions. Such evidence, according to a former Justice of the Supreme Court, is particularly untrustworthy. He declared in this connection that "all know that men who accept such employment commonly lack fine scruples, often willfully misrepresenting innocent conduct, and manufacturing charges."[21]

The point of importance is not that one side is basically more honest than the other in labor injunction proceedings. Both parties color their cases to suit their needs. This is to be expected. The chief objection is that the court must make an important decision, affecting the liberty and life of many people, on the basis of evidence that is often untrustworthy. On the basis of this conflicting evidence, the court must make its decision. One judge squarely pointed up the difficulty of the problem when he stated, "I confess my inability to determine with any satisfaction from an inspection of inanimate manuscript questions of veracity. In disposing of the present rule, I am compelled to find, as best I may from two hundred thirty-five lifeless, typewritten pages of conflicting evidence, the facts which must determine respondents' guilt or innocence on the quasi-criminal charge of contempt."[22]

Some people brush aside the importance of the issuance of labor injunctions on the basis of evidence of this character. It is contended that the labor union will be reimbursed for damages resulting from an injunction issued on the basis of employer evidence subsequently proved false. Actually, equity proceedings do recognize the possibility of injury to a defendant where an injunction is issued on the basis of unworthy evidence of the plaintiff. To provide for this possibility, the court will normally require the plaintiff to post a bond along with an application for an injunction. If an injunction is issued on the basis of the plaintiff's evidence and if the full injunction procedure reveals the plaintiff's evidence to be false, the court will award proceeds from the bond to the defendant. This award is supposed to compensate the defendant for damages occurring from the injunction proceedings.

Such an award has little bearing in labor injunction cases. The bond is not forfeited in any injunction case until the permanent injunction is denied. It has been pointed out that unions generally do not find it practicable to exhaust this procedure. In labor cases, the temporary restraining order or the temporary injunction is usually the final stage of injunction proceedings. The injury that occurred to a labor union in an injunction proceeding cannot be measured in dollars and cents. Much of the damage inflicted on unions by the labor injunction is of an intangible character. No monetary value can be placed on items such as loss of potential or actual membership, loss of prestige, undermining of the union, and the like. In actual labor injunction cases, some courts did not even require the posting of bonds, or they set the amount of bonds at very low levels. In the light of these factors, "it [was] not surprising that the recovery on the bond in labor cases [was] almost unknown."[23] Through 1928, unions were awarded damages in only three cases. And these awards only compensated the unions for court costs and attorney fees, not for the damages they actually sustained.

❦ THE YELLOW-DOG CONTRACT AND THE LABOR INJUNCTION

Organized labor in 1917 felt the full impact of the labor injunction on the right to self-organization and collective bargaining. In that year, the Supreme Court of the United States handed down the celebrated *Hitchman* decision.[24] The Court held that the labor injunction could be employed to enforce the *yellow-dog contract*.[25] The yellow-dog contract was a device utilized by antiunion employers to stop the progress of the union movement. Its chief characteristic was the promise of a worker not to join a labor union while in the hire of an employer. A typical yellow-dog contract was involved in the *Hitchman* case:

> I am employed by and work for the Hitchman Coal & Coke Company with the express understanding that I am not a member of the United Mine Workers of America, and will not become so while an employee of the Hitchman Coal & Coke Company; that the Hitchman Coal & Coke Company is run non-union and agrees with me that it will run non-union while I am in its employ. If at any time I am employed by the Hitchman Coal & Coke Company I want to become connected with the United Mine Workers of America, or any affiliated organization, I agree to withdraw from the employment of said company, and agree that while I am in the employ of that company I will not make any efforts amongst its employees to bring about the unionizing of that mine against the company's wish. I have either read the above or heard the same read.[26]

The yellow-dog contract was first used in the 1870s by the stone manufacturers when combating the Molders' Union.[27] The Supreme Court in 1908[28] and in 1915[29] declared unconstitutional a federal and state statute designed to outlaw the use of these agreements. An analysis of this development is reserved for a later chapter.[30] However, the instrument did not come into widespread use until after the *Hitchman* decision. The yellow-dog contract was used mainly when unionization was attempting to gain a foothold. It is difficult to state to what degree the union movement was retarded by the utilization of the instrument. One may be safe in concluding, however, that when it was employed, the progress of unionization was seriously retarded. Though the device was used most extensively in the bituminous coal mines of West Virginia, Tennessee, and Kentucky, the yellow-dog agreement served to hinder the progress of collective bargaining and unionization in the coal, shoe, glass, full-fashioned hosiery, clothing, metal trades, and the commercial printing industries.

Some may wonder why workers signed such agreements. Perhaps some signed because they were opposed to collective bargaining in principle and preferred to work in a nonunion shop. Another possible reason was that such contracts were signed under the force of economic necessity. Workers with families to support and no other employment opportunities would be expected to execute the agreement. It was largely a question of "sign or starve."

Such circumstances throw a considerable amount of doubt on the Supreme Court's declaration that the workers involved in the *Hitchman* case "voluntarily made the agreement and desired to continue working under it." Was it actually true, notwithstanding the language of the Court, that the yellow-dog contracts won the "unanimous approval of [the] employees"? Were these individual contracts really signed "with the free assent" of the employees?

On the face of it, the Court was correct in the belief that the contracts were "voluntarily made," but a deeper penetration of the problem leads to a different conclusion. A contract does not appear to be "voluntarily made" when one of the parties has no actual liberty to refuse to execute the agreement. One would expect a more profound analysis of the problem from a court of equity. Justice Pitney, who delivered the majority decision of the court in the *Hitchman* decision, remarked in this very case that "a court of equity ... looks to the substance and essence of things and disregards matters of form and technical nicety." It appears that the Court failed to fulfill this worthwhile function when it concluded that the workers had actual liberty to refuse to sign the yellow-dog contract.

In the minority opinion, joined in by Justices Brandeis, Holmes, and Clarke, recognition was made of the realities of the proceedings. These men were aware that the inquiry of "the substance and essence of things" required a more practical view of the matter. In this respect the minority opinion, written by Brandeis, states: "If it is coercion to threaten to strike unless plaintiff consents to a closed union shop, it is coercion also to threaten not to give one employment unless the applicant will consent to a closed non-union shop. The employer may sign the union agreement for fear that labor may not be otherwise obtainable; the workman may sign the individual agreement for fear that employment may not be otherwise obtainable."

Additional economic circumstances surrounded the *Hitchman* case. In 1907, the United Mine Workers of America, the defendant in the *Hitchman* decision, was organizing the miners in the states of Pennsylvania, Maryland, Virginia, and West Virginia. The union had successfully organized the mines in the so-called Central Competitive Area, which included the states of Illinois, Indiana, Ohio, and western Pennsylvania. Labor standards in the Central Competitive Area, however, were threatened by the unorganized mines of the eastern states. Unionized mines could not be expected to compete with the nonunion mines where labor standards were lower. Owners of unorganized mines could afford to sell coal more cheaply on the market than could the operators of the organized mines. Thus, the United Mine Workers of America were vitally concerned with organizing the eastern mines and raising labor standards. The very existence of the union depended on organizing the nonunion mines. Either this would be accomplished or the union in effect would be required to go out of business. Stimulated by these pressing circumstances, the United Mine Workers Union began an intensive organizing campaign in West Virginia. The Supreme Court was aware of these economic factors when it declared in the *Hitchman* case that "the plain effect of this action was to approve a policy which, as applied to the case, meant that in order to relieve the union mines of Ohio, Indiana, and Illinois from the competition of the cheaper product of the nonunion mines of West Virginia, the West Virginia mines should be organized." Apparently, the high court was fully conscious of these economic circumstances; nevertheless, this knowledge did not control its decision.

The union knew of the yellow-dog contracts at the Hitchman mine in West Virginia. Nonetheless, a labor organizer induced many of the miners to agree to join the union. Both the majority and minority of the Court made much of the difference of the terms "to join actually" and "to agree to join." Actually, the organizer did not "join up" miners who had signed the yellow-dog agreement. He merely requested them to agree to join. After a miner agreed to join, his name was written into a book. The plan of the union was first to gain the support of a majority of the miners, and then to call a strike at these mines. At the time of the strike, the union probably would have issued union cards and the miners would then be actual members of the union. Brandeis argued in this connection that "there is evidence of an attempt to induce plaintiff's employees to *agree* to join the union; but none whatever of any attempt to induce them to violate their contract." The majority of the Court held that no practical difference existed between "agreeing to join" and "actually joining." In this respect, the Court was perfectly correct. Its shortcoming lay in the fact that it did not extend its "practical" view of things to the broader implications of the *Hitchman* case. When it served its purpose, the Court employed practical reasoning and looked to the "substance and essence of things"; but, at the point of decision, the Court abandoned this procedure and interpreted the facts and law of the case in a most narrow and technical fashion.

In reaching its decision, the Court held that the union attempted to "subvert the system of employment at the mine by coverted breaches of the contract of employment known to be in force there." The contract, reasoned the Court, was voluntarily made by the workers and the employer. The right to freedom of contract is a liberty enjoyed by all. This right, as "any other legal right," is entitled to protection. By inducing a breach of contract, the labor organization was interfering with the right to contract. Hence the Court was constrained to enjoin the organization from further interference with the right to contract. The injunction was a proper remedy, and consequently this instrument was to be employed to protect and make effective the yellow-dog contract. Such was the reasoning of the Court. Not only was the yellow-dog agreement legal, but the Supreme Court was prepared to implement it through the injunctive process. What this meant to collective bargaining and unionization was indeed profound. Faced with an organization campaign, the employer made the execution of the yellow-dog contract a condition of employment. In periods of less than full employment, workers would be economically coerced into the agreement. The employer then applied for an injunction restraining any person who might encourage workers to join a union. Any disobedience to the injunction was punishable as contempt of court.

The *Hitchman* decision was the low-water mark of the attitude of the Court toward collective bargaining and unionization. Not until 1932 was the effect of this decision eradicated. Its reversal came not by a change of attitude in the courts, but by action of the legislative branch of government. From 1917 until 1932, the courts were a potent force against attempts to unionize. Not content with the fact that the bargaining power between employers and employees was inherently unequal, the Supreme Court in the *Hitchman* decision made the balance even less equal. The *Hitchman* doctrine clearly demonstrated the hostility of the courts to collective bargaining. It served clear notice that the courts were available to restrict union efforts at organization.

SUMMARY

The injunction is issued by equity courts. Normally, it is an order that directs a person and (where pertinent) his or her associates to refrain from pursuing a certain course of action. The application of the injunction to labor disputes stifled the growth and effective operation of unions. Through the injunction, the courts denied to workers the opportunity to resort to collective action to improve their economic lot. In the *Debs* case, the Supreme Court upheld the constitutionality of the labor injunction. The result was the widespread use of the instrument in labor disputes. Many union activities necessary for the effective operation of unionism were restrained by the courts. The judiciary served well the interests of the antiunion employer. The effects of the labor injunction on unionism were varied. However, organized labor felt the full impact of the labor injunction when the Supreme Court held that the instrument could be utilized to enforce the yellow-dog contract. The indiscriminate use of the injunction in labor disputes occurred along with the rapid progress of American industrialism. The courts via the injunction slowed down the drive toward collective action until society reacted to limit the legislative character of the courts.

DISCUSSION QUESTIONS

1. What is meant by a labor injunction? Explain how it was introduced in the United States.
2. Describe the various forms and procedures of injunctions.

3. What was the primary significance of the *Debs* case?
4. In what way did the concept of property affect issuance of injunctions?
5. Five abuses of injunctions have been identified. Discuss each type of abuse thoroughly.
6. Why did the courts approve of yellow-dog contracts? How could they have been important to employers?

🕿 NOTES

[1] 47 Stat. 70 (1932).
[2] Edwin E. Witte, *The Government in Labor Disputes* (New York: McGraw-Hill Book Company, 1932), p. 234.
[3] *Ibid.*, p. 92.
[4] *In re Debs*, Petitioner, 158 U.S. 564 (1895).
[5] The Constitution of the United States, Article I, Section 8, provides the federal government with the power "to regulate commerce ... among the several states....."
[6] Witte, *op. cit.*, p. 84. The use of the labor injunction was first noted in the 1880s. However, its utilization became widespread after the constitutional question was settled.
[7] *National Labor Relations Act of 1949, Senate Report to Accompany S. 249*, 81st Congress, 1st sess., p. 8; National Labor Relations Board, *Annual Reports*, 1949–1966.
[8] See J. P. Frey, *The Labor Injunction* (Cincinnati: Equity Publishing Company, 1927). Also Witte, *op. cit.*, pp. 105–106.
[9] The injunction was first used in labor disputes in England in 1868. Since that time, its application to labor disputes has been very infrequent there. One reason for this is the more restricted meaning attached to the property concept in England. In this connection, see Charles O. Gregory, *Labor and the Law* (New York: W. W. Norton & Company, 1946), p. 97.
[10] The Supreme Court in the *Debs* case sustained an injunction the terms of which forbade "all other persons whomsoever" from encouraging the strike.
[11] *Gompers v. Bucks Stove and Range Company*, 221 U.S. 418 (1911). This case is discussed in more detail in Chapter 3.
[12] Felix Frankfurter and Nathan Greene collaborated to bring out the definitive study dealing with the abuses of the labor injunction. It is called *The Labor Injunction* (New York: The Macmillan Company, 1930). At the time the book was written, Frankfurter was a professor of law at Harvard University. President Roosevelt subsequently appointed him to the Supreme Court of the United States. Undoubtedly, *The Labor Injunction* was a powerful force making for the enactment of labor injunction control legislation.
[13] Felix Frankfurter and Nathan Greene, "The Labor Injunction," *Encyclopedia of the Social Sciences*, VIII, p. 654.

[14] Frankfurter and Greene, *op. cit.*, p. 64, Appendix 1.

[15] P. F. Brissenden and C. O. Swayzee, "The Use of Injunctions in the New York Needle Trades," *Political Science Quarterly*, XLIV (1929), pp. 548, 563.

[16] Witte, *op. cit.*, p. 90.

[17] *Ibid.*, p. 90.

[18] *Encyclopedia of the Social Sciences, op cit.*, p. 655.

[19] *Ibid.*, p. 654.

[20] *Great Northern Railway Company* v. *Brosseau*, 286 Fed. 416 (1923).

[21] Justice McReynolds in *Sinclair* v. *U.S.*, 279 U.S. 749 (1929).

[22] *Long* v. *Bricklayers' Union*, 17 Pa. Dist. R. 984 (1929).

[23] Witte, *op. cit.*, p. 91.

[24] *Hitchman Coal Company* v. *Mitchell*, 245 U.S. 229 (1917).

[25] For a general treatment of the yellow-dog contract, see Joel Seidman, *The Yellow-Dog Contract* (Baltimore: Johns Hopkins Press, 1932).

[26] *Hitchman Coal Company* v. *Mitchell, op. cit.*

[27] Harry A. Millis and Royal E. Montgomery, *Organized Labor* (New York: McGraw-Hill Book Company, 1945), p. 511.

[28] *Adair* v. *U.S.*, 208 U.S. 161 (1908).

[29] *Coppage* v. *Kansas*, 236 U.S. 1 (1915).

[30] See Chapter 7.

CHAPTER THREE

UNIONS UNDER ANTITRUST STATUTES

During the first thirty years of the twentieth century, industry became the dominant feature of American economic life. By 1930, nonagricultural occupations accounted for about 80 percent of the labor force. The number of workers attached to manufacturing increased over the thirty-year period from about 4.5 million to more than 8 million. In 1900, the total value of goods produced by industry was $11 billion. By 1930, the figure had increased to $70 billion. The nation was business-oriented. Many believed that business, if left alone, would insure steady employment, an increased standard of living, and in general, a better life. Calvin Coolidge once remarked that "the business of the United States is business."[1] Few would deny that the current American position of world industrial leadership largely reflects the emphasis that public policy has traditionally placed on encouraging and strengthening competition.[2] The problem for debate—at the turn of the century as now—was how best to encourage and strengthen competition.

The early part of the twentieth century was an era of declining competition and increasing concentration of control of American industry. As markets became more fully exploited, business leaders rapidly saw the advantages of cooperation over competition. The result was the establishment of price agreements, trusts, pools, and trade associations. Each and every one of these devices was fashioned to stamp out

35

competition between rivals. When the economic environment permitted, the business community renounced rigid competition as the regulator of industrial life for the greater certainty of cooperative control by the few. The elimination of competition meant the growth of huge and powerful corporations more capable of plotting their own destinies without the interdependencies occasioned by competition among many small firms.

The situation can thus be described:

> Throughout the twentieth century the limitations upon economic opportunity and the concentration of economic power have increased rapidly in the United States. Economic individualism and personal freedom have declined. The language of free competition remains, but free competition has been circumscribed. Orthodox economics still speaks of *laissez faire*, but business itself has restricted the mechanism through which the principles of *laissez faire* can operate.[3]

The dominance of big business in American life did not go unnoticed. By the latter part of the nineteenth century, the public became somewhat concerned over the concentration of ownership into fewer hands. Business groups had formed huge trusts and combinations, the purpose of which was to monopolize the production and sale of vital products. Combinations operated in basic industries such as oil, sugar, tobacco, whiskey, and shoemaking machinery. The goal of the combinations was to eliminate competition. Once competition was stifled, it was a relatively simple matter to establish price levels that would maximize profit. To realize this objective, combinations regulated the rate of output, established market territories, imposed penalties on violators of combination policy, and eliminated outside sources of competition. Congress enacted the Sherman Antitrust Act in 1890 to eliminate monopolistic control of the nation's economy.[4] Predatory monopolistic practices endangered the traditional character of American economic life. Hence the law reflected the faith of the nation in free competition. It suggested that the American system of free enterprise did not exist for a few industrial giants. Rather, an economic system was to be maintained in which the small producer was to have an opportunity to enter into the economic affairs of the nation. The Sherman Act was based on the belief that competition, and not monopoly, advanced the interests of the nation.

❦ APPLICATION OF SHERMAN ACT TO LABOR UNIONS

Whatever the effect of the antitrust laws on the business structure, the fact remains that their operation retarded the development of trade unionism. After the passage of the Sherman Act, labor unions felt its impact on many occasions. Unions were to learn that the law limited a variety of vital union activities. The prosecution of labor unions under the antitrust provisions stimulated controversy, centering on the fact that Congress made no specific reference to labor unions in the Sherman Act. Sections 1 and 2 of the law state:

> Every contract, combination, ... or conspiracy, in restraint of trade or commerce among the several States, ... is ... illegal ... every person who shall monopolize, or attempt to monopolize, or combine or conspire with any other person or persons, to monopolize any part of the trade or commerce among the several States ... shall be guilty of a misdemeanor.[4]

Central to the controversy was the fact that the two key sections did not specifically exclude unions. The question of importance was whether the words "combination" or "person" referred to unions as well as to business enterprises. Did Congress, by not mentioning unions, intend by omission that unions were to be excluded from the operation of the statute? Much has been written on this controversy. One representative study concluded that the intent of Congress was to exclude unions from the scope of the statute.[5] On the other hand, another study supported the opposite point of view.[6] Examination here on the intent of Congress would be of little practical value. The controversy was eventually resolved by the Supreme Court of the United States. It would be a barren academic exercise to inquire whether or not the Court was correct in holding labor unions subject to the Sherman Act. The fact is that the Court for many years applied the Sherman Act to unions. It is of greater importance to examine the manner in which the antitrust laws affected labor unions. What economic circumstances were involved in the application of the Sherman law to labor union cases? What labor union activities were restrained by action of the high court? How did the application of the Sherman law to labor organizations affect the development of the union movement?

SHERMAN ACT PENALTIES

Before considering these problems, however, it is necessary to spell out the penalties provided for in the Sherman Act. Congress provided adequately for the enforcement of the law. The penalties were to apply equally to labor unions and to business enterprises convicted under the statute. The statute provides for three methods of enforcement. First, violators are guilty of a misdemeanor. Thus, the courts may punish violators on conviction of the statute "by fine not exceeding five thousand dollars, or by imprisonment not exceeding one year, or by both."[7] Second, the Sherman law empowers the district attorneys of the United States "to institute proceedings in equity to prevent and restrain such violations."

This means that the federal government may enforce the law by the injunction process. Finally, the law provides for damage suits against violators. Section 7 of the law states that "any person who shall be injured in his business or property by any other person or corporation, by reason of anything forbidden or declared to be unlawful by this Act, may sue therefor in any circuit court of the United States ... and shall recover threefold the damages by him sustained, and the costs of the suit, including a reasonable attorney's fee." It is noteworthy that Section 7 provides for damages that are three times the actual damage caused by the violation. Such a provision could serve as a deterrent to anyone aware of the possibility of such a judgment.

EARLIEST UNION CONVICTION UNDER ANTITRUST STATUTES

Prosecution of labor unions under the Sherman Act started shortly after its enactment. In 1893, a federal court in Louisiana applied the antitrust statute to labor unions for the first time.[8] A group of unions in New Orleans engaged in a sympathetic strike, the purpose of which was to further the position of a drayers union's strike. The lower court declared that one of the results of the strike was "the forced stagnation of commerce that flowed through New Orleans." It was held that the action of the workers restrained trade within the meaning of the Sherman Act. In handing down its decision, the court brushed aside the contention that unions were excluded from the terms of the antitrust law. On this score, the court held that although the statute had its origin in the "evils of massed capital," the intent of Congress was to "include combinations of labor, as well as capital: in fact, all combinations in restraint of commerce, without reference to the character of the persons who entered into them." The court issued an injunction that forbade further strike action. It is noteworthy that the injunction was the procedure utilized to enforce the Sherman Act in the first instance wherein the statute was applied to labor unions.

More commonly, the Sherman Act in 1893–1894 was applied to a series of strikes involving the railroad industry.[9] In one of these early cases, a federal district court suggested that any railroad strike was a violation of the Sherman Act. The court declared that

> in any conceivable strike upon the transportation lines of this country, whether main lines or branch lines or branch roads, there will be interference with and restraint of interstate or foreign commerce. This will be true also of strikes upon telegraph lines, for the exchange of telegraphic messages between people of different states is interstate commerce. In the presence of these statutes ... it will be practically impossible hereafter for a body of men to combine to hinder and delay the work of the transportation company without becoming amenable to the provision of these statutes.[10]

This was a very important judicial observation. If every railroad strike restrained trade within the meaning of the Sherman Act, railroad employees could not engage in a lawful strike. The district judge referred to all strikes. He did not distinguish between those conducted peacefully and those carried out violently. There was no inquiry into the purpose of the strike. If this doctrine had been established in law, it would have profoundly affected the character of industrial relations and collective bargaining in the railroad industry, and quite possibly in industry in general.

IN RE DEBS

The *In re Debs* case in 1895 provided the Supreme Court the opportunity to decide the applicability of the Sherman law to railroad strikes.[11] The high court upheld an injunction restraining the Pullman strike. However, the Court did not rule on the applicability of the Sherman Act to labor disputes. Before the Supreme Court reviewed the *Debs* case, some circuit courts of appeal had approved injunctions in the Pullman strike, basing their action mainly on the Sherman law. For example, one court declared that "on July 2, 1890, Congress enacted a law that enlarged the jurisdiction of the federal courts and authorized them to apply the restraining power of the law for the purpose of checking and arresting all lawless interference with ... the peaceful and orderly conduct of railroad business between the States."[12] Another court held that "it may be conceded that the controlling, objective point, in the mind of Congress, in enacting this statute, was to suppress what are known as 'trusts' and 'monopolies.' But, like a great many other enactments, the statute is made so comprehensive and far-reaching in its express terms as to extend to like incidents and acts clearly within the expression and spirit of the law."[13]

When the *Debs* case finally reached the attention of the Supreme Court, the injunction was sustained, as noted, but the Court based its action on the power of the federal government to regulate and promote interstate commerce. In this respect, the Supreme Court declared: "We enter into no examination of the act of July 2, 1890 [Sherman Antitrust Act], upon which the Circuit Court relied mainly to sustain its jurisdiction. It must not be understood from this that we dissent from the conclusions of that court in reference to the scope of that act, but simply that we prefer to rest our judgment on the broader ground."[14] A railroad strike of the Pullman variety, which involved a great deal of violence, was unlawful with or without the Sherman law. The Supreme Court upheld the injunction on the powers of the federal government to regulate interstate commerce, and not on the basis of the Sherman Act.

ECONOMIC ISSUES IN DANBURY HATTERS DOCTRINE

Labor unions may have drawn some comfort from the *Debs* case on the ground that the Supreme Court did not specifically hold the Sherman law applicable to labor unions. Thirteen years later, however, organized labor suffered a severe legal defeat in an antitrust case. In 1908, the Supreme Court of the United States decided the famous *Danbury Hatters* case,[15] and held that the Sherman law applied to labor unions. To the present time, the *Danbury Hatters* case remains a landmark in the law of collective bargaining.

The United Hatters of North America, the labor organization involved, claimed in 1908 a membership of about 9,000. The union was affiliated with the American Federation of Labor. In those days, the AFL possessed a total membership of approximately 1,400,000. The United Hatters in the early 1900s was in the process of organizing the felt hat industry. Out of the 82 firms manufacturing hats, the union had successfully organized 70. In the organized firms, management recognized the union as the bargaining agent of the workers. Wages, hours, and other conditions of employment were determined through collective bargaining.

Collective bargaining did not operate in the nonunion shops. Conditions of work there were not subject to negotiation. As a result, labor standards in the nonunion shops were presumably lower than those in the organized firms. These circumstances provided a distinct competitive advantage to the nonunion firms. Operating with nonunion labor, employers could sell hats more cheaply than those marketed by organized firms, since the unorganized firms had greater flexibility in adjusting wage costs. The organized firms were not capable of withstanding the competition of the more viable nonunion firms for any prolonged length of time. The United Hatters recognized the necessity of organizing the nonunion plants in order to place the burden of competition on other variables than wages. Labor standards in the unionized firms were threatened to the extent that the national union was in danger of disintegration. Survival for the union meant the standardization of employment conditions throughout the entire industry. Such an objective could not be attained short of the organization of each firm in the hat industry. The competitive advantages enjoyed by the nonunion firms, based on lower labor standards, could be erased only by expanding the collective bargaining process to the entire hat industry.

In 1902, the United Hatters undertook the task of organizing Loewe & Company, located in Danbury, Connecticut. The union requested that the company recognize it as the bargaining representative of its employees. Union officials further requested that only union members be permitted to work in the firm. The company refused the demands of the union. As a result, the union called 250 workers out on strike. The organizational strike fell short of its objective since the number of strikers constituted only a minor percentage of the entire workforce. In addition, the company found replacements for the striking workers and was able to operate successfully. The organizational strike alone was not enough to achieve the union goal.

Faced with such circumstances, the United Hatters resorted to indirect economic pressure. It instituted a nationwide boycott against the products of Loewe & Company. Through widespread publicity, the union induced retailers not to handle the firm's hats. Similar pressure was placed on wholesalers. In addition, the general public was requested not to purchase any item from retailers or wholesalers handling Loewe's products. Under such pressures, many retailers and wholesalers ceased doing business with the company. Eventually the cooperation of the American Federation of Labor was attained. The AFL promoted the boycott by giving it wide publicity in leaflets, labor papers, and the daily press. Labor organizers toured the nation inducing unionists and dealers not to purchase Loewe's hats. The boycott was very successful. In one year, the company claimed a loss of $85,000.

In the summer of 1903, the company sued the United Hatters and its members for damages under the Sherman law. After a circuit court of appeals found the union not in violation of the statute, the company appealed the case to the Supreme Court of the United States. On February 3, 1908, the Court handed down its decision. It held that the United Hatters and its members had violated the Sherman law. The boycott implemented by the union had the effect of restraining trade within the meaning of the Sherman law. On this score the Supreme Court declared:

> The combination described in the declaration is a combination "in restraint of trade or commerce among the several states" in the sense in which those words are used in the act ... and [this] conclusion rests on many judgments of this court, to the effect that the act prohibits any combination whatever to secure action which essentially obstructs the free flow of commerce between the States, or restricts in that regard, the liberty of a trader to engage in business.

The *Danbury Hatters* doctrine resulted in increased prosecution of labor unions under the Sherman law. Now that the Supreme Court held the law applicable to labor unions, a new weapon was available to combat trade unionism.

In addition, the doctrine established the principle that individual union members were responsible for the actions of their officers. On January 5, 1915, approximately seven years later, the Supreme Court sustained a judgment of $252,000 against the United Hatters and its members. Justice Holmes, who wrote the opinion for the Court, declared that since "members paid their dues and continued to delegate authority to their officers unlawfully to interfere with the plaintiffs' interstate commerce in such circumstances that they knew or ought to have known, and such officers were in the belief that they were acting in the matters within their delegated authority, then such members were jointly liable."[16] The practical significance of the 1915 decision was that rank-and-file members as well as the union and its officers had been held liable for the payment of the judgment. It is noteworthy that the Taft-Hartley Act, enacted in 1947, though providing for a variety of ways in which labor organizations can be sued for damages, provides that damages can be recovered only from the assets of the unions and not from union members.

The *Danbury Hatters* doctrine also outlawed secondary boycott activity. A *secondary boycott* may be defined as the pressure placed on one business unit to force the firm to cease doing business with another business enterprise. It will be recalled that the United Hatters exerted pressure on the retailers and wholesalers to force them to cease trading with Loewe & Company. This action of the United Hatters fell within the secondary boycott category. The outlawing of secondary boycott action of unions resulted in a decline of effectiveness of the collective bargaining process. A broad and effective mode of economic action was no longer legally available to labor organizations. The struggle for recognition in the *Danbury Hatters* case demonstrated that the resort to the secondary boycott could have been the only alternative to the extinction of the union and of collective bargaining throughout the industry. The Supreme Court, however, was not persuaded by the economic circumstances that stimulated the action of the United Hatters. It was not sensitive to the fact that the boycott was instigated as a last resort in an effort to establish a bargaining relationship with the United Hatters. Essentially, the high court was of the opinion that "the liberty of a trader to engage in business" was equal to the liberty of workers to move to other economic endeavors to improve their standard of life if a particular pursuit was deemed unsatisfactory.

💥 LABOR MOVEMENT AND POLITICAL ACTION

Organized labor vigorously condemned the *Danbury Hatters* doctrine. It was denounced in labor papers, leaflets, and at labor gatherings. Union leaders missed no opportunity to protest against the action of the Supreme Court. They objected to prosecution of organized labor under a statute that they considered had been enacted to curtail business monopolies. Organized labor did more than merely denounce the *Danbury Hatters* doctrine. They resolved to change it. They were unsuccessful in attempts to obtain Supreme Court opinions favorable to the collective bargaining process. Supreme Court justices hold life tenure, and as a consequence were relatively insulated from whatever political pressures unions could bring to bear. Unions became aware that political action to influence elective officials was the only effective weapon at their disposal. If the

CHAPTER THREE

Supreme Court held labor unions subject to the Sherman law, the proper course of action was to try to change the law to preclude prosecution of labor unions under the antitrust statute. This, of course, put unions into the political arena.

The American Federation of Labor became involved in politics at the beginning of the twentieth century. Legislation designed to promote a more favorable legal environment for collective bargaining was introduced regularly at sessions of Congress and state legislatures. Later discussion, however, will reveal that the courts nullified state laws favorable to organized labor.[17] On the federal level, it was reported that

> the labor bills were passed by the House of Representatives at several sessions of Congress, but invariably failed in the Senate. About 1904, owing to the activity of the National Association of Manufacturers and related organizations, labor influence was decreased in the House. The Federation resolved that it could no longer remain a purely economic organization. It was obliged to seek influence in elections.[18]

THE *GOMPERS* DECISION

After the *Danbury Hatters* decision, handed down in 1908, union efforts to influence elections were intensified. Reportedly, "in 1908 the method of 'questioning' was applied to the candidates of the two great parties, and the Democratic party was endorsed. At the elections of 1910 and 1912 the Democrats were again endorsed."[19] Stimulated to political activity by the Supreme Court's construction of the Sherman law, the labor movement in 1911 was further motivated to intensify its efforts. In that year, the Supreme Court handed down the famous *Gompers* decision.[20] The Bucks Stove and Range Company refused to bargain or to recognize the Molders & Foundry Workers Union of North America, an affiliate of the American Federation of Labor. As a result, the AFL placed the name of the company in the "We Don't Patronize" list of its publication, the *American Federationist*. The effect of the advertisement was to decrease the sales of the company's stoves. In addition, retail stores that handled Bucks' stoves were boycotted, and some retailers, to protect their own interests, refused to do business with the stove company. An injunction was obtained by the company against the officers of the AFL. Samuel Gompers, founder and first president of the AFL, along with the Federation, violated the injunction. The *American Federationist* continued to carry the company's name in the "We Don't Patronize" list.

For disobedience to the injunction, Gompers and two other AFL officers were sentenced to jail for terms ranging from six months to one year. The case was appealed to the Supreme Court. On purely technical grounds, the contempt charges against the union officials were dismissed. But the Supreme Court held that a boycott promoted by words and printed matter violated the Sherman Antitrust Act. The fact that the AFL spread the boycott by the exercise of speech and the use of printed matter did not make the action of the union officers any less unlawful. In this connection, the Court declared:

> The court's protective and restraining powers extend to every device whereby property is irreparably damaged or commerce is illegally restrained. To hold that the restraint of trade under the Sherman Anti-Trust Act ... could be enjoined but that the means through which the restraint was accomplished could not be enjoined, would be to render the law impotent.

The Supreme Court of the United States relegated the constitutional guarantee of free speech and press to a secondary right in labor cases involving the Sherman law. A boycott restraining trade within the meaning of the Sherman law was unlawful, and trade unionists who promoted such a boycott by either spoken or written words violated the Sherman law. They could not plead immunity on the ground that the exercise of free speech and press is protected by the Constitution of the United States.

The *Gompers* decision pushed unions toward greater efforts to influence election results. Unions intensified their political activities. In the congressional elections of 1908 and 1910, the unions managed to influence the election of some candidates who pledged their support to organized labor. In 1912, organized labor pledged its support to Woodrow Wilson for the presidency on the basis of campaign pledges approved by the AFL. In that year, Woodrow Wilson was elected President, and the Democratic party showed majorities in both houses of Congress. For the first time in twenty years, the Democratic party controlled the executive and legislative branches of the national government. The Democratic party acted swiftly to fulfill its obligations to organized labor. In October 1914, the Clayton Act became law.[21] Organized labor thought the Act was calculated to provide unions relief from the Sherman Antitrust Act. In the following section, the provisions of the Clayton Act that were applicable to labor organizations will be discussed, along with an assessment of the political intent of the Congress and President Wilson regarding the Clayton Act amendments to the Sherman Act.

❦ CLAYTON ACT: LABOR'S "MAGNA CHARTA" OR ENIGMA?

The celebrated Section 6 of the Clayton Act dealt with the application of antitrust statutes to labor unions. It provided the following modifications of the Sherman Act:

That the labor of a human being is not a commodity or article of commerce. Nothing contained in the anti-trust laws shall be construed to forbid the existence and operation of labor, agricultural, or horticultural organizations, instituted for the purpose of mutual help, and not having capital stock or conducted for profit, or to forbid or restrain individual members of such organizations, from lawfully carrying out the legitimate objects thereof; nor shall such organizations, or the members thereof, be held or construed to be illegal combinations or conspiracies in restraint of trade, under the anti-trust laws.

Labor leaders drew great comfort from Section 6. It stated that "the labor of a human being is not a commodity or article of commerce." It provided that "nothing contained in the anti-trust laws shall be construed to forbid the existence and operation of labor organizations." In addition, Section 6 proclaimed that labor organizations and their members shall not be held to be "illegal combinations or conspiracies in restraint of trade, under the anti-trust laws." There was a great celebration in the ranks of organized labor. Unionists felt that the courts no longer could apply the antitrust laws to labor unions. Samuel Gompers, president of the American Federation of Labor, jubilantly declared that Section 6 was labor's "Industrial Magna Charta upon which the working people will rear their construction of industrial freedom."[22]

Close consideration of Section 6 makes one wonder why labor leaders felt so jubilant about the Clayton Act. It is doubtful that President Wilson ever intended to exempt labor or any other group from the Sherman Act. He may have intended, during the campaign, to support government impartiality in labor disputes, but changed his mind after the election. One writer has argued that labor obtained minor gains during the early days of the administration, such as the Sundry Civil Appropriation Bill, which prevented the Justice Department from using appropriated funds for prosecuting labor violations under the Sherman Act.[23] However, such surface gains proved meaningless in reality since, for example, there was no law to keep the Justice Department from using other funds to prosecute unions. By 1913, the President was attempting to end the animosity between his administration and the business community, which had developed during the 1912 campaign. At the same time he wanted to strengthen the antitrust provisions of the Sherman law in order to foster greater competition in the economy. The President was not to be deterred from his drive to obtain stronger laws against business monopolies. At the same time, labor unions could not be ignored in the drive for better control over monopolies.[24] The political realities in the Congress would not have permitted both a stronger monopoly control law and a total exemption of unions from the antitrust provisions. Section 6 of the Clayton Act had the approval of organized labor when it was first introduced in the House, but union leaders later decided that the provision was not what they desired and sought amendment. There was no further support from the President, since he considered that the campaign pledges made to labor had been fulfilled. Indeed, the President and leaders of the House resisted union pressures for outright exemption from the Sherman law.[25]

Labor pressures in the House led to an attachment to Section 6 that stated:

> Nor shall such organizations, or the members thereof, be held or construed to be illegal combinations or conspiracies in restraint of trade, under the anti-trust laws.

Some of the House leaders, along with organized labor, interpreted this amendment to mean union exclusion from the provisions of antitrust laws. It is probable that the "Magna Charta" statement of Gompers stemmed from this construction. However, this interpretation was not accepted by President Wilson or the Committee on the Judiciary.[26] No general agreement was reached in the House on either the labor exemption controversy or the meaning of the injunction section. The President, along with the House and Senate, agreed that Section 6 did grant unions the right to exist, but Congress could not agree upon the interpretation of either Section 6, the exemption of labor from antitrust prosecution, or Section 20, the controversy over the power of the courts to issue injunctions. Therefore, "to him [Wilson] must go much of the responsibility for the failure of the Clayton Act to satisfy labor's demands."[27]

Organized labor wanted complete exemption from the antitrust laws. This could have been accomplished by a very simple provision: "Nothing contained in the antitrust laws shall be construed to apply to labor organizations." But Congress and the President did not intend to exempt unions from the antitrust laws, and the proposal was rejected. If that had been its intention, Congress would have adopted the proposal. Instead, a relatively meaningless provision was enacted. Indeed, the President was convinced that the Clayton Act merely granted unions the legal right to exist. Some of the early testimony of Gompers before Congress indicated that winning such a right was his major objective. In the *Danbury Hatters* and *Gompers* decisions, the Supreme Court did not hold unions subject to the antitrust laws because labor was considered a commodity or an article of commerce. Unions were held to have restrained trade within the meaning of the Sherman Act because their boycott activities interfered with the interstate shipment of hats and stoves. The first sentence of Section 6 therefore did not change labor law. It was an empty phrase devoid of practical importance. Additional statements in Section 6 likewise should have made organized labor suspicious of the Clayton Act. Courts since 1842 held labor unions in themselves to be lawful organizations. In antitrust cases, the Supreme Court did not deny that employees had the right to form labor unions. As a consequence, the statements "nothing contained in the antitrust laws shall be construed to forbid the existence and operation of labor organizations" and "nor shall such organizations or the members thereof, be held or construed to be illegal combinations or conspiracies in restraint of trade, under the antitrust laws" added nothing new to labor law. Labor unions were lawful organizations before the passage of the Sherman law, and they were lawful organizations after the Sherman Antitrust Act was passed. Add to these phrases the statement that unions may "lawfully carry out the legitimate aspects thereof," and Section 6 appears worthless as a protective measure to labor unions. Who but the courts was to spell out when unions were lawfully carrying out their legitimate objectives? That was the crux of the problem in the Sherman Act antitrust cases. The Supreme Court declared that the implementation of a boycott by a labor union did not constitute a lawful activity under the Sherman law. All Section 6 did in this respect was to affirm the right of the courts to decide the questions of lawful and unlawful union activities and objectives.

Not only was the Clayton Act to prove worthless to labor unions, but their position was made much worse by the measure. Under the Sherman law, only the government could obtain an injunction for the enforcement of that law. Employers had no right to obtain an injunction against a union on the ground of violation of the antitrust statute. They could sue unions for treble damages, but employers were not permitted to obtain injunctions under the 1890 law. The Clayton Act changed these circumstances. It provided that private parties as well as law-enforcement officers of the federal government could obtain injunctions in antitrust cases. This meant that the ability of employers to obtain injunctions against unions was considerably increased. If the government was not inclined to proceed against unions in injunction proceedings under the antitrust laws, employers after 1914 could petition the courts for injunctions themselves. Subsequently, unions were required to contest numerous antitrust injunction suits originating from employer action. One writer stated:

> Of a total of 64 proceedings of all kinds brought against labor under the Sherman Act after the passage of the Clayton Act, 34, or more than one-half, were private injunction suits. The law may thus be said to have more than doubled the chances that labor activities would be hampered by the Sherman Act. This is indeed a curious, though probably the most important consequence of a law which labor greeted as its great charter of industrial freedom.[28]

Actually, the changes of 1914 proved an enigma to organized labor.

❦ RULE OF REASON: DEVELOPMENT OF A DOUBLE STANDARD

The major purpose for the enactment of the Sherman Act was to deal with growing business monopolies. It will be recalled that labor unions were not excluded from the provisions of the antitrust laws despite the confusion that stemmed from the legislative history of both laws. It remained for the Supreme Court to construe the degree to which the laws would be applied to both business and labor cases. The *rule-of-reason doctrine* was established and applied in business cases, but ignored in nearly all labor cases. This prompted Justice Brandeis in a 1927 case to imply that a double standard had been developed between business and labor.[29] This section deals with the development of the double standard by focusing on the major business and labor cases that clearly point out the double treatment under the law.

RULE OF REASON: APPLICATION TO BUSINESS

In one of the first business cases arising under the Sherman law,[30] the Supreme Court served notice that the antitrust laws were not to prevent the growth of big business. The American Sugar Refining Company purchased the stock of independent refineries, and as a result, controlled 98 percent of all cane sugar refining capacity of the country. The Court held that the control of an industry gained by the purchase of stock did not restrain interstate commerce within the meaning of the Sherman law. In 1904, however, the Court ordered the dissolution of a railroad monopoly created through the purchase of stock.[31] A combination of two independent railroads was effected through stock acquisition manipulations. The Northern Securities Company, a holding company formed to effect the transaction, gained control of the Northern Pacific Railway and the Great Northern Railway. The roads had been competing with parallel lines, that served the northwestern states from St. Paul and Duluth to Seattle and Portland. In ordering the combination to dissolve, the Supreme Court held that the effect and purpose of the monopoly suppressed competition and restrained trade within the meaning of the antitrust law.

Those who supported the underlying philosophy of the Sherman law were pleased with the *Northern Securities Company* decision. They believed that the Supreme Court intended to interpret the antitrust statutes in a manner that would cut down industrial giants. The Supreme Court did not maintain a hard line, however, for in 1911, it established the celebrated rule-of-reason doctrine in the *Standard Oil* and *American Tobacco* decisions.[32] In those cases, the Supreme Court distinguished between "reasonable" and "unreasonable" restraint of trade. Combinations that reasonably restrained commerce were not unlawful under the Sherman

Act. Only those that unreasonably restrained trade were unlawful. Not *every* combination that suppressed competition was to be dissolved, but only those that unreasonably stamped out competition.

By introducing the rule-of-reason doctrine into the construction of the Sherman law, the Supreme Court precluded any possible objective interpretation of the statute. The terms *reasonable* and *unreasonable* admit no precise definition. Obviously, the construction to be placed on the terms could vary with different persons. What may be reasonable to one individual may be unreasonable to another. In the *Standard Oil* and *American Tobacco* cases, the Supreme Court did rule that the monopolies unreasonably restrained commerce. The Standard Oil Company in the early 1900s refined between 85 to 90 percent of the country's oil.[33] On its part, the American Tobacco Company controlled, at the time of the case, about 97 percent of the production of domestic cigarettes and had a monopoly over most of the supply of other tobacco items, such as cigars, smoking tobacco, and snuff.[34]

The application of the rule of reason in subsequent antitrust cases, however, brought different results. In a case involving the United States Steel Corporation, the Supreme Court did not find a violation of the Sherman law.[35] Prosecution of the company was sought on the basis of monopolization under Section 2, not restraint of trade under Section 1. The decision was reached not to prosecute, despite the fact that the steel corporation had been organized as a holding company in 1901 for the purpose of acquiring the stock of independent operating companies. By 1920, the corporation controlled at least 50 percent of steel production in the nation. In addition, "from 1901 to 1911, when the government proceedings were instituted, there had been no price competition in the steel industry."[36] It was reported that "every stage in the production of iron and steel from the mining of ore and the manufacture of coke to the production of pig iron, as well as the manufacture of rails, bars, plates, sheets, tubes, rods, and other finished products, are under the control of the holding company."[37] Despite the facts presented, the Supreme Court ruled that the United States Steel Corporation was not in violation of the antitrust law. This was quite a contrast to the *Northern Securities* case.

In 1913, the Court likewise refused to apply the Sherman law to a shoe machinery combination.[38] The United Shoe Machinery Company, the defendant in the case, produced about 90 to 95 percent of all shoe machinery used in the nation. Four independent companies were united into one combination by the corporation. Promoters of the combination openly avowed their intent to control the entire production of shoe machinery equipment. This combination discouraged its customers' use of any machine not controlled by the United Shoe Machinery Company. On the one occasion when the combination was threatened with competition, the assets of the would-be competitor were bought up by the combination.[39] Faced with this situation, the Supreme Court held that the combination merely effected a reasonable restraint of trade.

By now it appeared that the Supreme Court construed the term "reasonable" in a very broad manner. In addition, the Supreme Court, in a series of decisions, held that price and production control effected by trade associations did not violate the antitrust statute.[40] In this connection the Court declared:

> Persons who unite in gathering and disseminating information in trade journals and statistical reports on industry, who gather and publish statistics as to the amount of production of commodities in interstate commerce, and who report market prices, are not engaged in unlawful conspiracies or restraint of trade merely because the ultimate result of their efforts may be to stabilize prices or limit production.[41]

Thus the rule of reason protected trade associations, even though the net result of their activities resulted in artificial control of prices and production. After 1927, the application of the rule of reason in business cases was varied. The Court tended to rule illegal such activities as price fixing, market allocations, and the like without regard to the reasonable or unreasonable effect doctrine.

RULE OF REASON: APPLICATION TO LABOR ORGANIZATIONS

Neither the passage of the Clayton Act nor the development of the rule-of-reason doctrine in business antitrust cases alleviated the position of labor unions under the Sherman law. In 1921 the Supreme Court of the United States had its first opportunity to deal with the application of the antitrust law to labor unions following enactment of the Clayton Act and the establishment of the rule-of-reason doctrine.[42] The Court decided the case squarely on the precedent of the *Danbury Hatters* and *Gompers* decisions. Labor's so-called Magna Charta pronouncement and the rule of reason did not influence the Court in its interpretation of congressional intent to apply the Sherman law to organized labor.

The 1921 case involved the International Association of Machinists, then an affiliate of the American Federation of Labor, and the Duplex Printing Press Company of Battle Creek, Michigan. At that time, there were only three other companies manufacturing printing presses in the United States. All four firms were in active competition with each other. From 1909 until 1913, the machinists' union was successful in organizing all the firms with the exception of the Duplex Company. In the shops in which the union had won recognition, employers recognized the eight-hour day, established a minimum-wage scale, and generally complied with other employment practices demanded by the union. On the other hand, the

Chapter Three   51

Duplex Company, which refused to recognize the union, operated on a ten-hour-day basis, refused to establish a minimum-wage scale, and disregarded the standards of work demanded by the union. Operating with lower labor standards, the Duplex Company represented a formidable competitive threat to the organized firms. So severe was this competition that two of the organized firms notified the union that they would be obliged to terminate their agreements with it unless their competitor, the Duplex Company, also entered into an agreement with the union and thereby raised its labor standards. Organization of the Duplex Company was the prerequisite for standardization of labor costs and uniformity of competitive conditions within the industry.

Aware of the soundness of the argument of the organized firms, the International Association of Machinists attempted to organize the Duplex Company. Since the company refused to negotiate with the union on a voluntary basis, the IAM called an organizational strike. The strike proved totally unsuccessful because only a fraction of the workers responded to the strike call of the union. Out of the 250 employees of the Duplex Company, eleven engaged in the strike.

The union had two alternative courses of action. Either it could terminate its contract in the organized plants, thereby ending collective bargaining in the industry, or it could resort to economic action calculated to force the Duplex Company to recognize the organization. The union chose the latter course of conduct. Union action took the form of a secondary boycott directed against the products of the Duplex Company. Since New York City represented one of the most important markets for the products of Duplex, the International Association of Machinists aimed to prevent sale of the company's presses in the New York area. To accomplish its objective, the union implemented an elaborate program that included ordering members of the union located in New York not to install or repair Duplex presses; notifying a trucking company usually employed by Duplex customers to haul the presses not to do so; and warning customers not to purchase or install Duplex presses. These activities were designed to eliminate the Duplex Company from the New York market with the effect of encouraging Duplex customers to purchase presses manufactured by companies with which the union had contracts. The economic circumstances surrounding the *Duplex* case were strikingly similar to those involved in *Danbury Hatters*. And, as in the latter case, the Court held that the action of the union violated the terms of the Sherman law. In the opinion of the Court, there was no mention of the rule of reason that guided decisions in antitrust cases involving business enterprises.

Subsequent to the *Duplex* decision, the Court utilized the rule-of-reason doctrine in one case to find lawful a union activity that had the effect of restraining commerce.[43] Involved in the case with the labor organization was an employers' association, the National Association of

Window Glass Manufacturers. This association was composed of firms that produced handmade glass. The union was the National Association of Window Glass Workers, which represented the workers engaged in the handmade glass industry. As the result of the advent of the automatic glass machine, the supply of handmade glass workers, a highly skilled craft, decreased by such an amount that there were not enough craftworkers to run all the handmade glass plants on a full-time basis. An industry-wide agreement was executed between the labor organization and the employers' association. To solve the labor supply problem, the contract provided that half the factories would operate between September 15, 1922, and January 27, 1923, and the remaining half between January 29, 1923, and June 11, 1923.[44] After reviewing the economic factors involved in the case, the Court concluded that "we see no combination in unreasonable restraint of trade in the arrangement made to meet the short supply of men." With the exception of this one case, the Court never again utilized the rule of reason in labor cases.

The Court, though ignoring the rule-of-reason doctrine in the *Duplex* case, could scarcely bypass completely the Clayton Act. As stated previously, however, the law was interpreted in a fashion that afforded no relief to unions in antitrust cases. With respect to Section 6 of the Clayton Act, the Court in *Duplex* declared:

> There is nothing in the section to exempt such an organization or its members from accountability where it or they depart from its normal and legitimate objects and engage in an actual combination or conspiracy in restraint of trade. And by no fair or permissible construction can it be taken as authorizing any activity otherwise unlawful, or enabling a normally lawful organization to become a cloak for an illegal combination or conspiracy in restraint of trade as defined by the antitrust laws.

Thus the courts still claimed the power to determine whether or not a labor organization was "lawfully carrying out legitimate objects." Nothing in the Clayton Act, the Supreme Court contended, denied this right to the judiciary. As a consequence, the Court ordered an injunction stamping out the secondary boycott instigated by the International Association of Machinists. The *Duplex* decision meant that the position of organized labor under the Sherman law remained unchanged. Secondary boycott activities were still unlawful. The right to do business was still paramount to the right of workers to self-organization and effective collective bargaining.

After the decision was rendered, organized labor went before the Supreme Court of the United States in six antitrust cases.[45] Before 1921, the federal courts applied the antitrust statutes only to railroad strikes and union secondary boycott activities. After 1921, and the *Duplex* decision, courts applied the Sherman law to ordinary factory and coal strikes. The double standard between business and labor cases was to be developed further in the *Coronado* and *Bedford* cases.

CHAPTER THREE

THE *CORONADO* DOCTRINE: CONTINUED DEVELOPMENT OF THE DOUBLE STANDARD

In the early part of the twentieth century, the United Mine Workers of America was confronted with a serious economic problem. The gains it had won through collective bargaining were threatened by the operation of nonunion mines. Intensive competition characterized the bituminous coal industry; unionized mines paying comparatively high wages and maintaining union standards of employment could not compete on even terms with nonunion mines operating with lower labor standards and lower costs. This differential, the union recognized, could only be erased by organization of the nonunion mines. Previously, we noted how the judiciary hindered the United Mine Workers from carrying out its objective by enforcing the yellow-dog contract with the labor injunction.[46] Union efforts in the mines were further checked by the application of the Sherman law to its organizational activities. The *Coronado* cases were the outgrowth of union efforts to expand organization in the coal industry in the face of employer opposition.

The Coronado Coal Mine was controlled by the Bache-Denman Coal Company, a corporation that controlled several coal mines in Sebastian County, Arkansas. In the spring of 1914, the company decided to operate its properties on an open shop and nonunion basis. This decision was made despite the fact that the United Mine Workers of America had valid contracts with the coal companies controlled by Bache-Denman, including one with the Coronado Mine. To implement its decision, Bache-Denman closed down a number of unionized mines and planned to open them on a nonunion basis. Aware of the possibility of violence, the company, while the mines were shut down, laid plans to operate them as open shops. Such preparation included the hiring of guards from the Burns Detective Agency, the purchase of rifles and ammunition, eviction of union members from company houses, and the stretching of cable around the mines. The coal company was aware of the threat of violence when the decision was reached to operate the mines on a nonunion basis. In this connection, Bache said, "To do this means a bitter fight, but in my opinion it can be accomplished by proper organization."[47]

Workers at the Coronado Mine expected the same pattern of action as at other mines of the Bache-Denman Coal Company. To forestall such action, the workers at the Coronado Mine struck, but the company refused to submit to union demands and during the strike attempted to operate the Coronado Mine with nonunion workers. On April 6, 1914, about a month after the strike had begun, a union committee, along with a large crowd of union miners and sympathizers, visited the superintendent of the Coronado Mine with the intention of persuading the company to restore operations on a union basis. The company refused once again. As a result, the crowd injured a number of nonunion employees, ran the guards off the premises of the mine, and flooded the mine, causing the cessation of all operations.

Violence erupted on July 17 when the unionists, equipped with rifles, attacked the mine in force. After a few hours, the guards and nonunion employees were driven from the premises. Several of the nonunion employees were murdered. By the end of the day, the entire mine was destroyed by dynamite and fire. A dialogue between the parties, which is a substantial attribute in an established collective bargaining relationship, was not available to alleviate the conflict.

Almost immediately the operators brought suit against the United Mine Workers charging a violation under the Sherman law. They claimed that the union had caused $740,000 in damages, but asked for a judgment three times this sum, since the Sherman law provides for treble damages. After prolonged litigation in the lower federal courts, the Supreme Court of the United States decided the first *Coronado* case on June 5, 1922, or about eight years after the strike took place.[48] The Supreme Court denied the company the damages it requested and ruled that the United Mine Workers of America had not violated the Sherman law. In reaching this conclusion, the Court held that "coal mining [was] not interstate commerce, and the power of Congress [did] not extend to its regulation as such." Since coal mining was not considered interstate commerce, the Sherman law, a federal statute, had no application to a strike effected in a coal mine. Owners of the coal company contended that the antitrust law applied because 75 percent of the output of their mines was delivered outside the state of Arkansas. This argument was rejected by the Court on the basis that the entire production of the Bache-Denman mines, 5,000 tons weekly, constituted an infinitesimal portion of the nation's entire coal production, about 10 to 15 million tons weekly.

The acts of violence during the strike were deplored by the Court, but it held that such unlawfulness in itself does not establish the jurisdiction of the Sherman law over a situation in which, in the absence of violence, the Act would not apply. Moreover, the Court was not convinced that the operation of the mine on a nonunion basis would have resulted in the sale of more coal by virtue of lower prices based upon lower labor costs. In this connection, it declared that the company would not lower the price of coal, but "would probably pocket the profit" that a reduction of wages would make possible.

However, the main ground for the Court's decision in the *Coronado* case was that the company did not prove that the union intended to monopolize or restrain interstate commerce within the meaning of the Sherman law. It was not sufficient to show that a strike may have indirectly reduced the amount of coal in commerce, but proof had to be adduced that the unionists had conspired to restrain trade or suppress competition. This type of evidence, the Court contended, had not been produced by the plaintiff. The real purpose of the Coronado strike was well publicized. The

CHAPTER THREE 55

United Mine Workers of America was on a campaign to stop nonunion coal from competing with union-mined coal. Since the Bache-Denman Coal Company had taken action inconsistent with the union program, the union had retaliated with a strike to implement its economic program. The Court recognized this, for in the *Coronado* opinion it declared that union leaders were stimulated "to press their unionization of nonunion mines not only as a direct means of bettering the conditions and wages of their workers but also as a means of lessening interstate competition for union operators which in turn would lessen the pressure of those operators for reduction of the union scale or the resistance to an increase."

The awareness of the general economic program of the United Mine Workers, however, did not determine the *Coronado* decision. The Court held that no evidence had been produced to demonstrate that the strike itself was stimulated by a plot to suppress competition within the meaning of the Sherman law. If the union had in fact conspired to eliminate the marketing of nonunion coal, and hence to restrain trade, the company had not proven it. If the company could prove that the union had intended to eliminate the sale of nonunion products, the company, the Court suggested, would win the case. This observation was an invitation to the company to hunt for such new evidence, and the company undertook a search for it. That the search was fruitful was demonstrated in 1925 in the second *Coronado* case.[49] This time, the high court held that the 1914 strike at the Coronado Mine had violated the Sherman law. It reversed its 1922 decision on the ground that the company had now supplied "the links lacking at the first trial."

The company secured as a witness a former officer of the union who had been involved in the 1914 strike. This witness had been the secretary of the local union engaged in the strike, and worked as a checkweigher in the mine. He, along with others, was tried and imprisoned for engaging in the bloody 1914 strike. In his testimony, he claimed that the union undertook to prevent coal mined at the Coronado Mine while the strike was in progress "from getting into the market." He further testified that union officers and union members engaged in the Coronado strike had instigated the acts of violence because they were aware that "if Bache coal, scab-dug coal, got into the market it would only be a matter of time until every union operator in the country would have to close down his mine, and scab it, because the union operators could not meet Bache competition." This testimony convicted the union, for the Court now held, in direct contrast to its position in 1924, "that the purpose of the destruction of the mines was to stop the production of nonunion coal and prevent its shipment to markets in states other than Arkansas, where it would by competition tend to reduce the price of the commodity and affect injuriously the maintenance of wages for union labor in competing mines."

An additional bit of new evidence also influenced the change on the part of the high court. As noted, in the first *Coronado* case, the estimate of the output of the Bache-Denman mine had been placed at 5,000 tons weekly. In the second case, the company adduced evidence that supported its claim that the action of the union prevented the production of 5,000 tons of coal daily. The company proved to the satisfaction of the Court that this larger figure justified the application of the Sherman law to the labor dispute. It is significant to note, however, that, despite the larger production estimate, the Court did not declare outright that coal mining constituted interstate commerce. Many years later, the Supreme Court was again to rule that mining was not interstate commerce. Actually, the amount of coal in question was not too important in the *Coronado* case. When the Court concluded that a conspiracy had existed to reduce the amount of coal in commerce, the conviction of the labor union was assured. This same verdict would have been handed down, no doubt, regardless of the amount of coal in question.

The effect of the *Coronado* decision was to deter the organizational campaign of the United Mine Workers. After the decision, many nonunion operators, following the precedent of the Bache-Denman Coal Company, brought suit against the union when faced with organizational campaigns. Uniformly, the complaint was always that the union conspired to suppress competition within the meaning of the Sherman Act by eliminating from commerce coal produced under nonunion conditions. Records indicate that the United Mine Workers of America was a defendant in antitrust proceedings more frequently than any other labor organization.[50] Not only did the *Coronado* decision stand as an obstacle to the efforts of the United Mine Workers, to organize the coal industry, but it served to dampen efforts of the entire labor movement. The Court held that unions, though unincorporated, could be sued as a body in the federal courts. It was not necessary for a plaintiff to proceed against each member of the union. The union as a body could be attacked in damage suits.

Of much greater significance, the *Coronado* doctrine shed doubt on the legality of any important strike. It is of importance to note that secondary boycott activities were not involved in the *Coronado* affair. Under the *Danbury Hatters* and *Duplex* doctrines, repeated in *Gompers*, the Court applied the Sherman law because of the implementation of secondary boycott activity. In contrast, the union was convicted in the *Coronado* case because of a strike directed against the company immediately involved in the dispute. Organized labor was aware that every major strike had the effect of reducing the amount of products in commerce. The Supreme Court in the *Coronado* case declared that when the intent of those preventing "the manufacture of production is shown to be to restrain or to control the supply entering and moving in interstate commerce, or the price of it in interstate markets, their action is a direct violation of the Antitrust Act." So sweeping was this declaration that union leaders feared that any strike for any purpose that diminished the amount of products in interstate commerce would be unlawful under the Sherman law. Should a strike result in reduction of the supply of goods in commerce, all that remained to convict under the Sherman law would be to adduce evidence that the strikers "intended" to suppress interstate trade. To prove such intent, as the *Coronado* case indicated, would not be a very difficult task. Thus the testimony of a single witness was the chief ground for the conviction under the Sherman law of the union and workers involved in the *Coronado* affair. The decision generated uncertainty in the ranks of organized labor. Every important strike could be subject to the jurisdiction of the Sherman law by virtue of the sweeping implications of the *Coronado* doctrine.

In 1924, in another case, the legal atmosphere surrounding the application of the Sherman law to strikes against employers immediately involved in a labor dispute was somewhat clarified. In the spring of 1920 the United Leather Workers Union attempted to organize five Missouri corporations engaged in the manufacture and sale of leather goods and trunks. After the companies refused to bargain collectively, the labor organization called its members out on strike. Picket lines were thrown up at each of the factories for the purpose of persuading nonstriking workers to join in the strike and to force the company not to hire replacements for the strikers. Some of the tactics employed by the union to stop production in the plants were not lawful, but the record indicates that the strikers did not resort in any manner to the excess of lawlessness displayed by the workers in the *Coronado* case. In any event, the union was successful in curtailing the operation of the factories, and the companies charged that the effect of the strike and the publicity prevented the manufacture and shipment of the products of their factories in interstate commerce. As a result, the companies claimed that the union restrained trade within the meaning of the Sherman law.

Here indeed was a test case involving the application of the Sherman law to a strike instigated against employers directly involved in a labor dispute. The union did not engage in secondary boycott activities, nor was the strike conducted in a context of lawlessness exemplified in the *Coronado* affair. Before the Supreme Court took jurisdiction of the case in 1924, lower federal courts dealt with the case. In November 1920, a district court judge issued a permanent injunction under the terms of the Sherman law, stamping out the strike. The judge held that the union injured the interstate commerce of the companies within the meaning of the Act.[51] Upon appeal, the Eighth Circuit Court upheld the ruling of the district court judge by a 2–1 vote. The majority of the circuit court of appeals held that "the natural and inevitable effect of the prevention by the defendants of the making of the plaintiffs of the articles they had made interstate contracts to sell, make, and deliver, was the prevention of their performance of their contracts and the prevention or partial prevention of their interstate commerce, and this result was so evident and unavoidable that the defendants could not have failed to know, to propose, and to intend that this should be the result."[52] In short, any strike for any purpose was unlawful under the Sherman law, provided that the strike reduced the amount of goods in commerce. Particular evidence to show intent of the workers to restrain commerce, as was required in the *Coronado* case, was not essential for conviction under the Sherman law, for intent could be inferred from the action of the strikers. In effect, the district and circuit courts held that workers who struck and suppressed interstate commerce knew the result of their action.

Had the Supreme Court of the United States upheld the position of the lower court, the right of workers to strike would have been circumscribed to the degree of rendering their fundamental economic weapon virtually useless. But the Supreme Court in a 6–3 decision reversed the judgment of the lower federal courts. The majority of the Supreme Court concurred with the dissenting judge in the circuit court of appeals, who, in speaking of the majority opinion, had declared: "The natural, logical, and inevitable result will be that every strike in any industry or even in any single factory will be within the Sherman Act and subject to federal jurisdiction provided any appreciable amount of its products enters into interstate commerce." In commenting on this statement, the majority of the high court declared: "We cannot think that Congress intended any such result in the enactment of the Antitrust Act." The Supreme Court overruled the lower federal court on the ground that the employers produced no evidence to indicate that the workers intended by their strike and picketing to restrain commerce. Even though the effect of their activities caused the reduction in the supply of products for interstate commerce, the Court contended: "The record is entirely without evidence or circumstances to show that the defendants in their conspiracy to deprive the complainant of their workers were directing their scheme against interstate commerce."[53] Thus, six members of the Supreme Court prevented the application of the Sherman law to every important strike. It is interesting to note that thirteen federal judges handled the *Leather Workers* case. Six held that the Sherman law outlawed every strike of any consequence. In short, the *Coronado* doctrine dramatized the Supreme Court's double standard in its extreme form.

❦ THE BEDFORD STONE DECISION: EFFECT ON UNION TACTICS AND COMPLETION OF THE DOUBLE STANDARD

In 1927, organized labor felt the full measure of the double standard constructed under the Sherman law, for in that year, the Supreme Court of the United States handed down the famous *Bedford Stone* decision.[54] This decision was a landmark in labor cases arising under the antitrust statutes. If organized labor sensed a new direction in decisions because of the *Leather Workers* decision, this attitude changed when the high court handed down its ruling in *Bedford Stone*. That decision, perhaps more than any other labor antitrust case, demonstrated to organized labor that the Sherman provisions provided a potent weapon to combat unionism and collective bargaining.

Arrayed against each other in the *Bedford Stone* case were an association of employers and an international labor union. The employers' association was composed of twenty-four corporations engaged in the business of quarrying and fabricating limestone in the Bedford-Bloomington area in Indiana. Their combined investment was about $6 million, and their annual aggregate sales amounted to approximately $15 million. Together, the twenty-four corporations produced about 70 percent of all the cut stone in the nation. The local employers' association was affiliated with a national employers' organization, called the International Cut Stone & Quarryers Association. Thus the highly solvent employers in the *Bedford Stone* case banded together for their mutual benefit into an effective local employers' association, which was affiliated with a national employers' organization and dominated the cut stone industry of the nation. On the other hand, the labor organization, the Journeymen Stone Cutters Association, had a total membership of 5,000 members in fifty local unions. The union jurisdiction extended to workers employed in quarries and mills and covered workers who installed cut stone in buildings.

Before 1921, the Bedford-Bloomington quarry operators recognized the Journeymen Stone Cutters Association as the bargaining agent of the workers employed in their mills and quarries. As a result, stone was produced under collective bargaining conditions. In 1921, however, the employers' association refused to extend the labor agreement, and in its place set up a series of company-dominated unions. Later discussion will reveal that company-dominated unions do not perform the functions of collective bargaining. An effective union cannot serve the interests of employers and employees at the same time.[55] Company-dominated unions, under the influence of management, are not free to protect basic employment interests of workers. In spite of the protests of the Journeymen Stone Cutters Association, the operators resumed production under nonunion conditions. The Indiana quarries had to be organized once again, or the Journeymen Stone Cutters Association would for all intents and purposes disintegrate as a labor organization, since the Indiana area was the most important stone-producing region in the nation.

Stimulated by such considerations, the Journeymen Stone Cutters Association enacted a clause in its constitution that forbade its members to handle stone "cut by men working in opposition" to the labor organization. In other words, the members decided not to work with nonunion cut stone. This rule was implemented in states and cities in which the Bedford-Bloomington operators sold stone to building contractors. Customers of these operators were persuaded not to purchase Indiana stone, for they were aware that, once purchased, the stone would not be installed in buildings by union members. For example, a building contracting company in New York would hesitate to purchase nonunion Indiana stone when it knew the members of the Journeymen Stone Cutters Association would refuse to install the product.

The tactics of the Journeymen Stone Cutters Association were essentially the same as those employed by the labor organization involved in *Duplex*. Both unions implemented a secondary boycott to force antiunion employers to recognize labor unions. Pressure was exerted on firms for the purpose of forcing them to cease doing business with companies directly involved in the labor dispute. Such pressure constitutes a secondary boycott. So impressed was the Court with the similarity of the *Bedford Stone* case to the *Duplex* decision that it declared, "with a few changes in respect to the product involved, dates, names, and incidents, which would have no effect upon the principle established, the opinion in *Duplex Company* v. *Deering* might serve as an opinion in this case."

The Court was correct in establishing this similarity from the point of view of the weapon employed by the unions. Upon closer examination, the analogy is not as clear-cut as indicated by the majority opinion, since in the *Duplex* case the union marshalled its forces against only one employer, while in *Bedford Stone*, the union was arrayed against an employers' association of great wealth and power. In any event, the Court, in the *Bedford Stone* case, held that the conduct of the union violated the antitrust act because "the strikes ... preventing the use and installation of petitioners' products in other states, necessarily threatened to destroy and narrow petitioners' interstate trade by taking from them their customers."

BRANDEIS AND THE DOUBLE STANDARD

Organized labor suffered a reversal with the Supreme Court's decision in *Bedford Stone*. Before the Court reviewed the case, a district court and a circuit court of appeals refused to restrain the activities of the labor union. The high court's knowledge that the Journeymen Stone Cutters Association was pitted against a powerful employers' association did not affect the decision. The union conduct was peaceful, and no violence of any sort occurred in connection with the boycott. As a matter of fact, the union did not even engage in picketing. The sole activity of the workers was to refuse to handle nonunion stone for the purpose of defending their union against a powerful and wealthy employers' association. In addition, the union did not deter contractors from purchasing stone not quarried in the Bloomington-Bedford region. The boycott was instituted against nonunion stone, and there was no interference with the liberty of contractors to purchase union-made stone. The Court ruled that the union's action constituted an "unreasonable restraint of ... commerce within the meaning of the Antitrust Act ...," despite the character of the application of the rule of reason in business cases. Brandeis dissented vigorously from the majority on this issue and made it clear that the double standard had been fully developed and that its development stopped just short of prohibiting strikes entirely. Justice Brandeis declared:

> If, on the undisputed facts of this case, refusal to work can be enjoined, Congress created by the Sherman Law and the Clayton Act an instrument for imposing restraints upon labor which reminds of involuntary servitude. The Sherman Law was held in *United States* v. *United States Steel Corporation* ... to permit capitalists to combine in a single corporation 50 percent of the steel industry of the United States dominating the trade through its vast resources. The Sherman Law was held in *United States* v. *United Shoe Machinery Co.* ... to permit capitalists to combine in another corporation practically the whole shoe-machinery industry of the country, necessarily giving it a position of dominance over shoe manufacturing in America. It would, indeed, be strange if Congress had by the same Act willed to deny to members of a small craft of workingmen the right to co-operate in simply refraining from work, when that course was the only means of self-protection against a combination of militant and powerful employers. I cannot believe that Congress did so.[56]

With the *Bedford Stone* decision, the pattern of the application of the Sherman law to labor unions was completed. A law enacted presumably to check the growth of "big business" was more restrictive to union organization. It served as a fertile ground for the labor injunction and provided the basis for damage suits against labor unions. Secondary economic activity by unions when the alternative was disintegration of the labor organization was deemed unlawful. Such action was no less unlawful when its implementation was on a peaceful basis. The judiciary was prepared to coerce free workers into "involuntary servitude," even though the refusal to work had as its fundamental purpose the raising of standards of living of workers by establishing, retaining, or widening the collective bargaining process. Strikes against employers directly involved in a labor dispute were likewise unlawful when proof could be adduced that the "intent" of the union was to suppress the amount of goods in commerce. The rule-of-reason doctrine, which proved of enormous benefit to business, did not alleviate the stern application of the Sherman law to labor unions. One standard was set for business enterprises and another for labor unions. In addition, the high court brushed aside as unimportant the powerful economic and social forces that surrounded labor disputes in antitrust cases. Economic and social realism was rejected in favor of the standard of cold and legal formalism. This narrow legal approach invariably resulted in a restriction of the collective action that was intended to improve union members' economic and social status in life.

🌠 SUMMARY

The period around the turn of the twentieth century was one in which big business and monopolistic organization characterized the economic system. Congress became concerned with this turn of events and passed the Sherman Antitrust Act in 1890 and the Clayton Act in 1914 to legislate the nation's economy into a competitive pattern. The effort largely failed in terms of regulation of firm size, but had a stronger effect upon the activities of labor organizations. The application of the antitrust laws to organized labor made secondary boycotts illegal. This proved restrictive to union efforts to organize. The integration and interdependency of the economy made the secondary boycott a first-rate union weapon. The inability to use the weapon decreased union power to influence the outcome of economic struggles.

Out of the application of the antitrust laws to union activities arose several landmark labor cases: *Danbury Hatters, Gompers, Duplex, Coronado,* and *Bedford Stone*. A comparison of these cases with business cases such as *E. C. Knight, Northern Securities, Standard Oil,* and *United States Steel* makes it clear that the Supreme Court developed a double standard in the application of antitrust provisions to the two groups. On the one hand, the Supreme Court in effect held that unionism was incompatible with the antitrust statutes. On the other hand, it ruled that the rule of reason would be applied in each business case to determine if there had been a reasonable or unreasonable restraint of interstate trade. The Sherman Act, passed primarily to check big business, was more effective in the control of labor's collective bargaining process.

🌠 DISCUSSION QUESTIONS

1. Trace the development of the application of Sherman Act provisions to labor unions prior to 1908. What implication did these early cases have for the right to strike?
2. Compare the rules of *In re Debs* and *Danbury Hatters*. How did each case affect union growth and development?
3. What did labor expect from the Clayton Act, and what did that Act actually allow?
4. Explain the rule of reason, its application to business, and its application to unions.

CHAPTER THREE 63

5. Compare the *Coronado* cases to the *Bedford Stone* decision. In your comparison, show the similarities and differences in the surrounding circumstances.

🏵 NOTES

[1] Reported in Thomas C. Cochran and William Miller, *The Age of Enterprise* (New York: The Macmillan Company, 1943), p. 324.

[2] Reuben E. Slesinger, *National Economic Policy: The Presidential Reports* (Princeton, N.J.: D. Van Nostrand Co., Inc., 1968), p. 98.

[3] Cochran and Miller, *op. cit.*, p. 356.

[4] Sherman Anti-Trust Law, 26 Stat. 209, Act of July 2, 1890. On October 15, 1914, Congress enacted the Clayton Act, 38 Stat. 780, which in part purports to make the Sherman law more effective relative to the checking of monopoly control of industry.

[5] Edward Berman, *Labor and the Sherman Act* (New York: Harper & Brothers, 1930).

[6] A. T. Mason, *Organized Labor and the Law* (Durham, N.C.: Duke University Press, 1925).

[7] A 1955 amendment raised the maximum fine to $50,000.

[8] *United States v. Workingmen's Amalgamated Council*, 54 Fed. 994 (1893).

[9] Berman, *op. cit.*, p. 64.

[10] *Waterhouse v. Comer*, 55 Fed. 149 (1893).

[11] *In re Debs*, Petitioner, 158 U.S. 564 (1895).

[12] *United States v. Agler*, 62 Fed. 24 (1897).

[13] *United States v. Elliott*, 64 Fed. 27 (1898).

[14] *In re Debs, op. cit.*

[15] The official name is *Loewe v. Lawlor*, 208 U.S. 274 (1908). However, this landmark case is commonly referred to as the "Danbury Hatters" case, for the factory in question was located in Danbury, Connecticut. In 1915 the dispute was tried once more in the Supreme Court. The second case is officially cited as *Lawlor v. Loewe*, 235 U.S. 522 (1915).

[16] *Ibid.*

[17] See Chapter 7.

[18] J. R. Commons and Associates, *History of Labour in the United States* (New York: The Macmillan Company, 1926), p. 531.

[19] *Ibid.*, p. 532.

[20] *Gompers v. Bucks Stove and Range Company*, 221 U.S. 418 (1911).

[21] 38 Stat. 780 (1914).

[22] Edwin E. Witte, *The Government in Labor Disputes* (New York: McGraw-Hill Book Company, 1932), p. 68.

[23] Dallas L. Jones, "The Enigma of the Clayton Act," *Industrial and Labor Relations Review*, X, No. 2, January 1957, p. 31.

[24] *Ibid.*, p. 207.

[25] *Ibid.*, p. 209.

[26] *Ibid.*, pp. 211–212.
[27] *Ibid.*, p. 221.
[28] Berman, *op. cit.*, p. 103.
[29] *Bedford Cut Stone Company v. Journeymen Stone Cutters Association*, 274 U.S. 37 (1927).
[30] *United States v. E. C. Knight*, 156 U.S. 1 (1895).
[31] *Northern Securities Company v. United States*, 193 U.S. 199 (1904).
[32] *Standard Oil Company of New Jersey v. United States*, 221 U.S. 1 (1911). *United States v. American Tobacco Company*, 221 U.S. 106 (1911).
[33] Milton Handler, *Cases and Materials on Trade Regulations* (Chicago: The Foundation Press, 1937), p. 388.
[34] *Ibid.*, p. 401.
[35] *United States v. United States Steel Corporation*, 251 U.S. 417 (1920).
[36] Handler, *op. cit.*, p. 424.
[37] *Ibid.*, p. 422.
[38] *United States v. United Shoe Machinery Company*, 227 U.S. 32 (1913).
[39] Myron W. Watkins, "Trusts," *Encyclopedia of Social Sciences*, XV, p. 117.
[40] See Handler, *op. cit.*, pp. 256–385, for a discussion of the legal and economic aspects of trade associations.
[41] *Maple Flooring Manufacturers Association v. United States*, 268 U.S. 563 (1925).
[42] *Duplex Printing Press Company v. Deering*, 254 U.S. 443 (1921).
[43] *National Association of Window Glass Manufacturers v. United States*, 263 U.S. 403 (1923).
[44] Berman, *op. cit.*, p. 150.
[45] *Ibid.*, p. 118.
[46] See Chapter 2.
[47] *United Mine Workers v. Coronado Coal Company*, 259 U.S. 344 (1922).
[48] *Ibid.*
[49] *Coronado Coal Company v. United Mine Workers of America*, 268 U.S. 295 (1925).
[50] Berman, *op. cit.*, p. 119.
[51] *Herbert and Meisel Trunk Company v. United Leather Workers International Union*, 268 Fed. 662 (1920).
[52] *United Leather Workers International Union v. Herbert and Meisel Trunk Company*, 284 Fed. 446 (1922).
[53] *United Leather Workers International Union v. Herbert and Meisel Trunk Company*, 285 U.S. 457 (1925).
[54] *Bedford Cut Stone Company v. Journeymen Stone Cutters Association, supra.*
[55] See Chapter 6.
[56] *Bedford Cut Stone Company v. Journeymen Stone Cutters Association, supra.*

CHAPTER FOUR

CONTROL OF THE LABOR INJUNCTION

THE CHANGING ECONOMIC AND POLITICAL SCENE

As demonstrated, the legal climate surrounding the collective bargaining process in the period 1806–1932 was restrictive. Theoretically, unions were lawful organizations, workers were legally free to join unions, and the right to strike as such was lawful. In practice, however, the courts controlled the right of workers to join unions and the liberty of labor organizations to engage in activities designed to make collective bargaining effective. The use of the injunction in labor disputes proved a most formidable obstacle to the expansion and implementation of trade unionism. Frequently, labor unions had the economic strength to deal with the antiorganizational activities of employers, but fell before the labor injunction. When the courts held that the yellow-dog contract could be implemented by the labor injunction, the position of unions in an economic struggle was diminished immeasurably. The anomalous condition existed wherein workers legally free to join labor unions were prevented from doing so. Courts enforced the yellow-dog arrangement, which enabled employers to maintain shops closed to union workers. These same courts frequently outlawed union tactics calculated to obtain shops closed to nonunion labor. The wide application of the Sherman law to labor unions likewise operated to constrain the union movement. Union action aimed to enforce bargaining demands against employers was deemed unlawful under the antitrust laws. In their interpretation of the Sherman law, the courts took the position that workers had the right to collective bargaining only insofar as there was no infringement of the right to do business. This right of employers was considered more important than the liberty of workers to engage in action that would make collective bargaining work. For a time it appeared that all strikes of major proportions would be unlawful. That this condition did not result was attributable to the judgment of a few members of the Supreme Court. Had the composition of this Court been a shade different, it is likely that all strikes that suppressed the shipment of goods in interstate commerce would have been deemed unlawful. In the light of all this evidence, it can scarcely be denied that courts served well the interests of antiunion employers. The judiciary proved to be a willing ally to employers in labor-management disputes. As a result, the level of union membership in 1930 amounted to only about 3 million.[1]

Court limitations of worker rights to collective bargaining might have continued indefinitely had it not been for the economic collapse of the 1930s. The depression in this period constituted the most severe economic debacle ever suffered by the nation. Unemployment totaled about 25 percent of the labor force. Widespread bankruptcy of business enterprises and bank failures characterized the period. Foreclosures of firms, repossession of personal property, and loss of homes added to the difficulties of the nation. Fear and deprivation characterized the American people. Never before in the history of the nation was the faith of the people at such low ebb.

About 15 million people tramped the streets looking for work. Life savings disappeared in the whirlwind of financial ruin. Farmers did what they could to save their land, but farm after farm went on the auctioneer's block. Measures were supported to declare moratoriums on foreign debts, and the nation debated the possibility of applying the same principle to its own debtors, who were losing their homes, farms, and other worldly possessions. Rightly or wrongly, the average American identified the misery of the depression with business, perhaps because of the emphasis that had been placed on the role of capital in economic growth by students of the economic order.

The effects of the economic collapse could be multiplied indefinitely. School terms were reduced, and some schools and colleges even closed their doors. As educational appropriations were severely cut by economy-minded and debt-fearing legislators, teachers' salaries were usually decreased as far as possible. In Chicago, teachers worked for months without pay, many walking to and from school, not even having the pennies for carfare. More than one Chicago teacher went without lunch, still trying to do the job in the face of a bankrupt city government. At the college level, conditions were not much better. Scholars who had devoted their life to research and university-level instruction found themselves without jobs, or with salaries cut to such a degree that life was barely possible. Other professional groups suffered in equal or even worse fashion. People had no funds to purchase the services of musicians, lawyers, artists, or architects. These people, like industrial workers, tramped the streets looking for whatever work could be found. Disease increased, since money was not available for adequate—to say nothing of preventive—medicine. Ten thousand veterans of World War I marched on Washington in 1932, demanding immediate payment of their bonuses. They were dispersed with tanks, gas bombs, and bayonets. At that time, the national government was not politically capable of instituting a fiscal and monetary policy to deal with such disturbances in the economy.

Many aspects of the culture reflected the changes in social thought. The realities of the depression gave a new direction to literature and the arts. Books of social significance, such as *The Grapes of Wrath* and *Union Square*, claimed the public's attention. Such plays as *Waiting for Lefty* and *Of Mice and Men* highlighted the growing concern of the people with the imperfections of the economic order. The motion picture industry reflected somewhat the changing social thought. *The Grapes of Wrath* was filmed. *The River* and *The Plough That Broke the Plains* portrayed America in film. Depression-stimulated student organizations on college campuses concerned themselves with problems of social and economic significance. Opposition to birth control was largely overcome as an increasing number of parents doubted the wisdom of rearing families in an unfavorable economic environment. Thus the depression reached even to the structure and composition of family life. As never before, the economy was subjected to critical intellectual appraisal. One thing was certain: The concept of economic Darwinism was dead. Society recognized that millions of its most fit members could survive only imperfectly in a depression economy. An increasing number of people recognized that institutional defects in the economic environment rather than personal inadequacies caused business failure, unemployment, and poverty.

🌸 *EARLY REGULATION OF THE LABOR INJUNCTION*

Organized labor had had a long history of attempts to curb the use of injunctions prior to the period of turmoil of the 1930s. Political pressure by labor unions to obtain legislative relief from the labor injunction dates from the turn of the century. Impressed with the effects of the instrument in labor disputes, organized labor worked diligently to curtail the power of the courts to intervene in labor-management controversies. The spearhead of this legislative assault was the American Federation of Labor, the only national federation of labor unions still in existence prior to the CIO in the latter 1930s. Organized labor learned through experience the impact of the injunction on the collective bargaining process. Labor leaders pointed to the abuses of the instrument, asserting that the judiciary served as a potent ally to employers in labor disputes. These abuses and their implications in industrial relations were examined in Chapter 2.

The American Federation of Labor conducted its legislative campaign on national and state levels. Its objective was to engineer the passage of state and federal legislation designed to provide protection from the equity power of the courts. This was a logical and necessary approach, for both state and federal courts issued labor injunctions. State control of the labor injunction antedated federal regulation. Thus it was on the state level that organized labor first succeeded in influencing the enactment of anti-injunction legislation. The rewards, however, were not destined to endure. Prior to October 15, 1914, the date on which Congress enacted the Clayton Act (which in part regulated the labor injunction), only six states had passed legislation restricting the power of the state courts to issue injunctions in labor disputes. These states were California (1903), Oklahoma (1907), Massachusetts (1911), Kansas, Arizona, and Montana (1913).[2] The California and Oklahoma laws provided that acts that are not criminal when committed by a single person will not be subject to injunction when engaged in by a number of persons involved in a labor dispute. Massachusetts provided that its state courts could not enjoin peaceful picketing. The purpose of the Montana law was to prohibit discrimination against workers in equity proceedings. It provided that standards developed by the courts for the issuance of injunctions in nonlabor disputes should apply equally to labor disputes. In addition, the Oklahoma and Massachusetts laws granted persons involved in contempt cases the right to trial by jury.

Arizona and Kansas enacted legislation that closely resembled the injunction sections of the Clayton Act. The efforts of Arizona and Kansas may be regarded as the first genuine attempts to regulate by law the use of injunctions in labor disputes. While the laws of California, Oklahoma, Massachusetts, and Montana purported to control specific aspects of the labor injunction, Arizona and Kansas fashioned legislation calculated to remove the courts from this area of industrial relations. The laws of these two states prohibited judicial interference by injunction in controversies involving employers and employees when these controversies grew out of a dispute that concerned terms or conditions of employment. Such legislation removed the prerogative of the judiciary to declare what is lawful and unlawful in the carrying out of labor disputes. This restriction on the equity function of the courts marked a significant innovation in labor relations law. The judiciary had taken upon itself the full right to determine the legitimate boundaries of labor union activity. Arizona and Kansas had endeavored to check the courts from exercising such sweeping

CHAPTER FOUR

power in the area of industrial relations. It was legislation of this character that the American Federation of Labor championed and hoped to have enacted by all states and the federal government.

Although the first visible results of its efforts appeared in state legislation, the American Federation of Labor consistently attempted to promote the passage of a federal anti-injunction labor law. Indeed, the use of the injunction in labor disputes, along with the prosecution of unions under the Sherman law, stimulated the entrance of organized labor into national politics. To induce the passage of favorable national legislation, organized labor openly supported candidates sympathetic to its legislative program, and worked for the defeat of the "antilabor" politician. To this day, the union movement follows essentially this same political program, the foundation of which was laid down in the early 1900s. Organized labor had reason to believe that its efforts to obtain national anti-injunction legislation had borne fruit on October 15, 1914, for on this date Congress enacted the Clayton Act. Previously, we saw that labor's jubilation over the antitrust provisions of the Clayton Act was premature. A careful analysis of this act's Section 6 reveals that its terms added nothing new to the law of industrial relations. Actual experience with the law disclosed that the prosecution of labor organizations under the Sherman Act continued unabated.

The rejoicing of labor with respect to the injunction sections of the 1914 law appeared to be on firm ground. In general, the terms regulating the equity power of the federal courts in labor disputes seemed clear enough. The Clayton Act provided that the federal courts could not restrain employees involved in a labor dispute from engaging in peaceful picketing; from carrying out a strike in a peaceful manner; from engaging in a peaceful boycott; from attending any place where such employees may lawfully be; and from peacefully assembling in a lawful manner and for lawful purposes. These prohibitions are contained in Section 20 of the Clayton Act.[3] The terms "peaceful" and "lawful" defy objective construction and the Supreme Court was free to insert its own definition of what these terms meant. Patterns of union conduct previously interfered with by the federal courts were not immunized against the labor injunction.

Other sections of the Clayton Act closely regulated the procedure of issuing injunctions in labor disputes. Under circumstances wherein Section 20 did not operate to protect activities of labor unions, such as picketing attended with violence, the Clayton Act spelled out the procedure that had to be followed by the federal courts. A temporary restraining order could not be granted without notice to the labor union unless irreparable injury to property appeared imminent, for which injury there was no adequate remedy in law. In addition, a temporary restraining order issued without notice to the labor organization must by its terms expire within a period of ten days after issuance. No preliminary injunction could be issued without notice to the trade union. Persons accused of violation of injunctions might, if they desired, be tried by jury. Employers applying for an injunction had to post a bond for the indemnification of a union for court costs and damages if subsequent events proved that the organization had been wrongfully enjoined or restrained. Finally, the Clayton Act provided that every injunction or temporary restraining order must set forth in reasonable detail the specific acts to be enjoined.

Since on the one hand, the Clayton Act forbade completely under certain circumstances the issuance of labor injunctions, and on the other hand, outlined carefully the procedure to be followed in the issuance of injunctions, unions felt, —mistakenly—that the law adequately protected organized labor. Inspired by its apparent success on the federal level, organized labor then concentrated on the task of obtaining the passage of state anti-injunction laws. Once again, the record reveals that its efforts were only moderately rewarded. Although the American Federation of Labor advocated legislation patterned after the Clayton Act in every state legislature in the nation, only five states prior to 1921 enacted laws duplicating the terms of the federal anti-injunction statute.[4] No progress on the state level was made after 1921. The basic reason for this was that the Supreme Court of the United States declared the Arizona law unconstitutional. The action of the high court reduced the incentive to work for the passage of state anti-injunction laws. Of what use would it be to enact such laws if they could not stand the test of constitutionality? Since the role of the Supreme Court in shaping the character of labor injunction control legislation is of conclusive importance, attention must be directed to the reaction of the courts to such statutes.

❦ EARLY LABOR INJUNCTION LEGISLATION: COURT ATTITUDES

The Clayton Act, as noted, did not operate to preclude the application of the Sherman law to labor unions. Once the Supreme Court took this position, it affirmed the use of the labor injunction to restrain unions found in violation of the antitrust statutes. This was the essence of the *Duplex* decision of 1921 and of the *Bedford* doctrine of 1927. Thus, the principle was laid down that the injunction provisions of the Clayton Act were not operative if the judiciary found that labor unions had restrained trade within the meaning of the Sherman law. As a consequence, antitrust laws served as a basis for the issuance of labor injunctions for many years.

In addition, in 1917, the Supreme Court affirmed the use of the injunction to make effective yellow-dog contracts. Despite the provisions against the use of labor injunctions in the Clayton Act, the high court in

CHAPTER FOUR

Hitchman held that the equity power of the judiciary could be properly employed to implement agreements in which workers agreed not to join labor unions as a condition of employment. As a matter of fact, the Court did not make any reference to the Clayton Act in the *Hitchman* case, even though the terms of that law may have been reasonably construed to prohibit the issuance of labor injunctions in yellow-dog cases. The fundamental intent of the Clayton Act was to check the power of the federal courts to intervene by injunction in labor disputes that grew out of controversies that concerned terms and conditions of employment. A controversy as to whether or not workers could form labor organizations for the purpose of collective bargaining fell squarely within the meaning of the injunction sections of the Clayton Act. In addition, Section 20 of the Clayton Act forbade the use of the injunction in labor disputes where the effect of the instrument would enjoin persons from "communicating information" or "from attending at any place where such persons may lawfully be." Even granted that the term "lawfully" is subject to no precise definition, the courts may have been guided by the intent of the legislation, as demonstrated in Chapter 3. Of course, this approach was precluded when the Supreme Court chose to hold that interference with a yellow-dog contract transgressed rights vouchsafed in the Constitution.

The high court was required to resolve an additional question. What about the application of the Clayton Act to cases in which violations of the antitrust statutes or yellow-dog contracts were not involved? Would the Court now construe the statute in a manner that provided a degree of protection to labor unions against the labor injunction? The answer to this question was found in the *American Steel Foundries* and *Truax* cases.

ONE "MISSIONARY" PER ENTRANCE

In spite of the broad restrictions on the issuance of injunctions in labor disputes, the Supreme Court in the 1921 *American Steel Foundries* case[5] interpreted the law in a manner that sharply limited the application of injunctions to labor-management controversies. The high court construction of the Clayton Act in this case meant that the Act was to leave unchanged the law of industrial relations. This was subsequently recognized by the Court when it declared that the injunction sections of the Clayton Act "were merely declaratory of what had always been the law and the best practice in equity."

As a result of a strike over wages, a labor organization had picketed a steel plant. The company obtained an injunction from a federal district court that stamped out all picketing. On review of the case, the Supreme Court modified the order, but limited union picketing to one picket per entrance of the factory. On this score Chief Justice Taft declared: "We think that the strikers and their sympathizers engaged in the economic struggle should be limited to one representative for each point of ingress and egress in the plant or place of business and that all others be enjoined from congregating or loitering at the plant or in the neighboring street by which access is had to the plant....." Although these pickets (the Court termed them "missionaries") were to have the right of observation, communication, and persuasion, they could not approach nonstriking workers in groups, and their communication to these workers could not be abusive, libelous, or threatening. In addition, the Court held that a picket acting alone could not obstruct an unwilling listener by "dragging his step." It is noteworthy that the Court was concerned not only with the number of pickets, but also with their conduct on the picket line.

A further limitation was attached to the picketing activities of labor unions. According to the Court, the Clayton Act provisions protected the activities only of employees of an employer on strike, or of ex-employees who might reasonably be expected to return to work for the employer. Other workers directly involved in a labor dispute, who were not in the present or past employment of the company but who might still have had a real economic interest in the working conditions of the firm, could not lawfully picket. This doctrine, it will be recalled, was first laid down in the *Duplex* case wherein Section 20 of the Clayton Act did not operate to make lawful union activities carried on by employees in one city to bring economic pressure against an employer located in another city. On this point, the Court in the *Duplex* case declared: "Congress had in mind particular industrial controversies, not a general class war." Following the *Duplex* decision, a narrow construction was placed on the Clayton Act in *American Steel Foundries*.

Unions learned that the Clayton Act would not prevent the intervention of court injunctions in labor disputes. Regardless of the purpose of union economic pressure and notwithstanding the peacefulness of picketing, the Supreme Court was not prepared to construe the Clayton Act as providing a greater area of freedom to labor unions than posting one picket per entrance to a plant. Even though the Court was careful to point out that "each case must turn on its own circumstances," the doctrine established in the *American Steel Foundries* case was followed by many courts. After this case, the courts almost always limited the number of pickets that could be utilized in a labor dispute.

❦ LABOR INJUNCTION CONTROL LEGISLATION HELD UNCONSTITUTIONAL

Shortly after the *American Steel Foundries* case, the Supreme Court ruled on the lawfulness of a state labor injunction control law. In *Truax*,[6] the high court held unconstitutional the Arizona labor injunction law. Previously, the Supreme Court of Arizona had approved its state law. Despite the construction of the state court, the Supreme Court of the United States held that the Arizona law had violated the due process clause of the Fourteenth Amendment to the Constitution.[7]

Facts of the case disclose that the employees of a restaurant located in Bisbee, Arizona, became involved in a labor dispute with their employer over conditions and terms of employment. Since the employer refused to yield to their demands, some of the workers went on strike. The owners of the restaurant managed to operate without the strikers and, to retaliate, the striking employees carried on a vigorous boycott against the management. So successful was the boycott that the restaurant receipts dropped from $156 to $75 per day. The boycott was carried on by picketing the immediate premises of the restaurant. Although no violence was involved, the pickets carried banners containing statements against the restaurant and its owners, workers, and customers. According to the Supreme Court of the United States, the Arizona statute precluded the issuance of injunctions under circumstances of the *Truax* case. As a result, it held that the statute deprived the restaurant owners of their property without due process of law and accordingly violated the Constitution of the United States. "Property," of course, included the right to operate a business in a profitable manner, and a statute could not stand as a cloak behind which a labor organization could interfere with the employer's right to do business. On this score Chief Justice Taft, speaking for the majority of the Court, declared, "a law which operates to make lawful such a wrong as is described in plaintiff's complaint deprives the owner of the business and the premises of his property without due process, and cannot be held valid under the Fourteenth Amendment." This reasoning was the opposite of that employed by the Arizona Supreme Court in giving its definition of property. Union actions, it was argued, merely suggested to an owner the advisability of a change in business methods, but in no sense interfered with the methods of conducting business. The economic weapons could be both primary and secondary boycotts and, further, "moral intimidation and coercion of threatening a boycott could be employed."[8] As noted, this liberality was not destined for long life after appeal to the United States Supreme Court.

A second reason for the declaration of unconstitutionality was the claim of the United States Supreme Court that the statute denied employers equal protection of the law. It contended that the Arizona statute provided employees with a right not enjoyed by employers. The Court declared:

> The necessary effect of [the Arizona law] is that the plaintiffs would have had the right to an injunction against such a campaign as that conducted by the defendants, if it had been directed against the plaintiffs, business and

property in any kind of a controversy which was not a dispute between employer and former employees. If the competing restaurant-keepers in Bisbee had inaugurated such a campaign against the plaintiff and conducted it with banners and handbills of a similar character, an injunction would necessarily have been issued to protect the plaintiffs in the employment of their property and business.

"HOLMES AND BRANDEIS DISSENTING"

Holmes and Brandeis[9] teamed up to challenge the decision of the majority. Indeed, in many other circumstances, the dissenting opinions of these two men eventually became the holdings of the majority of the Court. On many matters of fundamental importance, the Supreme Court now refers to the dissenting opinions of Holmes and Brandeis. History has demonstrated the wisdom of their views on the utilization of social and economic data in legal proceedings, the proper relationship between the legislative and judicial branches of government, and their overall approach to constitutional matters.

Holmes in *Truax* reaffirmed his belief that the legislative power of government should be checked by the judiciary only under rare and unusual circumstances. He always held closely to the principle that state legislatures and Congress should be free from judicial restraint in their attempts to experiment in legislative matters. This position was grounded in the proposition that the legislative arm of government is subject to the direct control of the electorate. Representatives who enact unpopular laws cannot expect reelection. Holmes refused to accept the proposition that the judiciary should constitute a forum for the invalidation of laws passed by popularly elected legislators. Such an attitude squares with the viewpoint of those who would see the democratic process strengthened. The containment of the legislative process by the judiciary could result in the checking of progress. Judges are elected or appointed to their positions for comparatively long periods of time. For example, members of the federal judiciary may hold office for life or, as the Constitution points out: "The Judges, both of the supreme and inferior Courts, should hold their offices during good Behavior....." This means that the judiciary, insulated against changing personnel, could act as a permanent check against the legislative will of the people. Such a circumstance is clearly demonstrated in the area of labor law.

These considerations were underscored by Holmes in the *Truax* case when he declared that

> there is nothing that I more deprecate than the use of the Fourteenth Amendment beyond the absolute compulsion of its words to prevent the

making of social experiments that an important part of the community desires, in the insulated chambers afforded by the several states, even though the experiment may seem futile or even noxious to me and to those whose judgment I most respect.

Brandeis emphasized the principle that the legislative branch of the government could properly limit the equity power of the courts in labor disputes without violating the due process clause of the Constitution. He stressed the fact that injunction control laws represented a reasonable exercise of legislative power and hence did not deprive employers of their property without due process of law. Since experience with the use of the injunction in labor disputes revealed the need for legislative restriction, the enactment of such laws was neither unreasonable nor arbitrary. Changing needs of society require the changing character of legislative approach to social and economic problems. Workers chose to form labor unions to advance their economic welfare. The courts through the injunction process threw the weight of the law on the side of management in labor controversies. Legislators, aware of these circumstances and basing their action on a plethora of data, decided to reduce the role of government in collective bargaining by decreasing the power of courts to intervene.

The fact that many legislative bodies found that regulation of the injunction in labor disputes would serve the public interest was given great weight by Brandeis. He was deeply impressed by the careful accumulation of factual evidence that stimulated the advocacy and passage of injunction control legislation. As a matter of fact, the contribution of Brandeis to the judicial process was his insistence that the courts weigh carefully the circumstances that produced legislation. He encouraged the courts to consider laws in their socioeconomic context and not to pass judgment on the basis of legal niceties or judicial precedent. In this manner, Brandeis breathed life into the law. To him, the law was not a dead, unresponsive, or unchanging institution. Rather, he thought that courts had to be aware of the swiftly moving events in the area of economic and social affairs. A law that might have been arbitrary a century ago at present might be a reasonable legislative approach to a particular problem because of the changing character of the needs of the public. This then was the creed of Brandeis: to penetrate behind the complex and intricate apparatus of the law and attach controlling weight to empirical data showing the necessity for legislation. That Brandeis was fully aware of the numerous abuses growing out of the use of the injunction in labor disputes is amply demonstrated by his statement in *Truax*. He declared that in labor injunction proceedings:

> an alleged damage to property, always incidental and at times insignificant, was often laid hold of to enable the penalties of the criminal law to be

enforced expeditiously without that protection to the liberty of the individual which the Bill of Rights was designed to afford; that through such proceedings a single judge often usurped the functions not only of the jury but of the police department; that in prescribing the conditions under which strikes were permissible and how they might be carried out, he usurped also the powers of the legislature; and that incidentally he abridged the constitutional rights of individuals to free speech, to a free press and to peaceful assembly.

As for the "equal protection" argument of the majority of the Court, Brandeis contended that a state legislature might regulate the use of the labor injunction without violating the equal protection clause of the Constitution. Such a conclusion was grounded in the commonplace legal principle that the states may set up reasonable classifications for legislative purposes. A classification between employers and employees, according to Brandeis, appeared reasonable, and consequently, to deny the use of the injunction to protect property rights in employer-employee disputes did not violate the equal-protection section of the Constitution, even though the same property rights would be protected by the injunction when parties did not stand in an employer-employee relationship. Thus Brandeis felt that the Arizona law neither denied employers the equal protection of the law, nor deprived them of their property without due process of law. A labor injunction control law constituted a valid exercise of the legislative power of the states, for such a law was designed to correct a condition deemed evil by the collective judgment of the people of the commonwealth.

❦ *NORRIS–LA GUARDIA*

The action of the Supreme Court checked any progress in the area of injunction control legislation. For about a decade, no state attempted to regulate the use of the labor injunction. In addition, state supreme courts, following the precedent of the U.S. Supreme Court, construed those state anti-injunction labor laws passed after the Clayton Act in such a manner as to render them impotent. Since the rate of issuance of labor injunctions continued unabated, organized labor still desired legislative relief. The problem, however, was to fashion a law that would effectively limit the equity power of the courts in labor disputes *and* stand the test of constitutionality.

A congressional committee appointed a panel of experts to help in the drafting of legislation that would remove the abuses of the labor injunction, stand the test of constitutionality, and generally serve the cause of justice. In 1927, an anti-injunction bill was presented to the public for

CHAPTER FOUR 77

debate. In March 1932, the bill was finally passed by overwhelming majorities in both houses of Congress and shortly afterward was signed by President Hoover. This bill was popularly termed the Norris–La Guardia Federal Anti-Injunction Act. What was the nature of this law, and how was it received by the judiciary?

NORRIS–LA GUARDIA: UNDERLYING THEORY

Congress justified the Norris–La Guardia Act by pointing to the need for collective bargaining in modern society. This consideration is clearly stated in the provision of the law that spells out the public policy of the United States with respect to employer-employee relations. This section begins by pointing out that under prevailing economic conditions, developed with the aid of government authority for owners of property to organize in the corporate and other forms of ownership association, the individual unorganized worker is commonly helpless to exercise actual liberty of contract and freedom of labor. Such a statement was supposed to reflect the current industrial environment, suggesting that a job to a worker is infinitely more important than is a single worker to a corporation. The law assumed that business enterprise would not be greatly disturbed if any single worker quit because of dissatisfaction with working conditions. On the other hand, a job was seen to be of crucial importance to the worker and the family. To insure a flow of income, the individual worker might continue to work under conditions that he or she felt were unsuitable, and would be more prone to hold jobs regardless of working conditions when there were no alternative job opportunities. Under such conditions, it would be extremely difficult, if not impossible, to argue that a worker needed a job less than a corporation needed a single worker. Consequently, the law found that there existed no liberty of contract between single workers and employers in modern industry, as was assumed in litigated cases prior to 1932. If there was no actual liberty of contract, the single worker had little or no freedom in selling his or her labor, having to hold a job regardless of working conditions. This is not to say that some workers did not quit jobs because of dissatisfaction with working conditions. Nor did these considerations deny the fact that some enterprising workers prepare themselves for better jobs by study and training. Despite these qualifications, the fact remains that in modern society, the typical individual worker tends to hold a job as long as the employer permits.

Workers tend to raise their bargaining strength by forming labor unions. An employer, though not greatly disturbed when one worker leaves employment, must be vitally concerned when all workers cease working. Regardless of the rate of output, some costs of operation continue unabated. Production stoppage could result in the inability to fill orders and even in a permanent loss of customers. Since employers are aware that collective action of workers could result in the effective use of the strike, causing economic loss to the firm, they must listen with some degree of respect to the complaints and suggestions of organized workers. In short, by organizing into labor unions, workers are in a better position to sell their services in a manner that can be more in accordance with their conception of the standards of justice and fairness.

The Norris–La Guardia Act recognized the helplessness of the individual worker in the employment relationship. It suggested that the formation of labor unions could correct the inherent inequality of bargaining power between employers and employees. Finally, it affirmed that U.S. public policy sanctions collective bargaining and approves the formation and effective operation of labor unions.

PURPOSE OF NORRIS–LA GUARDIA ACT

Thus, the basic purpose of the Norris–La Guardia Act is easily understood. Collective bargaining is endorsed by the public policy of the United States. Consequently, logic would appear to demand that Congress implement this policy by checking a condition that had historically operated to retard the growth and effective operation of the union movement. The fundamental purpose of Norris–La Guardia is to circumscribe sharply the power of the courts to intervene in labor disputes.

Since experience had shown that the injunction constituted the means by which the courts had entered the area of labor-management relations, Congress checked the prerogative of the courts to issue labor injunctions. The regulation of the injunction was incidental to the main purpose of Congress: to insulate industrial relations from the influence of the courts. If the facts had indicated that the courts had interfered in labor-management relations in other ways, the approach of Congress might have been different. From the 1880s, however, the history of labor relations had revealed that the injunction constituted the *modus operandi* of the judiciary. Hence, the law found that regulation of the equity power of the courts was the proper approach to the problem.

It was the manner in which the courts wielded their power that stimulated congressional action. If evidence had revealed that the use of the injunction did not place government on the side of employers in labor disputes, there of course would have been no necessity for an anti-injunction law. However, close attention was directed to the abuses growing out of the labor injunction. These factors led to an unmistakable conclusion: the use of the injunction placed the power of government on the side of management in labor disputes. The statute indicated that justice is advanced when government remains impartial. Accordingly, the judiciary had to behave as a neutral, not as an ally, in labor disputes. These considerations would have been equally valid if the injunctive power of the courts had been utilized to make government an ally of trade unions in labor disputes. Regulation of the injunction under these circumstances would have been just as necessary as under the conditions that actually prevailed.

Norris–La Guardia did not provide labor unions with any new legal rights. It merely allowed them a greater area in which to operate free from court control. Naturally, this circumstance facilitated immeasurably the ability of labor unions to act as effective collective bargaining agencies. It is true that Norris–La Guardia encouraged the growth of the labor movement. The fact remains, however, that this growth was nurtured by the government only to the degree that Norris–La Guardia checked the power of the courts to interfere in labor-management disputes. The Act did not require workers to join unions, nor did it stop employers from preventing the development and operation of unions by methods other than the use of the injunction. Its underlying objective was to set up an area for industrial conflict in which the courts were forbidden to tread.

AREA OF INDUSTRIAL FREEDOM

Of all the abuses growing out of the use of the injunction in labor disputes, perhaps the outstanding one was that the courts had the power to make industrial relations law. Labor leaders denounced in no uncertain terms a procedure that permitted the judiciary to usurp the power of the legislature. In particular, they protested against an arrangement that empowered the courts to decide the lawful and unlawful areas of labor union activities. The cry of organized labor—"government by injunction!"—arose from the authority of the courts to decide by themselves, regardless of the existence of the legislative arm of government, the licit and illicit in industrial relations.

Such an arrangement served to raise the courts to a position of preeminence in the area of labor-management relations. By virtue of their authority to issue injunctions in labor disputes, the courts wielded a most extraordinary power over labor relations. The manner in which they exercised this power is a matter of public record. Overwhelming evidence indicates that the equity power of the courts served the interests of the employer in labor disputes. In light of these considerations, and if the philosophy of the Norris–La Guardia Act is understood, it should be clear why the law set up a system of self-determination for labor unions. Congress stripped the federal courts of the power to restrain certain forms of union conduct. Regardless of the objective of the labor union in carrying out these activities, the authority of the federal courts to restrain such conduct was neutralized. In short, Congress immunized certain union conduct from the review of the courts. What are these activities that are insulated against court intervention?

Section 4 of Norris–La Guardia begins by declaring that no federal court shall have the power to issue any form of injunctive relief in any case involving a labor dispute, the effect of which would prohibit any person or persons participating or interested in such a dispute from doing, whether singly or in concert, any of a series of acts. The first of these acts immunized from court review is the right of workers to cease or to refuse to perform any work. Hence, this provision is designed to deny federal courts the opportunity to interfere with the right of workers to strike. Illustrations were offered that revealed that some courts stamped out strikes when judges did not approve of the purpose for which the strikes were carried out. For example, many courts restrained strikes for union security. Under the terms of Norris–La Guardia, the federal courts could not substitute their own judgment for that of workers where strikes were concerned. Judges could not restrain any strike, regardless of its objective. This does not mean that strikes are never carried out for a purpose that is clearly antisocial. That such is the case is evidenced by the fact that some public-spirited labor leaders have advocated the outlawing of certain types of strikes. The point of importance here is that Norris–La Guardia deprived judges of the power to utilize their own standards of reference to decide the lawfulness or unlawfulness of strikes. If strike control was deemed necessary in the public interest, this curtailment was supposed to be the work of the legislative branch of government. This was considered a superior approach to one in which judges, basing their decisions on their own socioeconomic outlook, were empowered to limit the right of workers to strike.

Under the protection of the Norris–La Guardia Act, labor unions could provide workers engaged in a labor dispute with strike-relief funds or with anything else of value. In the past, some judges had forbidden labor unions from providing strikers with strike-relief funds. Such a condition, of course, decreased a union's chance to win a strike. Workers on strike soon exhaust what savings they may have accumulated while at work. During a strike, the worker still must meet household expenses, insurance policy premiums, medical bills, rent, and the like. Some unions attempt to ease this burden by providing strikers with modest strike benefits. In most cases, the sum is only a fraction of what the worker would have earned at the job. However, the money is of considerable importance in such a circumstance, even if it means nothing more than improving the morale of the strikers. When unions supplement strike-relief funds with food tickets or with food itself, the lot of the striker is improved. Norris–La Guardia meant that federal courts could no longer deny labor organizations the right to perform these functions.

Section 4 also checked the power of the courts to restrain the right of workers to picket or to give publicity to labor disputes. The law facilitated the ability of workers to win labor disputes by broadening considerably the

Chapter Four

lawful area of union publicity activities. No federal court could restrain picketing activities of unions as long as violence or fraud was not present. A comparison between the picketing sections of the Clayton Act and Norris–La Guardia is worthwhile. In the former law, there was no mention of the term *picketing* or words denoting a similar meaning. The Norris–La Guardia Act, however, specifically stated that nonviolent and fraud-free "patrolling" to publicize a labor dispute could not be enjoined. In *American Steel Foundries*, the Supreme Court had held that the Clayton Act protected workers' picketing only to the extent of "one picket per entrance." In establishing this point of view, the Court no doubt was persuaded in part by the fact that the Clayton Act avoided use of specific language to protect picketing activities. Norris–La Guardia prevented such a limited construction of its provisions by utilizing the term "patrolling."

The law also permitted workers engaged in labor disputes to advise and urge other employees to join the conflict. Frequently, some workers refuse to go out on strike even though a labor union may officially proclaim one. The position of the strikers would be greatly abetted if all workers joined the strike; for where all workers strike, the employer normally cannot produce at all, or can operate only at a very low rate of production. In the past, courts were very careful to protect nonstrikers from the overtures of the workers engaged in the conflict. The decision of the Supreme Court in *American Steel Foundries* highlights this proposition. The effect of Norris–La Guardia was to provide more freedom to unions and their members to encourage all workers to strike. The action of the union in this respect is limited by the general restrictions in Section 4. Thus, whenever a union urges nonstrikers to join in the conflict, such a campaign must be free from violence or fraud.

Section 4 further forbade the issuance of a labor injunction when it would keep a union from aiding any person participating in or interested in any labor dispute who was being proceeded against, or was prosecuting, any action or suit in any state or federal court. Thus, the resources of a labor organization could be utilized to defend members of the union, or the union itself, in court proceedings. Sometimes, as an outgrowth of a labor dispute, legal action is taken against the officers of the union. Under such conditions, the organization may decide to come to the support of its officers and provide them with the services of expert and expensive legal talent. After Norris–La Guardia, such an activity could no longer be enjoined by a federal labor injunction. Furthermore, under the protection of Norris–La Guardia, labor unions could conduct meetings or assemble peacefully to promote the interests of their members. There had been evidence that some courts actually forbade workers from holding peacefully conducted meetings. An injunction that produced such a result could cause irreparable damage to a labor organization involved in a labor dispute. During the course of a strike, a union frequently holds meetings involving all or a portion of the membership to discuss items of strike strategy or to vote on the issues of the conflict. Norris–La Guardia meant that the federal court could no longer restrain the right of a union to conduct such meetings.

To underscore the guarantees already discussed, Congress added a general provision to Section 4. It stated that no court could issue an injunction to prevent workers from agreeing with each other to do any of the acts allowed in Section 4. This section was intended to prevent the application of the conspiracy doctrine to those activities removed from the scope of the labor injunction. An act engaged in by one worker no longer could be ruled unlawful when carried out by a group of workers. It was noted previously that the conspiracy doctrine operated to make group action unlawful even though the same activity would be lawful if carried out by one person. This general "anti-conspiracy" clause of Section 4 is actually rather superfluous. The general intent of the Norris–La Guardia Act would in any case prevent the application of the conspiracy doctrine to labor activities protected from the injunction. However, in its zeal to block court intervention in labor disputes, Congress wrote this provision into Section 4. It wanted to be doubly sure that the right of workers to strike, give publicity to labor disputes, hold meetings to promote their interests, or come to the aid of their fellows by providing them with legal aid or strike benefits would not be circumscribed by the judiciary.

❦ CONCEPT OF "LABOR DISPUTE"

It is clear that Congress immunized a variety of trade union activities from the application of the federal injunction. By checking the power of the courts, the Norris–La Guardia Act expanded the freedom of action of labor unions. In addition, the law protected labor union activities on a much broader basis, extending beyond a labor dispute involving an employer and its own employees. The guarantees of the law not only extended to such a limited situation, but its immunities also operated when the disputants did not stand in a proximate relationship of employer and employee. In short, for purposes of Norris–La Guardia, a *labor dispute* included any controversy concerning terms of employment or concerning the representation of employees in collective bargaining, regardless of whether or not the disputants stood in the proximate relation of employer and employee.[10] By adopting a broad definition of a labor dispute, Congress expanded considerably the limits to which unions could lawfully operate. This conception of a labor dispute squared with the realities of modern industrial life. It recognized that the successful operation of collective bargaining frequently requires the implementation of union pressure on an industry-wide or craft basis. Moreover, it recognized that the brunt of union organizational activities of a plant may fall to workers other than those directly employed by the firm. No other concept of labor dispute would have made the anti-injunction law an effective check against the labor injunction. As an illustration, the Seventh Circuit Court of Appeals ruled in 1977 that a union group that used the name of an employer it sought to organize was protected from an injunction by Norris–La Guardia. The group called itself the Great America Service Trades Council, AFL-CIO, and ran an advertisement in a newspaper addressed to applicants and potential applicants asking them to report to the council's office to sign a bargaining authorization card. The company claimed the union infringed on its registered trademark of "Great America" and asked for an injunction in federal district court, which was granted. The court of appeals reversed the decision, holding that the union's action was a legitimate one of trying to organize workers and that the use of the company's name was to facilitate this aim.[11]

THE PASSING OF THE YELLOW-DOG CONTRACT

The Norris–La Guardia Act effected still another important change in the law of industrial relations. It declared that yellow-dog contracts are not enforceable in any court of the United States. In this manner, the architects of Norris–La Guardia nullified the effect of the *Hitchman* decision, the case in which the Supreme Court upheld the validity and enforceability of the yellow-dog contract. Thus fifteen years elapsed before organized labor was released from the yellow-dog contract. Just as important is the observation that such relief came not from a change of attitude of the judiciary but from action of the legislative branch of government.

If one is aware of the effects of the yellow-dog contract on the collective bargaining process, it should be easy to understand why the instrument was declared unenforceable by Norris–La Guardia. No other single measure could exceed the effectiveness of a yellow-dog contract when enforced by an injunction. Section 3 of the law condemned the yellow-dog contract as inconsistent with the public policy of the United States. Norris–La Guardia identified public policy as support and endorsement of the collective bargaining process. Since the yellow-dog contract conflicts with such public policy, Congress denied federal courts the authority to enforce such promises.

It is noteworthy that the Norris–La Guardia Act did not outlaw the yellow-dog contract. It only made the federal courts unavailable for the enforcement of the instrument. In later years, however, the National Labor Relations Board (NLRB) held that an employer engages in an unfair labor practice if it demanded that employees execute such agreements. Thus the yellow-dog contract, the most complete of all antiunion measures, was laid to rest by action of Congress. No federal court is available for the enforcement of a contract, the terms of which require that a worker give up employment on joining a union, nor can an employer require such agreements of employees.

🌒 LABOR INJUNCTION: PROCEDURAL LIMITATIONS

Nothing could be more inaccurate than to conclude that the Norris–La Guardia Act forbade under every circumstance the issuance of federal injunctions in labor-management controversies. Certainly the law circumscribed sharply the power of courts to intervene in labor disputes. On the other hand, Congress did not prohibit altogether the issuance of labor injunctions. If a labor-management controversy does not fall within the labor dispute concept, the exercise of the equity power of the federal courts is not precluded. Despite the broad definition of labor dispute in Norris–La Guardia, there are circumstances in which a labor-management conflict does not fall within the scope of the law.[12] Injunctions can also be issued when union activities involve fraud and violence. Since the law does not distinguish between tangible property and the right to do business under proper conditions, the federal courts may protect by injunction both forms of property. Before any injunction can be issued, however, Norris–La Guardia sets up certain standards that must be adhered to by the federal courts.

Temporary Restraining Orders. In the first place, the law set up several restrictions bearing on the issuance of temporary restraining orders. The authors of Norris–La Guardia were well aware of the abuses growing out of the use of the temporary restraining order. The law provided that a hearing must take place to determine whether or not the temporary restraining order should be issued. At such hearing, the defendants in the case must be provided with the opportunity to challenge the allegations of the complainant. On the other hand, Norris–La Guardia recognized the possibility that the issuance of the temporary restraining order without such a hearing might be the only procedure whereby property could be protected from substantial and irreparable injury. For example, there would be no time to notify the defendant and hold a hearing if workers were inflicting serious damage to an employer's plant or machinery. Such circumstances demand that court intervention take place without delay. Under such pressing circumstances, a court could issue a temporary restraining order without a hearing, and the complainant must adduce testimony under oath the character of which, if sustained, would justify the court in issuing a temporary injunction upon the basis of a hearing participated in by the defendant.

If a temporary restraining order is issued in the absence of a hearing, the order by its own terms must expire within five days. This time limit was included to prevent the possibility of a temporary restraining order remaining in effect for a prolonged period. As noted, some courts, without requiring a hearing, issued temporary restraining orders that remained in force for long periods of time. When this occurred, the labor union suffered irreparable injury. The full injustice of this practice came to light when subsequent investigation proved the union innocent of the crimes alleged by the complainant. Such a possibility was precluded under the Norris–La Guardia Act by virtue of the five-day limitation.

The law set up another limitation on the issuance of temporary restraining orders. It provided that no temporary restraining order could be issued except upon condition that the complainant submit a bond with the court to recompense those enjoined for any loss, expense, or damage caused by the erroneous issuance of such an order. The amount of the bond was to be fixed by the court. In this manner, Norris–La Guardia recognized that until a full investigation was made of a case, there was always the possibility that the defendants might be unjustly enjoined. If the court restrains a labor union from a course of conduct on the basis of employer-filed evidence and if subsequent investigation proves the evidence to be invalid, Norris–La Guardia provides for some compensation for the union.

Even though the posting of a bond may serve to deter employers from requesting temporary restraining orders based on false evidence, the fact remains that the baseless enjoinment of the labor union may result in irreparable damage to the organization, regardless of the subsequent recovery of money damages. Thus real protection of unions from the labor injunction is derived from other provisions of Norris–La Guardia, and only seemingly from the bond-posting requirement. Yet this feature makes for better injunction procedure than prevailed in the period before the Norris–La Guardia Act, when many courts failed to require the posting of any bond or set the figure at a very low level. Courts resorted to this practice even though the posting of bonds of reasonable amounts was required in nonlabor cases.

Temporary and Permanent Injunctions. Congress also established a series of standards to guide the federal courts in the issuance of temporary and permanent injunctions. Norris–La Guardia provided that no court could issue these forms of injunctive relief unless a hearing was held. Before the passage of the anti-injunction law, the courts held hearings prior to the issuance of temporary injunctions. However, the character of the hearing required by the terms of the Norris–La Guardia Act differed sharply from the typical hearing conducted prior to enactment. Under Norris–La Guardia, if an injunction was sought, witnesses had to be produced to support allegations in the complaint. Thus, federal courts could no longer issue temporary injunctions on the basis of mere sworn affidavits, a procedure proven inequitable in the pre-Norris–La Guardia period. In addition, the union had to be permitted to produce witnesses to challenge the allegations. Both sides had to be allowed the opportunity to cross-examine witnesses. Thus, the law gave the court a better basis to determine the facts of the case. An injunction issued after such precautions most likely is justified. It is important to note that these requirements apply equally to temporary and permanent injunction proceedings.

Federal courts may not grant injunctive relief unless the facts indicate that in the absence of the injunction, substantial and irreparable injury to property will result. Moreover, prior to the issuance of a temporary or permanent injunction, the court must be satisfied that greater injury will be inflicted upon the complainant by the denial of relief than will be inflicted upon the defendant by the granting of relief. This provision recognized that a labor union might suffer from the issuance of an injunction. It further recognized that an employer might be injured in the absence of an injunction. Only after the court balances these relative injuries may it exercise its equity power in labor disputes. Of course, the problem must be resolved largely on a subjective basis. In any event, the requirement of balancing the relative damages to the disputants was supposed to serve the cause of justice.

In addition, under the terms of Norris–La Guardia, the court prior to the granting of equity relief must be satisfied that the complainant has no adequate remedy at law. This means that no injunction will be issued against a labor union if the court finds that the employer may recover damages resulting from unlawful union activity in trial court proceedings. Considerations that would prompt a court to find that an employer has no adequate remedy at law include: (1) financial irresponsibility of the labor union; (2) the fact that an employer would be required to file a multiplicity of suits to recover damages; and (3) the possibility that it would be difficult to obtain a jury that would not be sympathetic to the labor union. The latter factor would be important in a community that is a stronghold of unionism—the so-called "union town."

Still another finding of fact must be made by the court before Norris–La Guardia sanctions the granting of a temporary or permanent injunction. The facts must reveal that local police officers charged with the duty to protect the complainant's property are unable or unwilling to furnish adequate protection. This provision threw the responsibility for the protection of property on the local community. Many people would agree that such protection is the primary concern of local police officers. If the local police force is capable of providing such protection, it is undesirable for the federal government to exercise its authority in labor disputes. Most labor-management disputes have a local setting. It appears that local control of the matter will advance the long-run cause of industrial relations harmony. Local police officers frequently know personally the people involved in the dispute. Such law enforcement officers, as a result of this personal relationship, can frequently contain violence by resort to mere moral suasion. However, provided the other requirements of Norris–La Guardia are satisfied, federal courts may issue injunctions in labor disputes when local protection of property is lacking.

Elimination of the Blanket Injunction. Previous discussion revealed that one of the most flagrant abuses growing out of labor injunctions involved the blanket injunction. The chief characteristic of this abuse relates to the all-inclusive scope of the court order. Courts enjoined lawful as well as unlawful acts and directed injunctions at people not committing unlawful acts as well as those engaging in such conduct. The blanket injunction resulted from the courts' utilization of catchall phrases. Unions found that the task of winning labor disputes was made difficult, if not impossible, when they were confronted with the blanket injunction.

Authors of Norris–La Guardia took these considerations into account when the provisions of the law were written. To eliminate the blanket injunction, the law required that all injunctions issued by federal courts had to be specific in their terminology. Persons or organizations enjoined in the carrying out of unlawful conduct had to be specified by name. This provision eliminated the use of the typical ambiguous phrase, frequently found in the labor injunction before Norris–La Guardia: "all other persons whomsoever." In addition, the federal courts now had to state clearly the unlawful acts to be enjoined. Thus, the law required that the labor injunction prohibit only "specific acts as may be expressedly complained of in the bill of complaint filed" as a result of a labor dispute. This standard eliminated the catchall phrase: "in any way interfering with the operation of the complainant's business." Such vague clauses were frequently contained in injunctions issued prior to the passage of Norris–La Guardia. The law recognized that in the course of some labor disputes, some actions of unionists and their sympathizers might be unlawful while others might be lawful. The purpose of requiring specific wording by courts in injunctions was to eliminate only the performance of illegal conduct. The requirement for specific terminology applied equally to the temporary restraining order and the temporary or permanent injunction.

Promotion of the Collective Bargaining Process. Norris–La Guardia rests on the assumption that labor peace can best be achieved through the acceptance in good faith of the collective bargaining process. This feature of the law is best exemplified by its provision denying parties to a labor dispute the opportunity to obtain injunctive relief unless all possibilities of settling their controversies through collective bargaining have been exhausted. In short, the law places the primary responsibility for achieving industrial peace on management and labor. The equity powers of the judiciary are not available to any party to a labor dispute if the court finds that the party has not made reasonable efforts to settle the dispute by direct negotiation. When direct negotiation fails, the disputants are expected to make use, whenever appropriate, of mediation and voluntary arbitration.[13] Good faith in collective bargaining must further be demonstrated by the willingness of the parties to comply with any law controlling the collective bargaining process. For example, a union does not qualify for injunctive relief if it has violated legislation regulating the collective bargaining process. Although labor unions make few applications for injunctions, the fact remains that a labor organization cannot avail itself of the advantages of the equity power of the judiciary when facts indicate that it has not complied with a law applicable to a labor dispute. Under Taft-Hartley, for instance, it is an unfair labor practice for a labor union to refuse to bargain collectively. If a union fails to fulfill this responsibility, the federal courts must act unfavorably on its application for equity relief.

Few people will find fault with this requirement of Norris–La Guardia. It is unwise to make available injunctive relief when facts indicate that the applicant has violated a law applicable to the labor dispute. Successful collective bargaining requires an honest attempt by both sides to reach a peaceful agreement. If any party to a labor dispute fails to bargain in good faith or refuses to comply with laws bearing on the collective bargaining process, it appears reasonable to deny to this party injunctive relief.

Violations of Injunctions. Two significant innovations for contempt of court proceedings are found in Norris–La Guardia. If a person is charged with contempt of court, the accused has the right to a "speedy trial and public trial by an impartial jury." Previously, it was pointed out that persons charged with contempt before Norris–La Guardia had no right to a jury trial. Such a procedure meant that the same judge who issued an injunction had the power to decide whether that injunction had been violated and what the punishment should be. In many cases, judges abused this prerogative and imposed penalties on highly questionable grounds. Particular abuse resulted when judges were biased against trade unions. After Norris–La Guardia was passed, a person charged with violation of a labor injunction could be tried by a jury of peers. Such an opportunity is denied defendants in a labor injunction proceeding when contempt is committed in the presence of the court or so near thereto as to interfere directly with the administration of justice. But a person charged with contempt of court can request a change of judge if demand for the withdrawal of the judge is made prior to the hearing on the contempt proceeding. Upon the demand for the retirement of a judge, the judge must

Chapter Four

withdraw from the case and another judge must be designated to conduct the proceeding. Obviously, this provision was inserted in the Norris–La Guardia Act to eliminate from contempt proceedings a judge possessing a strong antiunion bias. Persons charged with the violation of a labor injunction had no such privilege before Norris–La Guardia was passed.

JUDICIAL CONSTRUCTION OF NORRIS–LA GUARDIA

Historical evidence demonstrated that when the equity power of the courts was exercised in labor disputes, the power of government was on the side of employers. Norris–La Guardia was passed to eliminate this condition. By freeing certain union practices from the impact of the injunction and by regulating closely the procedure of issuing injunctions, Congress implemented its desire to neutralize the influence of the courts in labor-management controversies. Despite the law's clear terms, the judicial interpretation of the Norris–La Guardia Act was awaited with high interest, particularly by organized labor and employers. Both were aware of the possibility that the judiciary might nullify the second attempt of Congress to regulate the use of injunctions in labor disputes.

The first indication of the judicial fate of Norris–La Guardia involved the Supreme Court's construction of the Wisconsin anti-injunction law. In 1931, Wisconsin enacted an injunction law that foreshadowed Norris–La Guardia. In many respects, the Wisconsin law was similar to the federal anti-injunction measure. The terms of the state law were just as protective of labor unions as were those subsequently contained in Norris–La Guardia. Consequently, what the Supreme Court had to say about the Wisconsin law would be applicable to Norris–La Guardia. If the Court found the state law unconstitutional, or interpreted it in a manner that would drastically reduce its applicability, the same fate would be in store for the federal anti-injunction law. If, on the other hand, the high court upheld the constitutionality of the Wisconsin law and construed its terms in a liberal manner, the supporters of the federal law would be encouraged.

In addition, the character of the construction of the Wisconsin law would influence profoundly the effectiveness and progress of state anti-injunction laws. Passage of the Norris–La Guardia Act encouraged many state legislatures to enact laws patterned after the federal statute. If the high court treated the Wisconsin law unfavorably, these state laws would be rendered useless. Other states that might have been inclined to enact anti-injunction laws would be discouraged by an adverse construction of the Wisconsin statute. Thus, from the state and federal point of view, the nation awaited with deep interest the Supreme Court construction of the Wisconsin anti-injunction law.

THE TILE-LAYING INDUSTRY CASE

The Wisconsin law was tested in 1937 in a case involving the tile-laying industry of Milwaukee.[14] For many years this industry had been in a depressed condition. Lack of building operations had resulted in serious unemployment among tile layers. Severe competition also added to the problems of the industry. Some of the workers of the industry were organized and others were not. Labor standards in the unionized section were higher than those prevailing in the nonunion portion. To protect the union worker, the Tile Layers Union had insisted that each employer with whom it had a contract employ only members of the union. In addition, the union required that no employer work on the job. This requirement was embodied in the following clause contained in each agreement:

> ARTICLE III. It is definitely understood that no individual, member of a partnership, or corporation engaged in the Tile Contracting Business shall work with the tools or act as Helper but that the installation of material...shall be done by journeymen members of the Tile Layers Union Local #5.

Obviously, the objective of the prohibition was to provide more jobs for union members. Widespread unemployment among tile layers and the fact that the tile-laying industry contained many employers who hired only a small number of employees induced the union to adopt a program to increase job opportunities for its members. A Mr. Senn became involved in a dispute with the union over the restriction contained in Article III.

Senn was in the contracting business in Milwaukee. His operations were very small. At peak seasons, he employed only two journey tile layers and two helpers. He worked along with his employees and performed on-the-job work normally done by a journey tile layer or helper. The union wanted Senn to become a union contractor, and requested that he sign an agreement that would deny him the opportunity to work personally on the job. He claimed that he would execute a union agreement provided that Article III did not appear in the agreement.

As expected, the union refused such a request. It pointed out the reasons for Article III and further declared that the granting of Senn's request would discriminate against all contractors who signed agreements that included Article III. Since the union could not grant Senn's request, he refused to sign the agreement or to allow his small shop to be unionized. As a result of his refusal, the union picketed his place of business. According to the record, the picketing was peaceful and was conducted without violence. The objective of the picketing was to persuade the public to cease doing business with Senn and to encourage the people of Milwaukee to take their business to employers under contract with the labor union.

Chapter Four

The Wisconsin anti-injunction law, the statute in question, operated to protect the picketing activities of the union. Senn sought an injunction from the state courts to enjoin further picketing. He claimed that the picketing was injuring his business and that the objective of the union—to require him to refrain from working with his own hands—was unlawful. The state courts of Wisconsin refused his request, pointing to the provisions of the Wisconsin statute forbidding the courts to issue injunctions to enjoin peaceful picketing. Not content with the decision of the state court, Senn appealed his case to the Supreme Court of the United States. He claimed that the Wisconsin law was unconstitutional on the ground that it deprived him of his property without due process of law. As such, the charge against the Wisconsin statute duplicated the one leveled against the Arizona anti-injunction law, which had been held unconstitutional in *Truax* v. *Corrigan*.

By a 5–4 vote, the Supreme Court upheld the constitutionality of the Wisconsin law. Brandeis delivered the majority opinion of the Court. He pointed out that the end sought by the union was not malicious or unlawful, for the union rule was reasonable and "adopted by the defendant out of the necessities of employment within the industry and for the protection of themselves as workers and craftsmen in the industry." Brandeis conceded that the disclosure of the existence of the labor dispute by the union might be annoying to Senn. But, he declared, "such annoyance, like that often suffered from publicity in other connections, is not an invasion of the liberty guaranteed by the Constitution. Unions may request by picketing that the public withhold patronage from an employer 'unfair to organized labor' and bestow it on unionized firms." Brandeis showed the similarity of such union picketing to the advertisements of merchants who compete with one another by means of the press, by circulars, or by window displays. If the latter form of advertising does not violate the Constitution, Brandeis believed that a union publicity campaign, carried on peacefully and truthfully, was likewise lawful.

Other arguments were presented by Brandeis to support the Court's position. Both members of the union and Senn had the right to strive to earn a living. Senn sought to do so through exercise of his individual skill and planning. It was not unlawful if workers by combination sought the same objective. The union did not desire to injure Senn, but the picketing was carried on to "acquaint the public with the facts, and, by gaining its support, to induce Senn to unionize his shop." Brandeis pointed out that Senn had the equal opportunity to "disclose the facts in such manner and in such detail as he deemed desirable, and on the strength of the facts to seek the patronage of the public." In any event, if the effect of the picketing prevented Senn from securing jobs, there was no invasion of constitutional rights, for "a hoped-for job is not properly guaranteed by the Constitution."

Since the means of the union and the end it sought did not violate the Constitution, the Supreme Court held that the Wisconsin law that insulated the union activities from the injunction did not deprive Senn of his property without due process of law. In this connection, Brandeis declared: "If the end sought by the unions is not forbidden by the Federal constitution the state may authorize working men to seek to attain it by combining as pickets, just as it permits corporations and employers to combine in other ways to attain their desired economic ends."

The *Senn* decision marked a significant change in attitude on the part of the Supreme Court. Workers could take effective action to achieve their economic objectives. Such a program was not unlawful merely because it interfered with the right to run a business. Not only business people could organize for their mutual protection, but workers likewise could join in association and undertake action designed to implement the objectives of their associations. The *Seen* decision, which reflected the Brandeis philosophy, stands as a landmark in industrial relations law. It was the forerunner of a long line of court decisions that constructed a more favorable climate for the operation of effective collective bargaining.

THE *LAUF* DOCTRINE: WIDE APPLICATION OF NORRIS–LA GUARDIA ASSURED

One year after the *Senn* decision, the Supreme Court decided the fate of Norris–La Guardia. For a time it appeared that the federal judiciary would repeat the Clayton Act performance and destroy the effectiveness of Norris–La Guardia. In spite of the unmistakable intent and written mandate of Congress, the lower federal courts held that the terms of the Norris–La Guardia Act did not apply to labor disputes when the disputants did not stand in a proximate relationship of employer and employee. Such an interpretation, wholly inconsistent with the terms of the law, if sustained by the Supreme Court, would have destroyed the effectiveness of Norris–La Guardia. It would have allowed a wide basis for the issuance of the labor injunction. The result would have been a nullification of the second attempt of Congress to provide labor unions with a measure of relief from the restraining hand of the judiciary.

For these reasons, all interested parties awaited the Supreme Court's ruling in the *Lauf* case with deep interest.[15] Like the tile-laying case, the locale was Milwaukee. Unlike that case, however, the industry was the retail meat markets of the city. The company in the dispute operated five meat markets. About thirty-five employees worked in them. None belonged to Local No. 73 of the AFL Butchers Union, the labor organization in question. The labor union attempted to organize the five stores. The union conducted an extensive picketing program, the objective of which was to condemn the company in the public's eyes as unfair to organized labor. Previously, the company had refused the union demand to compel its workers to join the union as a condition of employment. It contended that its employees had their "own association and were perfectly well satisfied." There was speculation that the company had sponsored the inside union with the objective of keeping it out of a nationally affiliated labor organization.

In any event, the picketing continued, and subsequently the lower federal courts enjoined all picketing activities of the Butchers Union. The terms of the injunction provided that the union and its members were forbidden from (1) in any way picketing the premises of the complainant; (2) advertising, stating, or pretending that the complainant was in any way unfair to said defendants or organized labor generally; and (3) persuading or soliciting any customers or prospective customers of the said complainant to cease patronizing the complainant at its meat markets.[16] As noted, the lower federal courts issued the injunction on the ground that the pickets were not employees of the company.

If the Supreme Court had sustained the injunction, Norris–La Guardia would not have afforded much protection to labor unions conducting organizing campaigns. Unions grow through the organization of the unorganized. The job of organizing a nonunion plant is at times very difficult. For this reason, experienced representatives of established international unions frequently spearhead organizational campaigns. Such international representatives are not actual employees of the plants that are being organized. For this reason, the lower federal courts that handled the *Lauf* case enjoined these representatives' activities. It follows from such a doctrine that nationally affiliated unions would not have been able to organize a nonunion area or a plant in which a company-dominated union is operating. Under such a construction of Norris–La Guardia, the public policy expressed in the statute—encouragement of the collective bargaining process—could not have been implemented.

The Supreme Court refused to sustain the ruling of the lower federal courts. It found that a labor dispute existed in the *Lauf* case, even though the disputants did not stand in proximate relationship of employer and employee. Such an interpretation is demanded by the terms of Norris–La Guardia. The members of the Butchers Union had a real economic interest in the outcome of the organizational drive of the nonunion retail meat markets. Higher labor standards prevailing in the union shops were imperiled to the extent that nonunion shops operated. If the Butchers Union did not organize each nonunion shop, it could be expected that union stores, once their collective bargaining contracts expired, would resist the execution of new ones, claiming inability to meet nonunion competition. As a result of these considerations, the Supreme Court held that a labor dispute within the meaning of Norris–La Guardia existed. Since the controversy constituted a labor dispute, the high court ordered dissolved the injunction which restrained the picketing. The Butchers

Union was free to picket the nonunion meat markets even though they had no members working in the shops.

The *Lauf* decision affirmed the power of Congress to define and limit the jurisdiction of the federal courts. It demonstrated that Norris–La Guardia was to apply to a wide area of industrial relations. Unions were to be protected in their activities regardless of whether the disputants were in the proximate relationship of employer and employee. The *Lauf* decision served to emphasize the fact that the way was clear for Congress to regulate the collective bargaining process.

❦ THE IMPACT OF NORRIS–LA GUARDIA

Approval by the Supreme Court of Norris–La Guardia checked the use of the federal labor injunction. The action of the high court also stimulated the passage of state labor injunction control legislation. By 1967, twenty-five states and Puerto Rico had enacted injunction control legislation.[17] The state statutes vary, but all have similarities to Norris–La Guardia. It is likely that labor injunction procedures in these states have improved because of the existence of the federal law. However, the fact remains that the absence of state injunction control legislation provides the springboard for court intervention in labor disputes. Experience has conclusively demonstrated that such intervention has resulted in the placing of government on the side of employers in labor-management controversies. For example, some early experience in Ohio indicates that the equity power of the state courts has proven harmful to the growth and effective operation of the collective bargaining process.[18]

If a great deal of labor violence had followed the Norris–La Guardia Act, the legislation would not have been effective. Some people were fearful that this condition would result from the passage of the statute. However, there is no evidence that more violence accompanied labor disputes after Norris–La Guardia than took place before this law was passed. As a matter of fact, some of the U.S.'s most bloody strikes, such as Pullman and Homestead, occurred before 1932. It is noteworthy that in England, labor violence has been less extensive than in the United States. This remains true even though the use of the labor injunction in Great Britain has been comparatively infrequent. It must be emphasized that violence is unlawful with or without injunctions. Overturning of automobiles, beatings, damage to machinery, and the like are not less unlawful because of the nonexistence of the injunction. On the other hand, as remarked previously, it is doubtful that an injunction will prevent violence if workers are bent on it.

One must be careful to distinguish between the violence of labor disputes and the use of organized labor's economic weapons. Implementation of the strike, picketing, and the boycott do not signify labor violence. In fact, Norris–La Guardia was passed to free these normal expressions of collective action from the restraining hand of the judiciary. The point of importance is that the anti-injunction law has not encouraged the carrying out of these trade union functions within a context of lawlessness and violence.

Nor should one point to the growth of the union movement as grounds for the condemnation of Norris–La Guardia. Indeed, the statute was passed to promote the union movement and collective bargaining. By regulating the use of the injunction in labor disputes, Norris–La Guardia provided a legal environment favorable to the growth of the union movement. One may quarrel with the objective of the law, but one scarcely can criticize the legislation because it has accomplished its goal. It is extremely doubtful that the growth of the union movement could have taken place in the absence of an effective law controlling the use of injunctions in labor disputes.

SUMMARY

The Great Depression of the thirties resulted in a profound change in the climate of social thought about the place of unions in contemporary society. As a result, Congress and some state governments passed legislation to provide a more favorable legal structure for the operation of unionism. The Norris–La Guardia Act was the first expression of this new legislative policy. It served to neutralize the power of the courts in labor disputes by regulating the substance and procedure of the labor injunction. Whereas the Clayton Act was interpreted into ineffectiveness by the Supreme Court, Norris–La Guardia was treated favorably by the courts. This was expected, because the judiciary could not very well isolate itself from the forces of social thought.

Congress justified Norris–La Guardia by pointing to the need for collective bargaining in modern society. Since the abuse of the labor injunction operated to forestall unionism, it was proper to pass legislation to deprive employers of the opportunity to utilize the judiciary as an ally in labor-management disputes. The effect of Norris–La Guardia was to provide unions with a larger area in which to carry on their activities without interference by the courts. As such, the law conferred no new rights on workers. It merely neutralized the federal courts in labor disputes. The Supreme Court has been diligent in carrying out the congressional intent even in cases where it considered justice would have been better served by deviation from that intent.

The passage of Norris–La Guardia served to implement its basic objective: the containment of the influence of the courts in labor disputes.

Among other things, it deprived the federal courts of the power to enforce the yellow-dog contract; denied them the right to enjoin peaceful and truthful picketing regardless of the purpose of the picketing; forbade courts to enjoin peaceful strikes regardless of the purpose of the strike; and established a carefully drawn-up procedure to regulate the issuance of the injunction in labor disputes when the law did not forbid the instrument. Some states passed "little" Norris–La Guardia acts to protect workers not covered by the national statute.

❦ DISCUSSION QUESTIONS

1. What impact did the Supreme Court's rule regarding Wisconsin's anti-injunction law have on the various states in their attempts to control use of the labor injunction?
2. How did the Supreme Court construe Section 20 of the Clayton Act, and what effect did that have on unions?
3. What was the intent of Congress in the passage of the Norris–La Guardia Act?
4. Explain how Norris–La Guardia dealt with the following issues:
    (a) court neutrality in labor disputes
    (b) definition of a labor dispute
    (c) yellow-dog contracts.
    Were important court decisions overturned by Congress in these categories?
5. Congress placed procedural limitations on court issuance of injunctions. When could the courts use injunctions in labor cases under these procedural restrictions?
6. Demonstrate, with reference to appropriate court cases, how the Supreme Court interpreted the Norris–La Guardia Act.
7. How might the provisions of Norris–La Guardia be applied to nonlabor organizations? Is there adequate court authority to provide an answer to this question?

❦ NOTES

[1] Florence Peterson, *American Labor Unions* (New York: Harper & Brothers, 1935), p. 56.

[2] Edwin E. Witte, *The Government in Labor Disputes* (New York: McGraw-Hill Book Company, 1932), pp. 270–273.

[3] Section 20, Clayton Act, reads as follows: "That no restraining order or injunction shall be granted by any court of the United States, or a judge or the judges thereof, in any case between an employer and employees, or between employers and employees, or between employees, or between persons employed and persons seeking employment, involving, or growing out of a dispute concerning terms or conditions of employment, unless necessary to

prevent irreparable injury to property, or to a property right, of the party making the application, for which injury there is no adequate remedy at law, and such property or property right must be described with particularity in the application, which must be in writing and sworn to by the applicant or by his agent or attorney."

"And no such restraining order or injunction shall prohibit any person or persons, whether singly or in concert, from terminating any relation of employment, or from ceasing to perform any work or labor or from recommending, advising or persuading others by peaceful means so to do; or from attending at any place where any such person or persons may lawfully be, for the purpose of peacefully obtaining or communicating information, or from peacefully persuading any person to work or to abstain from working; or from ceasing to patronize or to employ any party to such dispute, or recommending, advising, or persuading others by peaceful and lawful means so to do; or from paying or giving to, or withholding from, any person engaged in such dispute, any strike benefits or other moneys or things of value; or from peaceably assembling in a lawful manner, and for lawful purposes; or from doing any act or thing which might lawfully be done in the absence of such dispute by any party thereto; nor shall any of the acts specified in this paragraph be considered or held to be violations of any law of the United States."

[4] These states were Oregon, North Dakota, Utah, Washington, and Wisconsin.

[5] *American Steel Foundries* v. *Tri-City Central Trades Council*, 257 U.S. 312 (1921).

[6] *Truax* v. *Corrigan*, 257 U.S. 312 (1921).

[7] The Fourteenth Amendment to the Constitution states: "Nor shall any State deprive any person of life, liberty, or property, without due process of law; nor deny to any person within its jurisdiction the equal protection of the laws."

[8] Benjamin J. Taylor, *Arizona Labor Relations Law* (Tempe: Arizona State University, Occasional Paper No. 2, Bureau of Business and Economic Research, College of Business Administration, 1967), pp. 14–15.

[9] For an interesting and stimulating account of the life of Louis Dembitz Brandeis, see A. T. Mason, *Brandeis: A Free Man's Life* (New York: The Viking Press, 1946). On the life of Oliver Wendell Holmes, Jr., see Silas Bent, *Justice Oliver Wendell Holmes* (New York: Vanguard Press, 1932).

[10] See Chapter 5 for a discussion of the importance of the concept of labor dispute established in Norris–La Guardia relative to the application of antitrust laws to labor activities. Section 13 of Norris–La Guardia spells out the meaning of "labor dispute."

[11] *Marriott Corp.* v. *Great America Service Trades Council*, AFL-CIO, 552 Fed. 2nd 176.

[12] See, for example, *Carpenters and Joiners Union* v. *Ritter's Cafe*, 315 U.S. 722 (1942). The principle of the case is that picketing must be confined to the industry in which the labor dispute has arisen if the picketing is to be protected from the labor injunction.

[13] Voluntary arbitration means the employer and union mutually select an impartial person to decide the dispute. Most important, they agree to the

finality of the decision. Arbitration is used extensively to resolve disputes arising under an existing labor agreement. It is used infrequently to determine disputes arising in the negotiation of a new contract.

[14] *Senn v. Tile Layers*, 301 U.S. 468 (1937).

[15] *Lauf v. Shinner & Company*, 303 U.S. 323 (1938).

[16] Harry A. Millis and Royal E. Montgomery, *Organized Labor* (New York: McGraw-Hill Book Company, 1945), p. 624.

[17] United States Department of Labor, *Growth of Labor Law in the United States* (Washington, D.C.: U.S. Government Printing Office, 1967), p. 207.

[18] Glenn W. Miller, *American Labor and the Government* (Englewood Cliffs, N.J.: Prentice-Hall, Inc., 1948), pp. 107, 112.

CHAPTER FIVE

ANTITRUST PROSECUTION UNDER NORRIS–LA GUARDIA

NORRIS–LA GUARDIA AND LABOR PROTECTION

Norris–La Guardia did more than curb the labor injunction. It served to restrict labor union prosecution under the antitrust laws. Although the terms "Sherman Act" or "antitrust laws" do not appear in Norris–La Guardia, the background of the law reveals that this was the unmistakable intention of Congress. It was enacted to provide unions with the benefits they had hoped for under the Clayton Act. On this score the authors of the statute declared, "The purpose of the bill is to protect the right of labor in the same manner the Congress intended when it enacted the Clayton Act, which act, by reason of its construction and application by the Federal Courts, is ineffectual to accomplish the Congressional intent."[1] Along the same lines, the Supreme Court subsequently affirmed that "the Norris–La Guardia Act was a disapproval of *Duplex Printing Press* v. *Deering* and *Bedford Cut Stone Company* v. *Journeymen Stone Cutters Association* as the authoritative interpretation of Section 20 of the Clayton Act."[2] Thus, the Norris–La Guardia Act granted protection to labor unions from the application of the Sherman Act. How did Norris–La Guardia accomplish this purpose? How did the Supreme Court react to this new effort of Congress? What developments indicate a possible change in direction on the part of the Court regarding the extent of permissible union action in the pursuit of its own interests?

🌿 LABOR DISPUTE DEFINED BROADLY IN NORRIS–LA GUARDIA

In writing Norris–La Guardia, Congress remedied the labor provisions of the Clayton Act. Section 20[3] of the latter statute prohibited the federal courts from restraining certain activities of unions growing out of a labor dispute. However, in the Clayton Act, Congress failed to define the meaning of *labor dispute*. The judiciary was obliged to define the term. The character of the construction was of paramount importance, for the labor dispute definition determined the practical effects of the Clayton Act. Thus an activity of a union growing out of a labor dispute could not be enjoined. But the very same activity—say, peaceful picketing or an orderly strike—not arising out of a labor dispute was subject to the injunction.[4] The concept of a labor dispute had particular importance for unions involved in antitrust proceedings. The last sentence of Section 20 provided that an activity of a labor union immunized by the statute could not be held to constitute a violation of *any law* of the United States. For practical purposes, this meant that where Section 20 protects a union activity from a labor injunction, the federal judiciary may not find such conduct to be a violation of any law of the United States, including the Sherman Act. On the other hand, this immunity does not apply when the act of the labor organization does not arise out of a labor dispute as that term has meaning for the purposes of the Clayton Act.

In the *Duplex* decision, it was necessary for the Supreme Court to construe the meaning of labor dispute. Much to the disappointment of organized labor, the Court defined the concept in a very narrow fashion. It held that for a labor controversy to fall within the meaning of a labor dispute for purposes of the Clayton Act, the parties to the dispute had to stand in proximate relationship of employer and employee. It will be recalled that with the exception of *Coronado*, the major antitrust cases resulting in legal setbacks to organized labor centered on secondary boycotts. In a secondary boycott, a union exerts pressure against employers who have no direct controversy with the organization. Labor organizations have often exerted pressure on other firms for the purpose of winning their dispute with the employer with whom the union is embroiled in a controversy. Such was the logic of the secondary boycott activities instigated by unions in *Danbury Hatters, Bucks Stove, Duplex,* and *Bedford Stone*.

Organized labor hoped the Clayton Act would be interpreted to forbid the issuance of an injunction to restrain secondary boycott picketing. The courts would then have been required to hold that the secondary economic pressure of unions did not violate any federal law, including the Sherman Act. These hopes were not realized; the high court excluded union secondary pressure activities from the protection of Section 20 because the parties to the controversy did not stand in proximate relationship of employer and employee. The limitations in Section 20, the

Court said, applied only to disputants in a labor controversy "who are proximately and substantially concerned as parties to an actual dispute respecting the terms or conditions of their own employment, past, present, or prospective." The Court refused to protect union activity directed against firms "wholly unconnected" with a company with which a union has a dispute over conditions of employment except "in the way of purchasing its products in the ordinary course of interstate commerce."

Brandeis vigorously denounced this point of view of the majority of the Supreme Court. He argued that the fundamental purpose of the Clayton Act was to broaden the legitimate area of union activities. Brandeis felt that Section 20 of the Clayton Act protected a secondary boycott from the injunction, and hence from the application of the Sherman Act, for "a statute of the United States declares the right of industrial combatants to push their struggle to the limit of the justification of self interest."

The authors of Norris–La Guardia were well aware of the various constructions placed on the term *labor dispute* by the judiciary. In the absence of legislative action, labor unions could not engage in secondary economic pressure activities, for the parties involved in such disputes do not stand in a proximate relationship of employer and employee. The task of Congress was to write a definition of labor dispute that would nullify the effect of the *Duplex* decision. It was necessary to spell out the concept in a manner that would legalize union secondary boycott activities. To accomplish this objective, Norris–La Guardia defined a labor dispute as any controversy concerning conditions of employment, *regardless of whether the disputants stand in proximate relationship of employee and employer.*

❦ JUDICIAL REACTION

In spite of the clear terms of Norris–La Guardia, organized labor was fearful that the courts would find some way to nullify the intent of Congress. Union leaders remembered the fate of the Clayton Act. Court construction would determine whether or not the new law was to provide benefits to labor unions. For these reasons, the judicial construction of the law was awaited with much interest. The Supreme Court of the United States interpreted the Norris–La Guardia Act so as to conform with the intent of Congress. Its terms were broad enough, the Court held, to forbid the issuance of labor injunctions to restrain union secondary pressure tactics.

This principle was first established in *Milk Wagon Drivers Union* in 1940, and reaffirmed the next year in the more widely known *Hutcheson* decision. The members of the Milk Wagon Drivers Union, an American Federation of Labor affiliate, handled the bulk of the home milk deliveries in Chicago. With the advent of the depression, however, the "vendor system" of milk distribution was established. Under this depression-stimulated method, vendors purchased milk from nonunion dairies and sold the product to retail stores. As a result, the stores were able to sell milk at a price below that prevailing for milk delivered at home. To complicate the whole affair, the vendors organized themselves into a CIO union, but this feature of interunion rivalry did not influence the subsequent decision of the Supreme Court. The members of the Milk Wagon Drivers Union picketed the retail stores that handled milk under the new milk distribution method.

The action of the Milk Wagon Drivers Union constituted a secondary boycott, for pressure was placed on the retail stores not to deal with the vendors, with the intent of encouraging the vendors not to purchase milk from nonunion dairies. Interstate commerce was involved because the Chicago milk area included the state of Wisconsin. After a federal district court refused to enjoin the action of the labor organization, an appeal was made to the Seventh Circuit Court of Appeals.[5] This court reversed the district court and held that the AFL union, by engaging in a secondary boycott, violated the terms of the Sherman Act. Finally, the Supreme Court, in a unanimous decision, held that Norris–La Guardia protected the action of the AFL union, for the union was engaged in a labor dispute within the meaning of the law.[6]

In *Hutcheson*, Norris–La Guardia was once more interpreted in a manner that protected union secondary boycott activities.[7] In this matter, an interunion jurisdictional problem was involved. It centered on a controversy involving the United Brotherhood of Carpenters and Joiners of America and the International Association of Machinists. Both these labor organizations were affiliated with the AFL at the time of the conflict. The dispute was over the issue of which of these unions was to install and dismantle machinery in the Anheuser-Busch property in St. Louis.

When the Machinists Union was awarded the job by the company, the Carpenters Union called a strike, picketed the plant, and refused to permit its members to work on new construction taking place on Anheuser-Busch property. In addition, through letters and labor journals, the union called upon its members and friends to refrain from purchasing or selling Anheuser-Busch beer. In a split decision, three jurists dissenting, the Supreme Court held that the action of the Carpenters Union was protected by Norris–La Guardia. Despite the fact that the secondary boycott grew out of a jurisdictional dispute between two unions, the high court held that the terms of Norris–La Guardia were applicable. The controversy was a labor dispute within the meaning of the Act, and for this reason the federal courts were not permitted to restrain the activities of the labor organizations. Not only did the term *labor dispute* include controversies between an employer and its own employees, but the term was elastic enough to prohibit prosecution of a union involved in an interunion jurisdictional dispute.

CHAPTER FIVE

Roberts wrote the dissenting opinion in the *Hutcheson* case, contending that Norris–La Guardia did not preclude the application of the Sherman Act to union secondary boycott action. His position was that even though Norris–La Guardia might serve to protect unions against injunctions in such controversies, the union could be sued for damages or tried under the criminal provisions of the Sherman Act. It will be recalled that the Sherman Act provided for its enforcement along three lines—injunction, damage suits, and criminal prosecution. According to Roberts, the fact that the injunction might be prohibited in labor cases did not mean that the other two methods of enforcement could not be employed. He declared that

> what a reading of the [Norris–La Guardia] Act makes letter clear, is that the prosecution of actions for damages authorized by the Sherman Act, and of the criminal offenses denounced by the Act, are not touched by the Norris–La Guardia Act. By a process of construction never, as I think, heretofore indulged by this court, it is now found that, because Congress forbade the issuing of injunctions to restrain certain conduct, it intended to repeal the provisions of the Sherman Act authorizing actions at law and criminal prosecutions for the commission of torts and crimes defined by the antitrust laws.

Roberts's viewpoint, though on the surface tenable, appears wholly inconsistent with the intent of Norris–La Guardia. It is doubtful that Congress meant to restrain the issuance of injunctions in labor cases arising under the Sherman Act, only to permit unions to be attacked through damage suits and criminal prosecution. If the position of Roberts had prevailed, unions would have lost whatever benefits Congress had intended them to have from the operation of Norris–La Guardia in antitrust cases. Also, the law would have protected secondary boycott activities from the labor injunction, but the government or employers could have proceeded against unions engaging in such conduct by initiating damage suits or criminal prosecutions under the Sherman Act.

The viewpoint of Roberts was brushed aside by the majority of the Court as constituting an erroneous interpretation of the Norris–La Guardia Act. Frankfurter, the jurist who wrote the majority opinion of the Court, contended that Norris–La Guardia reasserted the purpose of the Clayton Act and broadened its terms. If the judiciary had not interpreted the Clayton Act so as to immunize labor union secondary boycott activities, Congress, by expanding the concept of labor dispute in the Norris–La Guardia Act, had certainly meant to forbid the courts to enjoin such union conduct. If a secondary boycott could no longer be enjoined under the Norris–La Guardia Act, such an activity must not violate any law of the United States, including the Sherman Act. Frankfurter pointed out that Section 20 of the Clayton Act immunizes labor unions from prosecution under any federal law when the judiciary may not restrain the conduct of the labor union by the labor injunction. Finally, Frankfurter challenged the view of Roberts that unions could still be subject to damage suits and criminal proceedings under the Sherman Act, even though Norris–La Guardia forbids the issuance of injunctions to restrain a particular pattern of union conduct. On this score, Frankfurter declared:

> Congress expressed this national policy and determined the bounds of a labor dispute in an act explicitly dealing with the further withdrawal of injunctions in labor controversies. But to argue, as it was urged before us, that the *Duplex* case still governs for purposes of a criminal prosecution is to say that that which on the equity side of the court is allowable conduct may in a criminal proceeding become the road to prison. It would be strange indeed that although neither the Government nor Anheuser-Busch could have sought an injunction against the act here challenged, the elaborate efforts to permit such conduct failed to prevent criminal liability punishable with imprisonment and heavy fines.

🎕 THE APEX DOCTRINE NULLIFIES EFFECT OF CORONADO DECISION

Organized labor was permitted by the principles affirmed in *Hutcheson* and *Milk Wagon Drivers Union* to undertake economic activities to expand the area of collective bargaining. Doctrines established by the Supreme Court in *Danbury Hatters, Bucks Stove, Duplex,* and *Bedford Stone* were swept away by the impact of Norris–La Guardia. Only the *Coronado* cases appeared as a threat to labor unions in their Sherman Act relationship. In these cases, it will be recalled, the Supreme Court held that a labor union violated the antitrust provisions when it engaged in a strike, the effect and intent of which was to reduce the amount of goods in interstate commerce.

In 1940 the Supreme Court decided the *Apex* case,[8] a proceeding that in many respects duplicated *Coronado*. Similar to *Coronado*, a great deal of violence surrounded the strike directed against the Apex Company of Philadelphia. The strike also had the effect of reducing the amount of nonunion goods in interstate commerce. The Apex Company engaged in the manufacture of hosiery, producing annually merchandise valued at approximately $5 million. It shipped in interstate commerce about 80 percent of its finished product. The company operated a nonunion shop, and in April 1937 the hosiery workers' union demanded that the firm recognize the labor organization as the bargaining agent of its workers and employ only union members.

On May 6, 1937, about a month after the company refused to agree to the union's demands, members of the hosiery workers' union employed in the Apex plant, along with other members of the union employed in other hosiery factories in Philadelphia, gathered at the factory. Once more, the union officers demanded that the company operate the plant on a union basis. When this last ultimatum was refused, the officers of the union declared a sit-down strike. Beyond causing damage to plant and machinery, the union prevented the shipment of 130,000 dozen pairs of finished hosiery, of a value of about $800,000. Evidence proved that about 80 percent of this merchandise was scheduled for shipment outside the state of Pennsylvania. The company sued the union under the Sherman Act provisions and a trial court awarded it damages of $237,310. The trial judge, utilizing his prerogative under the antitrust provisions, trebled this figure to a sum exceeding $700,000. In 1940, after extensive litigation in the lower federal court, the case was finally reviewed by the Supreme Court.

The *Apex* decision was awaited with deep interest. After the district court had awarded the Apex Company approximately $700,000 damages, a wave of similar damage suits against labor unions was instituted under the Sherman Act. Professor E. B. McNatt stated:

> Two days after the Federal District Court awarded the $711,932 to the Apex Company in Philadelphia, three New England trucking companies filed an antitrust action against the International Brotherhood of Teamsters, asking for $90,000 damages resulting from a strike. And a few weeks later, on May 22, the Republic Steel Corporation filed a similar suit against the CIO and some 700 individuals asking for $7,500,000 treble damages under the Sherman Act for injuries suffered as a result of the Little Steel strike of 1937.[9]

In addition to deciding the outcome of these and other damage suits, the *Apex* decision would determine whether or not the Court would reaffirm the *Coronado* doctrine in a period of "liberalism." Would the Supreme Court, despite the enactment of legislation to encourage collective bargaining, utilize the Sherman Act to outlaw strikes carried out to force companies to recognize and bargain with labor unions?

The issue in the *Apex* case was not whether the action of the union was lawful. As indicated, the Supreme Court spoke of the conduct of the unionists in terms of "lawless invasion of petitioner's plant and destruction of its property by force and violence of the most brutal and wanton character." Clearly, the union's conduct was unlawful. The state courts undoubtedly would have served as a forum in which the union could have been sued for damages. However, the company chose to sue the union for damages under the Sherman Act. Consequently, a fundamental question of the *Apex* case was whether violence made the Sherman Act applicable to a labor dispute, when, in the absence of violence, the statute would not have been applicable. The Supreme Court replied in the negative, for "restraints not within the [Sherman] Act when achieved by peaceful means are not brought within its sweep merely because, without other differences, they are attended by violence."

With this question clarified, the Court then proceeded to determine whether the Apex strike constituted restraint of trade within the meaning of the Sherman Act. Again the Court reached a negative conclusion and ordered the suit against the union dismissed. To support this decision, it declared that labor unions to function effectively must eliminate nonunion competition, and that action undertaken to achieve this objective does not violate the Sherman Act. The Court ruled that the intent of a labor union to eliminate nonunion competition by collective economic action did not violate the Sherman Act since "an elimination of price competition based on differences in labor standards is the objective of any national labor organization. But this effect in competition has not been considered to be the kind of curtailment of price competition prohibited by the Sherman Act."

In addition, the Court declared lawful for purposes of the Sherman Act strikes that have the effect of suppressing the amount of goods in commerce. Labor unions intend to stop production when they strike. Stoppage of production and a strike are one and the same thing. If a firm is engaged in interstate commerce, the amount of such commerce during the strike is reduced. Unions strike, however, not to reduce deliberately the amount of goods in commerce or to influence their price, but to win disputes with companies. As the Supreme Court declared in the *Apex* case, if the lawfulness of strikes resulting in a diminution to commerce were questioned, the Sherman Act would threaten the legality of "practically every strike in modern industry."

Thus the effect of the *Apex* decision was to destroy the doctrine established in the *Coronado* cases. In this connection, it is noteworthy that even though the circumstances of *Apex* and *Coronado* were strikingly similar, the Supreme Court ruled on the action of the hosiery union without specifically overruling the *Coronado* doctrine. Even so, the *Apex* case established the principle that a strike, the effect and the intent of which is to reduce the goods in commerce, does not violate the Sherman Act, provided the strike is carried out for the purpose of furthering the interests of the labor organization.

IMPACT OF *ALLEN-BRADLEY*

The position of the Supreme Court in the 1940–1941 antitrust labor cases improved the legal position of organized bargaining agencies. The judiciary no longer utilized the Sherman Act to block organizing activities of unions. Secondary boycotts were deemed lawful, and the antitrust provisions no longer threatened the legality of major strikes undertaken to enforce demands against employers. On the other hand, labor unions were still subject to prosecution under the Sherman Act. In the *Apex* case, the Court reaffirmed the principle that the antitrust statutes do apply to labor organizations. In this connection, it was stated that for thirty-two years, the

Court in its efforts to determine the true meaning and application of the Sherman Act had held that its terms "do enclose to some extent and in some circumstances labor unions and their activities."

At present, however, the Sherman Act outlaws union activities only when labor organizations combine with business groups to promote monopoly, and it is illegal for a contractor that the union has no interest in organizing to agree with a labor organization to boycott nonunion subcontractors that the union does have an interest in organizing.[10] The principle was emphasized in 1945 when the Supreme Court handed down its decision in *Allen Bradley*.[11] Local No. 3, affiliated with the International Brotherhood of Electrical Workers (AFL), had jurisdiction covering workers engaged in the manufacture of electrical equipment and in the installation of electrical products. Contractors operating in New York City had agreed not to purchase electrical equipment from suppliers not under contract with Local No. 3. This meant that electrical products manufactured outside of the city were excluded from a profitable market. For their part, manufacturers agreed not to sell electrical products to any contractor unless the contractor employed members of Local No. 3.

After a time, the combination among the three groups proved highly successful to all concerned. The business of New York City electrical manufacturers increased sharply since they did not face any out-of-city competition. Jobs were available for members of Local No. 3 and their wages increased through the tripartite arrangement. Contractors likewise benefited from the arrangement. The effect of the arrangement is further indicated by the fact that the New York manufacturers sold their goods in the protected city market at one price and sold identical goods outside of New York City at a far lower price. All parties to the arrangement thereby benefited. But the tripartite agreement caused much hardship to the consuming public, to those electrical manufacturers denied the opportunity to sell in the New York market, and to electrical workers outside the city.

Such an arrangement, the Court held, violated the Sherman Act. It stated that "Congress never intended that unions could, consistent with the Sherman Act, aid nonlabor groups to create business monopolies and to control the mobility of goods and services." However, it is important to note that if the labor union alone, by strike or boycott, accomplished the same results, the Sherman Act would not be applicable. Thus one jurist of the Court stated, "If the union in this instance had acted alone in self-interest, resulting in a restraint of interstate trade, the Sherman Act concededly would be inapplicable." The violation of the law occurred when the union, manufacturers, and contractors of New York City combined to exclude from use in the city electrical equipment manufactured outside the city of New York. The *Allen Bradley* doctrine did not overrule the principles established in the *Hutcheson* and *Apex* decisions. Unions are free from prosecution under the Sherman Act, provided the

Court is convinced that their activities are carried out for the sole purpose of advancing their own interests. The crime of the union in *Allen Bradley* was to combine with nonlabor groups for the purpose of monopolizing markets and increasing profits.

❦ ADDITIONAL APPLICATION OF ANTITRUST VIOLATIONS

Additional labor cases before the Supreme Court highlight the broadening of the zone in which labor organizations can apparently violate the Sherman Act. A new era of interpretation of labor union liabilities under the antitrust statutes appears to be developing. Two opinions were handed down on the same day, June 7, 1965, dealing with (1) limitations placed on the marketing hours of employers' products (*Jewel Tea* case)[12] and (2) industry elimination of small employers (*Pennington* cases).[13] A third case (*Connell*) involved using a contractor whom unions had no intent to organize, to get at subcontractors for organizational purposes.[14]

THE *JEWEL TEA* CASE

In the *Jewel Tea* case, collective bargaining negotiations involved a multiemployer association. The 1957 negotiations concluded with the signing of a pact by employers other than Jewel Tea and the National Tea Company to refrain from selling meat between the hours of 6:00 P.M. and 9:00 A.M. Jewel Tea contended that it signed the contract under duress of a union strike.

Jewel Tea brought suit in July 1958, seeking invalidation of the agreement under Sections 1 and 2 of the Sherman Act. It argued that the employer association and union had agreed among themselves that all collective bargaining agreements would contain the same provisions. Further, the company contended it was placed under the duress of a strike vote, since the rest of the industry had signed with the union. It argued that this amounted to a conspiracy to force agreement that meat would not be sold between 6:00 P.M. and 9:00 A.M., with or without union members working. Jewel Tea argued that it had been given no choice in the matter, since a strike would have hampered its competitive position within the region. A federal district court ruled that the union had only acted in its own self-interest, since the record was devoid of evidence of a conspiracy. The court of appeals, however, reversed the trial court and ruled that the agreement was a conspiracy whether it was called an agreement or a contract.

Upon review, the U.S. Supreme Court upheld the trial court, reversing the court of appeals. In a three-way split among the Justices, it held that the parties were required to bargain on subjects intimately tied to wages, hours, and working conditions. The antitrust exemptions applied, since the union action to limit marketing hours had been undertaken in the union's own self-interest. The Court reviewed the history of bargaining in the industry to arrive at its decision. Historically, the union had bargained on both working hours and operation hours of companies. It was reasoned that operations that continued beyond the agreed-upon working hours of union members would require someone other than union members to serve customers. Even if a self-service market was involved, union workers would be required to carry a heavier burden during working hours because of the increased demand to clean the work areas and package meat.

Justice Douglas entered a vigorous dissenting opinion. He argued that the collective bargaining agreement itself was clear proof of a conspiracy between the union and employers to restrain operations in the product market. He saw no difference between an agreement to sell at fixed prices and one to limit the hours during which a store could market its products. In his opinion, the *Allen Bradley* case had foreclosed the expansive view of labor exemption from the antitrust provisions. It was not necessary to review the bargaining history of the industry or to look at the effect that expanding marketing hours to between 6:00 P.M. and 9:00 A.M. would have on the work standards of union members. In effect, he reasoned that any agreement that employers could not make between themselves under antitrust, could not be justified by the existence of a collective bargaining agreement.

THE *PENNINGTON* CASE

The *Pennington* case was decided by the Supreme Court on June 7, 1965, the same day as the *Jewel Tea* decision. It involved an antitrust suit for treble damages by a small coal-mining employer whose argument stemmed from the National Coal Wage Agreement of 1950. Prior to 1950, the industry had been notorious for its frequent strikes and the government seizure of mines. Relative peace was brought to the industry when the pact was signed in 1950.

An amendment to the 1950 agreement was negotiated in 1958 whereby company signatories agreed to pay 80 cents per ton on each ton produced if the required 40 cents per ton had not already been paid into the United Mine Workers (UMW) Welfare and Retirement Fund. This clause was to discourage the leasing of coal fields to firms operating under wage standards inferior to those established by collective bargaining. But Pennington argued that the UMW had collusively agreed to support mechanization of the large mines and to impose the terms of the wage agreement on all mines without regard to ability to pay. As support, the plaintiff identified the large investment outlays the union made to mechanize some of the mines.

Additionally, the UMW was accused of persuading the Secretary of Labor to influence a prevailing wage determination under the Walsh-Healey Act that would eliminate small operators from supplying coal to the Tennessee Valley Authority (TVA). It was argued that the small operators could not effectively enter competitive bids if they were forced to pay prevailing union wage rates.

When some of the operators failed to meet their payments to the Welfare Fund, the UMW brought suit for violation of the wage agreement. Several small firms retaliated by bringing suit against the UMW for entering into a conspiracy with the large operators to settle the general problem of overproduction by eliminating the marginal firms.

The Supreme Court upon review remanded the case for retrial in a federal district court in accordance with its decision on the case. It held that not every agreement arising out of collective provisions was exempt from the Sherman Act provisions merely because it involved a mandatory subject for bargaining. Exemption could not be claimed "when it is clearly shown that it [the union] has agreed with one set of employers to impose a certain wage scale on other bargaining units." This position was justified by holding that such an agreement restricted the freedom of unions to "respond to each bargaining situation as the individual circumstance might warrant." Justice White, in a footnote to his opinion for the Court, remarked that a union, if acting unilaterally, could seek to impose uniform wage standards on the entire industry even if it suspected that some marginal operators could not compete if required to pay the union scale. The mere act of attempting to impose a uniform wage standard was not sufficient evidence to uphold a union-employer conspiracy charge. The intent to eliminate marginal firms had to be supported by specific and concrete evidence.

Justice Douglas, in a concurring opinion joined in by two other Justices, interpreted the Court's opinion as meaning that an industry-wide collective bargaining agreement was obvious evidence of the existence of a conspiracy with no further investigation required. He also wrote that a union could not agree on a wage scale in excess of the ability of some employers to pay when such agreement was for the purpose of forcing some of them out of business.

RETRIAL IN TENNESSEE DISTRICT COURT

The 1965 retrial provided the guidelines within which the U.S. district court was required to solve the mining cases. The trial court reviewed the entire history of bargaining in the bituminous coal industry, similar to the *Jewel Tea* review, including the possibility of collusion on TVA bids to determine whether the UMW was guilty of Sherman Act violations. It was found that the union was not in violation of the antitrust law. The trial court held on the basis of the *Hutcheson* case that a union, if acting alone and not in concert with nonlabor groups, was not in violation of the antitrust act. The concurring opinion of Justice Douglas was construed to mean that, to be found illegal, the wage agreement had to exceed the ability of some firms to pay, and even then it had to be made expressly for the purpose of putting some employers out of business. Also, the union investment in some companies did not in itself show collusive bidding. The trial court was convinced that the bids entered by the large companies were justified on the basis of productivity gains. Several studies have verified the validity of this position.[15]

ANOTHER COURT'S VIEW

In 1968, two small coal operators sued the United Mine Workers in a federal district court, charging they could not operate profitably under the terms of a contract imposed on them by the union and Bituminous Coal Operators Association. A jury decided that the UMW had engaged in a conspiracy and intended to contract with the two small companies only on the terms provided in the national agreement. Thus, it was held that the union had forfeited its exemption under the Sherman Act. Triple damages were awarded in the amount of $1,432,500 for one company and $67,500 for the other.

The decision was upheld by a federal appeals court. Unfavorable union treatment in the appellate court prompted the UMW to appeal to the U.S. Supreme Court. Review was denied without comment.

The trial court's action makes it clear that the UMW's motives were considered to be different from those of the 1965 case. The jury was convinced that the union had combined with an association of companies to prevent effective competition from a third party.

"CLEAR PROOF" NOT REQUIRED

The Supreme Court took another run at the antitrust implication of the 1950 Coal Agreement in *Ramsey* v. *Mineworkers*,[16] which was decided in 1971. In this case, the high court took the position that union antitrust liability did not require the meeting of the standard of "clear proof" that is clearly specified in the Norris–La Guardia Act, but required only that parties making a complaint establish their case by a preponderance of the evidence. The Norris–La Guardia Act required that no union shall be liable for acts of its officers who violated the antitrust laws, except on "clear proof" of the officers' "actual participation in or actual authorization of, such acts." In this respect, then, the standard of proof requirement to find unions in violation of the antitrust statutes had been eased.

Eighteen small coal mine operators in Tennessee filed suit in federal district court alleging UMW violation of the Sherman Act. It was charged that the UMW had agreed not to oppose mine mechanization and that, in turn, the large producers with whom the union dealt had agreed to give wage increases and to make royalty payments to the union welfare fund. Basically, the charge was that there was a conspiracy with the large operators to drive the small unmechanized mines out of business by forcing them to pay wages and other benefits that they could not afford. The 1958 Protective Wage Clause Amendment to the 1950 Soft Coal Wage Agreement required the UMW not to enter into wage agreements applicable to employees covered by the contract on any basis other than those specified in the contract. In other words, the agreement was that the union would not permit other employers to sign a collective bargaining agreement with the UMW on terms different from those agreed to by the multiemployer group. The employer group constituted the larger mechanized operators in the industry.

The federal district court in Chattanooga, Tennessee, dismissed the suit. In doing so, the judge interpreted the 1958 amendment in the context of Norris–La Guardia Act language. He decided that the law required "clear proof" not only that UMW officers had actually participated in writing the amendment, but also that the amendment itself constituted a violation of the Sherman Act. In the decision, the judge remarked that under the "preponderance of the evidence" rule that is applied to most antitrust cases, the UMW had implied agreement to an illegal conspiracy, but that when the "clear proof" standard was applied, the UMW was not held to be liable under the antitrust laws. The trial court's opinion was affirmed by an appellate court.

The Supreme Court agreed to review the case. It held that the lower court was in error and remanded the case for retrial. The majority opinion was that the lower courts "read far too much" into the Norris–La Guardia Act's "clear proof" standard, which applies only to showing that union officers had authority to perform allegedly illegal acts. The acts themselves are to be judged on the preponderance of the evidence rule.

Justice Douglas, in dissent, was of the opinion that Congress intended that the "clear proof" standard should be applied broadly in antitrust suits dealing with the unions, and that because the majority of the Court did not agree, their opinion amounted to a drastic rewriting of a part of the Norris–La Guardia Act.

The retrial held later in 1971 resulted in the trial judge instructing the jury that while the agreement between the UMW and the major operators was not in itself illegal, the agreement would on its face be a violation of the Sherman Act if the jury found proof that the agreement had been entered into with the intent of driving some coal mine operators out of business, or with the knowledge that it would have that effect.

The jury returned a "guilty" verdict requiring the UMW and one large company to pay triple damages. The lower court's decision was upheld by an appellate court, and a request for review before the United States Supreme Court was refused without comment. The union and company had asked the high court to decide the ultimate question of whether an agreement is on its face illegal when a union and an employer or group of employers agree to a basic contract that requires the union to insist on the same terms in its negotiations with other employers that have been imposed on the signatory employers.

THE *CONNELL* CASE

The *Connell* case, in 1975, involved an employer signing an agreement to subcontract its plumbing and mechanical work only to employers with whom the union had a contract. The contract was signed under protest, and the employer went to federal court to request an injunction to halt enforcement of the agreement on the ground that it was in violation of the antitrust laws. In a 5–4 decision, the Court overruled the Fifth Circuit Court of Appeals, rejecting the NLRB's position that the agreement was not subject to federal antitrust laws. The Court's majority held that the contract constituted a "direct restraint of the business market [with] substantial anti-competitive effects, both actual and potential, that would not follow naturally from the elimination of competition over wages and working conditions." Even the construction industry proviso to Section 8 (e) of the National Labor Relations Act did not privilege the agreement, because, the Court held, the "proviso extended only to agreements in the context of collective bargaining relationships and possibly to common-situs relationships on particular job sites as well."

A key factor in the 5–4 decision was the union's lack of desire to represent the general contractor's employees. The Court then charged the lower courts to decide whether the arrangement violated the antitrust laws. It does not appear that the agreement in *Connell* would have prompted the Court to rule as it did if the union had had an interest in Connell's employees.

👺 *CONSEQUENCES OF SUPREME COURT ACTION*

The *Allen Bradley* case had made it clear that unions could not act "in combination with non-labor groups" to influence the product-market-prohibited businesses through the antitrust laws. Unions, therefore, had restrictions placed on their favored Norris–La Guardia Act positions.

The *Pennington* case narrowed the assumption contained in *Allen Bradley* that any union wage agreement with employers was exempt from antitrust. *Pennington* provided that a union could legally agree with an employer or group of employers on wages, hours, and other terms and conditions of employment. However, those agreements are still subject to antitrust prosecution if the union agrees to impose those same provisions on other employers. The trial court left to the jury a question of whether the actual purpose of the national union contract was in fact to drive small producers from the market.

Jewel Tea opened the gate to antitrust action against unions a little wider. The Court held that a jury's or judge's findings of fact could impose antitrust liability on unions, even though the issue involved was one that unions might reasonably believe to be a proper subject for bargaining.

The *Connell* case attacked a previously acceptable and legal union organizing tactic, bringing court surveillance of union organizing activity within the context of the antitrust laws. If a union was not trying to organize a contractor, the Court found in *Connell*, it could compel the contractor to boycott subcontractors that the union desired to organize.

A considerable amount of uncertainty has been thrust upon the legality of multiemployer bargaining because of these Supreme Court rulings. The most serious consequence is that the high court in particular has served notice that the judiciary is going to determine the motives of the parties to collective agreements on subjects of mandatory bargaining. The vigorous dissent of Justice Goldberg in *Pennington* indicates that the judiciary may once again have been moving in the direction of setting up its own socioeconomic philosophies over the congressional intent of how collective bargaining should work.

It is possible for both juries and trial judges to determine the motives of unions in seeking uniform contracts throughout an industry by imposing their own philosophies on whether a union acts unilaterally or in collusion with an employer group. To some, mere discussion at the bargaining table of the possible competitive effect of a wage package may be sufficient to prove the existence of a conspiracy. The development of such an application would in effect place the collective bargaining process in approximately the same state in which it existed prior to Norris–La Guardia. It has already been explained that unions do attempt to standardize wage settlements throughout an entire industry. Such a condition has generally accompanied successful union organization in several industries, one of which is coal. Although the UMW has had only limited success in such efforts, it does make continued bids to standardize agreements throughout the areas it represents. Widening the area of judicial action might seriously hinder this UMW effort.

Another possible consequence of these cases is that the collective bargaining process itself could be put in danger. Guy Farmer, former chair of the National Labor Relations Board, "reported that between 80 and 100 percent of the workers covered by union contracts" in several industries are under multiemployer contracts.[17] The concurring opinion of Justice Douglas indicated that both unions and employers are liable when restraint-of-trade violations grow out of such agreements. If the one is found in violation, then the other cannot expect to escape. It is possible that employers will resist entering into multiemployer agreements with unions if marginal firms are permitted to resist signing agreements by bringing charges of collusion in the courts and collecting treble damages levied against both unions and large employers. Such a development would endanger the entire collective bargaining process. As mentioned, unions cannot organize successfully in the absence of a wage standard that they seek to impose on all units in a particular competitive sphere.

The task is to fashion legislation that will protect the interest of the public without endangering the ability of labor unions to act as effective collective bargaining agents. The vehicle to accomplish this worthwhile objective should be in the form of new and proper labor legislation. As a matter of fact, Congress adopted this procedure when it amended the National Labor Relations Act in 1947 and 1959. It has been suggested that measures to amend the existing labor laws dealing with union abuses in the product market may lose support. It is argued that Congress is unlikely to proceed if the Court deals firmly with the subjects of their debate. It may be that political expediency would be furthered by a lack of legislative action if the felt abuses are cleared away by new antitrust applications in the federal courts.

❦ SUMMARY

Other than curbing the labor injunction, Norris–La Guardia relieved labor unions from prosecution under the antitrust laws. To accomplish this objective, Congress defined the term *labor dispute* in a very broad fashion. It did this to overcome the basic shortcoming of the Clayton Act. Congress had failed to define the term in that law, and the Supreme Court had thence construed the meaning of labor dispute in a way that deprived unions of any protection in antitrust suits.

Some people felt, however, that the Supreme Court would nullify Norris–La Guardia, so that the position of organized labor would be no better than it was before the Act's passage. These fears proved groundless, for in the *Apex* and *Hutcheson* cases, the Court broadly construed Norris–La Guardia, providing unions with the opportunity to engage in activities calculated to effectuate the collective bargaining process.

Although Norris–LaGuardia legalized union tactics formerly held objectionable under the antitrust laws, the Supreme Court in the *Allen Bradley* decision found that the Sherman Act still applied to unions when they conspired with employers to monopolize markets. Cases decided since 1965 have broadened the base of the antitrust laws so as to cover a wider area of labor activities. A great deal of uncertainty and speculation as to the eventual effect of these decisions has been generated. It seems very possible that the judiciary will take on an expanded role in determining how collective bargaining will work, at least in industries covered by multiemployer contracts.

🌞 DISCUSSION QUESTIONS

1. The judiciary was required to define the meaning of labor dispute contained in Section 20 of the Clayton Act. What was the judicial response to the congressional definition provided in Norris–La Guardia?
2. Compare the Supreme Court's *Apex* decision of 1940 to its *Coronado* rule. What standard of union conduct was established by *Apex*, and how durable has it been?
3. Did *Allen Bradley* alter *Apex* standards in any way? Do you agree with the *Allen Bradley* decision? Why or why not?
4. Does the Court permit too much latitude in labor cases as evidenced by its tolerance in the *Jewel Tea* case? Why or why not?
5. Review the facts surrounding the *Pennington* case. Did the Court's decision in *Pennington* constitute a narrowing of its vision in *Apex*, or do you think the decision was consistent with *Apex* and subsequent cases including *Jewel Tea*?
6. With the *Ramsey* v. *Mineworkers* case in mind, do you think the Court's understanding of union responsibility in the labor market is realistic? Support your position with historical and legal facts concerning the responsibilities of unions under collective bargaining.
7. What changes, if any, could be made by labor law amendments to provide more realistic coverage of unions under antitrust legislation? Include in your answer an assessment of union economic power.

🌞 NOTES

[1] House of Representatives, *Document No. 669*, 72d Congress, 1st sess., p. 3.
[2] *United States* v. *Hutcheson*, 321 U.S. 219 (1941).
[3] See Chapter #4, Note 3 for the text of Section 20 of the Clayton Act.
[4] *American Federation of Musicians* v. *Stein*, 218 F. (2d) 679 (1954); cert. denied 348 U.S. 873 (1955).
[5] *Milk Wagon Drivers Union* v. *Lake Valley Farm Products*, 108 Fed. (2d) 436 (1939).
[6] *Milk Wagon Drivers Union* v. *Lake Valley Farm Products*, 311 U.S. 91 (1940).
[7] *Hutcheson, supra.*
[8] *Apex Hosiery Company* v. *Leader*, 310 U.S. 409 (1940).
[9] E. B. McNatt, "Labor Again Menaced by the Sherman Act," *The Southern Economic Journal*, VI, 2 (October 1939), p. 208.

CHAPTER FIVE

[10] *Connell Construction Co., Inc.* v. *Plumbers, Local 100, Plumbers and Steamfitters*, 421 U.S. 616 (1975).

[11] *Allen Bradley Company* v. *Local Union No. 3, IBEW*, 325 U.S. 797 (1945).

[12] *Local Union 189, Amalgamated Meat Cutters and Butcher Workmen of North America, AFL-CIO* v. *Jewel Tea Company Inc.*, 381 U.S. 676 (1965).

[13] *United Mine Workers of America* v. *James M. Pennington*, 381 U.S. 657 (1965); *Pennington* v. *United Mine Workers*, 257 F. Supp. 815 (1966).

[14] *Connell Construction Co., Inc., supra.* (1975).

[15] See Carroll L. Christenson and Richard A. Myren, *Wage Policy Under the Walsh-Healey Public Contracts Act: A Critical Review* (Bloomington, Indiana: Indiana University Press, 1966), pp. 194–198.

[16] *Ramsey* v. *Mineworkers*, 401 U.S. 302 (1971).

[17] John Scott and Edwin S. Rockefeller, *Antitrust and Trade Regulation Today; 1967*, (Washington, D.C.: The Bureau of National Affairs, Inc., 1967), p.43.

CHAPTER SIX

EMPLOYER ANTIUNION CONDUCT: NEED FOR GOVERNMENT PROTECTION

THE PROBLEM

Commonwealth v. *Hunt* dissolved the identity between the conspiracy doctrine and the labor union. The decision established the lawfulness of labor organizations. However, by no means did the decision impose a respect for the right of workers to self-organization and collective bargaining. Workers were free to join labor unions, but there was no guarantee that they could effectively exercise that right. In this connection, it should also be noted that Norris–La Guardia did not prevent employer interference with the collective bargaining rights of workers. The law restricted the power of courts in labor disputes, but set up no prohibition on their interfering with workers' rights to engage in collective bargaining activities.

If employers are free to utilize their superior economic strength to prevent the organization and operation of labor unions, the fact that workers have the legal right to self-organization and collective bargaining has little practical value. A right, to be meaningful, must be respected. A democratic system provides for the right to freedom of worship. But if this right were not respected, the right to that freedom would have little practical significance. The same principle applies to the field of industrial

CHAPTER SIX

relations. Of what value to workers is their right to collective bargaining if they are not free to exercise that right? Should the evidence reveal that there have been practices calculated to prevent workers from the enjoyment of this right, it would appear logical that government should protect the right of workers to self-organization and collective bargaining. Just as government has taken positive action to prevent the nullification of other rights enjoyed by citizens of the nation, it would seem equally valid for government to protect the right of workers to collective bargaining. If, on the other hand, the record indicates that the right of workers to self-organization and collective bargaining has been respected, there is no occasion for government control.

Organs of government have declared that workers have the right to self-organization and collective bargaining. This recognition is grounded in the fact that labor unions fulfill a proper function in our economy. These considerations are underscored in a powerful statement made by former Chief Justice Taft:

> Labor unions are recognized...as legal when instituted for mutual help and lawfully carrying out their legitimate objects. They have long been thus recognized by the court. They were organized out of the necessities of the situation. A single employee was helpless in dealing with an employer. He was dependent on his daily wage for the maintenance of himself and family. If the employer refused to pay him the wages he thought fair, he was nevertheless unable to leave the employer and resist arbitrary and unfair treatment. Union was essential to give laborers an opportunity to deal on equality with their employer. They united to exert influence upon him and to leave him in a body in order by this inconvenience to induce him to make better terms with them. They were withholding their labor of economic value to make him pay what they thought it was worth. The right to combine for such a lawful purpose has in many years not been denied by any court.[1]

What remains to be seen is the extent to which the right of employees to self-organization and collective bargaining has been respected. Such an investigation must precede any recommendations for legislation calculated to protect this right of workers.

THE LA FOLLETTE COMMITTEE

Studies have dealt with efforts undertaken to forestall unionization of employees.[2] The most complete study dealing with antiunion tactics was conducted by the La Follette Committee. On June 6, 1936, Congress ordered a full-scale investigation of these antiunion techniques. Senator La Follette of Wisconsin headed the committee authorized to make the study. The committee published 14 volumes of testimony. It conducted 58 days of hearings, at which some 245 witnesses testified. The committee later published a series of summary documents, which organizes and makes more readable the mass of evidence collected at the hearings.[3] Its findings highlight the intensity and thoroughness with which the union movement was challenged.

Care was taken by the committee to insure the accuracy of its reports. In the hearings of the committee, all of which were open to the public, witnesses were summoned from every group having an interest in the proceedings. The committee was careful not to accept at face value testimony of questionable truthfulness unless it could be verified from other sources. Consequently, its findings appear to be of unquestionable accuracy. Space limitations render it impossible to make a thorough report of the group's investigation. However, this volume—and, particularly, this chapter—could not be complete unless some consideration were given to the work of the La Follette Committee. Accordingly, while highlighting the patterns of antiunion conduct, we shall direct attention to its results. Under present labor laws, many of the antiunion tactics disclosed by the La Follette group are unlawful. This, however, does not render this investigation any less important. Appreciation of present public policy rests upon the understanding of the factors producing such control.

❦ PATTERNS OF ANTIUNION CONDUCT: INDUSTRIAL ESPIONAGE

The La Follette Committee reported that industrial espionage was a common, if not universal, practice in American industry. The purpose of industrial espionage was to prevent the organization and operation of a labor union. The industrial spy centered his or her work in the local union. A chief function of the spy was to provide the company with the names of union members. In particular, the employer wanted to ascertain the names of the workers most active in the labor union. Such information provided the basis for discharging these workers or otherwise isolating them from other employees. That these lists were used to influence the results of organizing campaigns is underscored by the following testimony of a former member of the National Labor Relations Board:

> I have never listened to anything more tragically un-American than stories of the discharged employees of the Fruehauf Trailer Co., victims of a labor spy. More often men in the prime of life, of obvious character and courage, came before us to tell of the blows that had fallen on him for his crime of having joined a union. Here they were—family men with wives and children—on public relief, blacklisted from employment, so they claimed, in the city of Detroit, citizens whose only offense was that they ventured in the land of the free to organize as employees to improve their working conditions. Their reward, as workers who had given their best to their employer, was to be

hunted down by a hired spy like the lowest of criminals, and thereafter tossed like useless metal on the scrap heap.[4]

To obtain membership data, the spy could attend union meetings. A more effective method consisted of election to some official position in the union, such as financial or recording secretary. In this capacity, the spy could learn of every applicant for membership. At times, gathering the names of union members proved difficult. But, as the La Follette Committee reported, "In this, his initial task, the spy must not fail. If need be, therefore, he will bribe janitors or custodians, rifle files or desks, and burglarize offices to secure access to union records."[5]

Obviously, the operation of the industrial spy impaired the effective operation of a labor union. Workers were fearful that participation in union affairs—even the attendance at union meetings—might cost them their jobs. The following bit of testimony highlights this:

> *Senator La Follette:* As a result of your experience, what would you say caused this fear of your organization when they became suspicious that a spy was in their midst?
>
> *Mr. Robertson* (a labor leader): Because they felt to have their membership in our organization known to the company would place their jobs in jeopardy.[6]

Spy D-11, who operated in a plant in Hopewell, Virginia, also pointed out how spy activities result in union disintegration. After the workers of the plant became aware of his operations, he claimed that most of the workers felt "they would get out of the union if they knew just how to go about it."[7]

Industrial spies could cause the destruction of labor unions in ways other than by ascertaining the names on union membership lists. Another effective method was to discredit union leaders in the eyes of the rank and file. A labor union's strength was sapped after the membership lost confidence in its officers. A classic example in this connection was the action of one spy who faked a photograph of the local union president leaning on the bar of a saloon and then preferred charges of drunkenness.[8] In another instance, a spy who managed election to the secretaryship of a local union affiliated with the International Association of Machinists brought charges of embezzlement of union funds against organizers of the union. Subsequently, the charges were proved to be false, but not until the local union had begun to disintegrate.[9] In addition, the spy might attack union officials on the basis of religion or nationality.

The industrial spy frequently assumed the role of an *agent provocateur*. In this role, "he incites the union to violence, preaches strikes, inflames the hot-headed and leads the union to disaster."[10] Many examples of this procedure are available. One spy sat in the meetings of the strike strategy committee of the Dodge local of the United Automobile Workers in 1936 and urged the use of force and violence.[11] Another spy, operating in Kent, Ohio, in 1936, urged the unionists to dynamite a plant involved in a strike.[12] The strategy of these tactics, of course, was to goad the union into unlawful conduct, the effect being the stimulation of adverse public opinion, legal and military reprisal, and general disintegration of the labor union.

What was the source of supply of labor spies? A large number were furnished by private detective agencies. From 1933 to 1936, the Pinkerton Detective Agency claimed 309 industrial clients; Corporation Auxiliary Company, 499; National Corporation Service, 196; and the Burns Detective Agency, 440. Smaller detective agencies reported serving 497 clients. The La Follette Committee reports, "From motion-picture producers to steel makers, from hookless fasteners to automobiles, from small units to giant enterprises—scarcely an industry that is not fully represented in the list of clients of the detective agencies. Large corporations rely on spies. No firm is too small to employ them."[13] In the period 1933–1937, a total of $9,440,132.12 was expended by American firms to combat unions by means of industrial espionage and strikebreaking.[14]

Frequently, ordinary workers were trapped by detective agencies into spying on the union activities of their fellow workers. In spy jargon, such an individual was known as a "hooked man [sic]," an individual engaged in industrial espionage without knowledge that he or she was reporting to a detective agency or that the reports were going to an employer. Detective agency representatives who lured workers into spy activities were known as "hookers," and the process of entrapping workers to engage in spy activities was referred to as "hooking." Since most workers would refuse to spy on their fellow employees, the hooker used some pretext to induce a worker to write reports for the detective agency. The bait that the hooker usually used was money. A worker in financial difficulties would be an excellent prospect. The hooker might use a variety of pretexts to entrap an innocent worker. An outstanding example was the attempt of a representative of the Pinkerton Agency to hook the chairman of the grievance committee of a United Automobile Workers local. The representative posed as a federal officer to win the confidence of the worker. He asserted that he was an official of the government making an investigation of plant conditions.[15] Other hookers, to win the confidence of workers, posed as representatives of "minority stockholders," the "insurance setup," and the "financial house." One hooker even posed as a representative of a philanthropic agency that was working in the interests of the workers of the plant.

Employers' use of industrial spies was one factor that made government protection of the right to collective bargaining appear reasonable. After industrial espionage was outlawed, the professional detective agencies terminated such activities. For example, after the passage of the National Labor Relations Act, the Pinkerton Agency directed all its branch offices "to discontinue the furnishing of information to anyone concerning the lawful attempts of labor unions or employees to organize and bargain collectively, and not to undertake hereafter to furnish such information."[16] In addition, once industrial espionage was outlawed, the law was generally respected and its use declined. It is important to note, however, that spying terminated only after the passage of legislation. It is unlikely that industrial espionage would have ceased if it had not been outlawed.

🐭 PATTERNS OF ANTIUNION CONDUCT: ATTACK ON UNION LEADERSHIP

As in every other organization, the successful functioning of labor unions depends in large part on leadership. How well labor union officials carry out their tasks will determine the success or failure of the trade union. Union leaders must of necessity bear the major burden of organizing drives. They are likewise instrumental in the successful implementation of strikes. In short, union leaders are the driving force of the union movement. If union leadership could be coerced into inactivity, the labor organization itself would become functionless and in time would wither away. Repeated attacks against union leadership could destroy the leadership's effectiveness while discouraging others from assuming the role of the union leader.

The record is clear that union leaders have experienced both physical violence and intimidation. In addition, the record is equally clear that these individuals have been subjected to constant attacks against their character. The purpose of both of these approaches is to reduce the effectiveness of union leaders by frightening them into inactivity. Some people frighten more easily than others. This is as true of the union leader as of any other person. Consequently, it is difficult, if not impossible, to measure objectively the effect of the attacks on union leadership on the union movement. However, available evidence pointing up the character of the attacks would indicate that they have seriously retarded the progress of the union movement.

In Cleveland, on September 21, 1937, at about 11:45 P.M., Vincent Favorito approached his parked automobile. He had just attended a union council meeting. The purpose of the meeting was to deal with problems arising in the "Little Steel" strike of 1937. Before he reached his automobile, Favorito was attacked by three men. He described this attack as follows:

> As I was walking toward my car, approaching my car I was about five feet from it there, I turned off the sidewalk to go to my car which was facing north on West Tenth. The man that was on my right side, the man that was walking toward me, hit me with a blackjack on the back of my head and the fellow that was coming toward me from the back end of my car hit me on the face

with a gun, and I felt the man in back of me grapple me by the neck and put his knee on my back, and immediately then something come into my mouth like a gag, we can call it a gag because it was a rag, and I couldn't say a peep; and I was held on both arms by these two men that evidently wanted to knock me out, and didn't do it, and we struggled there. I happened to get loose some way and I get this man here that was in back of me and I throws him over me, but he went right on top of me, and I happened to hit the ground, and him on top of me, and I held him there.

I was afraid that if I would get kicked in the head that it would be the end of me. I held onto him, and while I was holding onto him these other blokes or thugs were hitting me, kicking me, and swearing. While this was going on they also kicked the fellow that was up on top of me and he happened to let go and I hollered. As I hollered my brother-in-law and my sister heard me and come to my rescue.[17]

On December 13, 1936, Charles Doyle, a member of the Steel Workers Organizing Committee, was attacked. The assault took place after Doyle attended a union meeting in the back room of Marie's Grill on South Park Avenue in Buffalo, New York. According to Doyle, he was pounced on by four men after he left the restaurant. He testified to the La Follette Committee that "someone hit me in the mouth from the front with his fist and immediately after that something hit me from behind, right on the ear at the side of the jaw."[18]

Testimony presented before the La Follette Committee also pointed up another attack in Cleveland against a union leader. This victim was Gerald Breads, an employee of the Otis Steel Company. Breads was active in organization work. His testimony is revealing:

Mr. Breads: I was at the Bohemian National Hall on Broadway, I wouldn't know what number it was, it is right there at Pershing Road.

Senator La Follette: When was that?

Mr. Breads: That was on the night July 13, 1937. I had to go to work that night at 11 o'clock so I left that hall about 9 and another fellow by the name of Paul Chocky was with me. We started away from the hall to get the dinky that runs across the Clark Avenue Bridge, and just as we was going across Broadway—

Senator La Follette (interposing): Was this while the strike was on?

Mr. Breads: There was a car pulled away from the curb. I stepped in front of the car and got out in the streetcar tracks and I seen Dewey Jones and another fellow jumping in the car alongside.

Senator La Follette: Did you recognize the other man?

Mr. Breads: I couldn't; no. So I started through the gas station with the idea that if I got on the dinky they wouldn't follow me into there. I had an idea what was going to happen. Before I got to the dinky they had cut me off. Dewey Jones and the other fellow in the back seat jumped out and pulled revolvers on me.

One of them stuck one in the back of my neck and Jones was in front of me holding one in my stomach.

Well, words passed both ways, they called me names and I called them back, I guess, and I asked them what it was all about. They told me to never mind that I would get mine, that I would get what was coming to me, and they wanted to put me in the car and I said no. They tried to force me in the car and shoved me right against the car and the fellow who was riding in the back seat with Jones at the time the car stopped, he grabbed me and shoved me farther in. Then there was nothing I could do but get up on the seat. I don't know what route we took, or where we was, but I come to under the Clark Avenue Bridge, after I got bashed over the head a couple of times with a blackjack and revolver butt, and I was also hit on the arm too.[19]

Rough shadowing was also employed to intimidate union leadership. Rough shadowing was the practice of keeping union leaders under open surveillance. As such, the procedure differed from industrial espionage, which was surreptitious in character. The objective of rough shadowing was to instill fear in the minds of union leaders. It also served the purpose of creating fear in the minds of workers who might have wanted to talk to union leaders. Rough shadowing may have been carried on during strikes, but was most frequently employed during preparation for strikes. One organizer claimed he was followed wherever he went. Another testified that even his home was kept under surveillance. This latter individual, attempting to lose his "shadowers," moved his residence and even changed his name. But this defense measure was only temporarily successful. He testified as follows:

When we started our organizing campaign it was practically impossible to carry on any activity at the headquarters of our union. It was necessary to use our homes as secret places where workers would be able to gather for the purpose of discussing the organizational problems. I lived at the time on the West Side, and about a week after I became a member of the staff several carloads of Republic stool pigeons were parking at my house. They were there from 7 o'clock in the morning until about midnight and they had a special crew on some occasions that remained there overnight. I realized that my home cannot be used any more as a place where workers can be invited to come to talk about labor questions, so I had to move out of there. I also knew if I moved out of that place under my own name they would discover it just as soon. So I moved into another apartment under a different name, under "Stevens," and I was there about 2 weeks and these same people that were shadowing me before discovered the home where I lived and I had to move again, and from "Stevens" I stretched it to "Stevenson," and that is how I used that alias of "Stevenson" in order to make sure that my home will not be discovered.[20]

In addition to physical violence and intimidating tactics, union leaders endured attacks against their character. The purpose of such attacks was to break down the will of union leaders and to destroy the loyalty which connected the rank and file with union leadership. Nothing could be more damaging to a union than the discrediting of union leaders in the eyes of the membership. This objective could be achieved by the circulation of false rumors and stories about union leaders. As is well known, a rumor is difficult to combat. Attacks against the character of a labor leader might take many forms. He might be denounced as a "communist," "foreign element," "agitator," or "labor racketeer." During World War II, notices posted throughout one plant suggested that union organizers were a group of "intimidators" who threatened the "substitution of Nazi-ism for Americanism."[21] In another case, also taking advantage of the wartime environment, the assertion was made that a union was "backed by Germans," the intent being to discourage membership in the labor union.[22]

🌣 PATTERNS OF ANTIUNION CONDUCT: STRIKEBREAKING TACTICS

The purpose of strikebreaking was to destroy a union once it was formed. To carry out effective collective bargaining, a labor union must be able to strike successfully. Both the employer and the workers must be aware of this union capability. If a union cannot wage an effective strike, the employer need not pay much attention to its demands. Moreover, workers soon lose respect and interest in such an organization. This does not mean that unions should or do resort to the strike at every opportunity. Mature collective bargaining should diminish the need for industrial warfare. However, to function effectively at any stage of the collective bargaining process, a union must be capable of implementing an effective strike.

In light of these considerations, it should occasion no surprise to learn that employers bent on the destruction of a labor union utilized every possible tactic to break a strike. Crushing the strike dealt an irreparable blow to the labor union. This was particularly true where the issue in the strike was union recognition. Labor unions must first be recognized by employers as collective bargaining agencies before they can bargain collectively over economic issues. Since this is true, tactics were frequently calculated to break union-recognition strikes.

This section points up some procedures that have been used to destroy labor unions by crushing strikes. Again, it must be kept in mind

CHAPTER SIX 127

that many, if not all, of these practices are now illegal. This fact, however, does not lessen the need for an analysis of strikebreaking procedures.

There are three major lines of approach to break strikes: (1) the fortification of a plant with munitions and private plant police, the latter hired not to protect property against theft, fire, and the like, but for the purpose of intimidating workers who would strike; (2) the hiring of professional strikebreakers; and (3) the breaking down of strikers' morale by instituting back-to-work movements.

A series of events that occurred in the spring of 1935 in Canton, Ohio, demonstrates the first procedure. The employees of a steel corporation had organized a labor union. The corporation refused to recognize or bargain with the representatives of the union. As a result, the union prepared to strike for recognition. Among other things, this strike illustrated the propensity of workers to resort to economic force when other efforts to gain recognition have failed. It also demonstrated the lack of a procedure to eliminate the need for those strikes called to force recognition of labor unions for collective bargaining purposes.

Aware of the imminence of the strike, the steel corporation made preparations to break it. The La Follette Committee describes the general character of these preparations as follows:

> The police department of [the] steel corporation reached the height of its activity during periods of union organization and in times of strike. As the first line of defense against labor organizations, it mobilized all the paraphernalia of military warfare. Manpower, munitions, and spies were all concentrated, deployed, and maneuvered with the objective of defeating organizing efforts, and of ambushing the union when it undertook the desperate step of calling a strike.[23]

More specific observations demonstrate the elaborate preparations for the strikebreaking. A few days before the strike, the corporation mobilized its plant police from other cities. Thus, fourteen men arrived from Buffalo; nineteen from Youngstown; one from Chicago; twenty-five from Massillon; and twenty-one from Warren. The munitions arsenal of the corporation was also increased. A day or so before the strike, the corporation purchased sickening gas and gas equipment for $8,804.30.[24] In addition, the company laid in a supply of pipes cut to club length, shotguns, small arms, and tear gas.

This preparation for a strike by a corporation was not an isolated example. The La Follette Committee reported even more extensive preparations, including the setting up of floodlights, the erection of electrically charged barbed wire around plant boundaries, and the use of armored trucks for the transportation of strikebreakers through picket lines. In addition, a corporation aware of an impending strike might work the plant overtime to build up inventory. If the company could fill orders during the course of the strike, it had a better chance to break the work stoppage.

The use of professional strikebreakers figured prominently in the pattern of strikebreaking. There is a considerable difference between the professional strikebreaker and the worker who merely refuses to strike. Workers should have the right to refrain from participating in a strike. If a union calls a strike and some employees refuse to strike, their decision should be respected. Although these workers tend to break a strike, they certainly are not professional strikebreakers. Individuals in this latter category, the La Follette Committee reported, had been supplied by the same agencies furnishing industrial spies.[25] In many cases, the professional strikebreaker possessed a criminal record. Sam "Chowderhead" Cohen, a famous strikebreaker, commenting on his long criminal record, declared, "You see, in this line of work they never asked for no references."[26] The job of the professional strikebreaker was to smash picket lines, to give the appearance that the plant was operating, and to incite violence so that the public authorities would take action against the unionists. For example, the strikebreaker might burn paper in a plant furnace so that the smoke of the chimney would give the appearance of plant production. The driving of empty trucks to and from the plant for the same purpose might also be performed by the strikebreaker. Actually, the professional strikebreaker was frequently incapable of carrying out the actual production duties performed by the ordinary worker. Generally, strikebreakers would merely amuse themselves in the plant to while away the time.

The record shows that the professional strikebreaker frequently provoked violence during strikes. Unionists or strikers recall being spit at by such people. Stones were hurled into picket lines and other disorderly acts executed to incite the strikers to violence. If the strikers were goaded into violent action, the employer could then appeal to the public authorities. Frequently, arrests followed, jail sentences and fines were imposed, and in some cases the state militia or the National Guard were called to the scene of the strike. The presence of these groups was very demoralizing to the unionists. Moreover, action of public authorities against strikers condemned the unionists as lawbreakers in the eyes of the public.

Wages paid to strikebreakers ranged from $5 to $15 per day; at least, these were the wage levels at the time that the La Follette Committee conducted its investigations. As stated, it was rare for strikebreakers to perform the duties of regular workers. Since this was the case, the employer realized no immediate profit from the use of strikebreakers. However, if the employment of these individuals could break a union, the employer presumably would profit in the long run. No union meant no collective bargaining. This in turn meant lower wages and lower labor standards.

Strikebreaking could be accomplished by pointing to the possibility of violence and to the effects of the strike on the business of the community, or by encouraging antilabor newspapers. All of these techniques, as well as others, were included in the celebrated "Mohawk Valley Formula." This organized system of strikebreaking was devised by James H. Rand, Jr., president of Remington Rand. By utilization of this formula, he was able to break strikes in six of his plants. The breaking of the strikes resulted in the destruction of the unions, for in each case the purpose of the strike had been to try to force the company to bargain collectively. Since the formula proved so successful, the National Association of Manufacturers circulated its principles among its members.

The Mohawk Valley Formula was developed in meticulous detail. It represented careful thinking and showed a deep insight into social processes. It serves as one illustration of the extent to which union organization met resistance. Such tactics have since been condemned in the nation's labor laws.

❦ PATTERNS OF ANTIUNION CONDUCT: COMPANY UNIONS

The record of industrial relations indicates that some companies used more moderate procedures to forestall the development and operation of collective bargaining. One such technique consisted of the sponsoring of company unions.[27] The formation of such organizations, often referred to as employee representation plans, was due to the recognition by management of the workers' desire to determine by organized action some of the elements of the employment relationship. Company unions provided for the expression of this deep-seated drive of workers. They also served to channel its implementation in a manner that lessened the threat to decision making, which some firms consider a managerial prerogative. This was the case because company unions were not independent from the control of management.

Company unions were not part of the labor union movement. They were not affiliated with either the AFL or the CIO. They were limited in membership to the workers in one company or one plant. Since company unions depended on their own resources, they could not utilize the resources, financial and otherwise, of international unions. They did not possess the backing of established and effective affiliates. Unlike regular unions, they could not avail themselves of experienced and capable labor leaders for the purpose of representation.

Collective bargaining implies the existence of labor unions free to act independently from the control of management. The process culminates in the execution of collective bargaining agreements, which are to be respected by both the labor union and the company. In addition, the collective bargaining function sometimes results in a strike. None of these basic features of real collective bargaining is found in company unions. On the contrary, employers dominated company unions by influencing the selection of their officers, supervising their functions, and directing their activities to suit the interests of management. Collective bargaining contracts between company unions and the company did not exist. At most, the activities of company unions consisted of calling minor grievances of workers to the attention of management. Officers of company unions had to take care that these unions did not vigorously prosecute major issues—such as the demand for higher wages, seniority systems, vacations, paid holidays, and the like. Such officers had to be careful how they spoke and acted before management representatives. If they appeared "unreasonable," management might discriminate against them with respect to layoffs, transfers, and promotions. In a regular labor union, union representatives are protected by collective bargaining agreements, and more effectively, by the organization itself.

In still another respect, the company union failed to function as a true collective bargaining agent. In regular labor unions, officers hold their positions as long as they satisfy the rank and file. Union leaders must be responsive to the demands of the membership. To do otherwise would mean jeopardizing their positions. This is essentially true at both the local and international levels. Such responsiveness to the demands of the rank and file does not characterize the company union. Representatives of such an organization, enjoying little or no protection from possible discriminatory reprisal by management, had of necessity to curry the favor and good will of company officials. Since this was the case, company union representatives would grant desires of the rank and file only to the extent that their implementation did not conflict seriously with company policy. Such a situation scarcely constitutes true collective bargaining.

Company unions were the creatures of management. If the interests of management would be advanced by their elimination, this could be accomplished without much difficulty. In short, the continuity of company unions depended upon the pleasure of management. Company unions possessed no sovereignty and exerted only that authority bestowed on them by the employer. Since company unions attempted to serve two masters—the company and the workers—such organizations could not function as effective collective bargaining agencies. Labor unions, as defined by national labor policy, must represent and be responsible to their membership. This element was lacking in company unions. Consequently, they fell short of providing effective vehicles through which workers could engage in collective bargaining in accordance with national policy.

At times, an independent local labor organization, free from the control of management, may function at the company or plant level. Such organizations have no affiliation with federations or international unions, but unlike company unions, these independent unions can perform the collective bargaining function. This is true because, though independent from federations or international unions, they are not subject to the control of the company. Such independent labor unions are controlled directly by the membership. Independent unions execute labor contracts, hold regular membership meetings, collect dues, elect their officers independent from the influence of management, and when necessary, call strikes. Independent unions have at times affiliated with the international unions of the AFL-CIO. These international unions have not, of course, issued charters to unions dominated by employers. Before application for such a charter can be considered favorably, the company union has to rid itself of all evidences of employer control. As a matter of fact, in many cases, company unions became regular labor unions by asserting their independence from management.

👁 *NEED FOR PUBLIC CONTROL*

The foregoing brief discussion, based largely on government documentation, discloses that a variety of techniques have been used to interfere with the formation of labor unions and the exercise of the collective bargaining process. Thus workers have often been denied the right to engage in collective bargaining. Such a right has been recognized by the government as lawful. Indeed, the Norris–La Guardia Act identifies collective bargaining with public policy. If the collective bargaining process was socially desirable, the utilization of antiunion techniques defeated the public purpose. It was necessary that society protect the right of workers to engage in collective bargaining. The alternative would result in an incongruous situation: on the one hand, public policy grants workers the right to self-organization and collective bargaining, and on the other hand, society silently approves by inaction employers' antiunion techniques. Consistency demanded that the government take appropriate action to provide protection to workers in the exercise of their right to collective bargaining. It appeared necessary that the government should either adopt this course of action, or else denounce collective bargaining as an antisocial and unlawful institution.

An additional consideration highlighted the need for public protection of the workers' right to collective bargaining. Even though confronted with hostile opposition, some employees were still determined to engage in concerted activities. To check interference with organizational efforts, workers made use of their economic weapon—the strike. Employees resorted to the strike to force management to recognize their unions, to bargain collectively with their representatives, and to cease interfering with the organization and functioning of their unions. The record of industrial relations demonstrates that workers frequently made use of the organizational strike. During the period 1919–1933, union organizational issues, such as refusal to recognize or bargain with labor unions, alone or in combination with other causes, accounted for 24 percent of all strikes. In 1934, 45.9 percent of all strikes resulted from those causes.[28] It is noteworthy that the Supreme Court of the United States recognized the seriousness of this problem in industrial relations. The Court in 1937 declared: "Refusal to confer and to negotiate has been one of the most prolific causes of strife. This is such an outstanding fact in the history of labor disturbances that it is a proper subject of judicial notice and requires no citation of instances."[29] In a 1967 study, one of the authors found that 94 percent of unfair labor practices filed against employers in one district office of the National Labor Relations Board stemmed from conduct arising directly out of union organizing campaigns.[30] Resistance to union organization was the single most important cause of strife in the labor relations area.

Organizational strikes, like economic strikes (that is, strikes for wages, hours, vacations, and so on), interfere with the effective operation of the national economy. A democratic government, responsive to the needs of the country, is expected to deal with the problem. To reduce the frequency of organizational strikes, the nation could outlaw strikes calculated to force management to permit union organization and collective bargaining. Such an approach obviously would be more appropriate for nations in which freedom of association is more restricted than for a democratic society. Outlawing of organizational strikes would be repugnant to a democracy. If legislation of this character were to stand the test of constitutionality, the law of industrial relations would be turned back considerably. If workers were not permitted to strike for union recognition, the union movement could make little progress, and, indeed, would likely disintegrate into ineffectual units. In such a legal environment, the employer would need only to refuse to bargain with a union. If a labor organization, as a result of such conduct, would dare to strike, the penalties of law would come into operation. It appears clear enough that outlawing of union organizational strikes would result in the eventual destruction of the labor union movement.

Instead of outlawing the organizational strike, the public interest might be better served by legislation prohibiting the causes and abuses of such strikes. Specifically, Congress and state legislatures could forbid resistance to union organizational efforts. In addition, such legislation could require that employers bargain collectively with workers' unions when a majority of employees express such a desire through democratic standards of expression. Due care should be taken to balance the rights of both groups. Laws of this character do not confer any new rights or impose any new restrictions on anyone if properly administered by an impartial agency. Such legislation requires merely the respect of a right already possessed by both groups.

Such an approach would be in the public interest. Strikes for organizational purposes could be made unnecessary. Workers could utilize the remedial processes of the government if there were interference with their right to self-organization and collective bargaining. Since the frequency of such strikes should decrease, the public would be relieved from the inconveniences following in the wake of organizational strikes. Moreover, labor history demonstrates clearly that strikes for recognition purposes are usually bitter in character. Such strikes are frequently contested because management and workers are fully aware that the breaking of a recognition strike will result in the elimination of the labor union. The story of industrial relations is replete with instances of the bloody nature of the organizational strike. The circumstances of Memorial Day, 1937 in Chicago highlight the point. Growing out of the context of an organizational strike carried out against a steel corporation, the record reveals a tragic pattern of events. Police attempted to disperse a large group of strikers and their sympathizers, and the result was violence. When the struggle ended, 10 strikers had been killed, 90 other unionists had been injured (30 by gunfire), and 35 of the police had sustained injury.[31]

Another example points up the violence that frequently followed in the wake of strikes undertaken to force management to recognize unions as representatives of their employees. On Monday, February 18, 1935, a union struck against an Ohio rubber company. The La Follette Committee reported that the strike resulted from the labor relations policy of the company, which was "based upon a refusal either to enter into a written agreement with the union of its employees or to recognize that union as exclusive bargaining agent for its employees."[32] The company prepared to break the strike. Industrial spies were hired from professional detective agencies. At the time of the strike, the company had available a guard force of 133 men, a good share of whom were professional strikebreakers. About nine hundred workers were employed in the factory, the result being a ratio of about one guard to seven employees. This led one worker to draw a parallel between the environment of a prison and the company. He complained that a "free-born American citizen trying to work and make a living for my [sic] family" had to work in a "plant being infested with guards walking among us...."[33] In addition, a supply of munitions was purchased. For $3,340.69 the company received tear gas and gas equipment, jumper-repeater tear gas rifles, three long-range field guns, and a large supply of shells.[34]

Such preparations were hardly conducive to peaceful strike conditions. As the La Follette Committee reported: "The company had created an explosive situation. The course of its activities preceding the strike can justly be construed as incendiary."[35] Despite the fact that strikers were given instructions "to conduct themselves in an orderly manner," violence characterized the strike from the beginning. When guards started shooting tear gas into the union's picket line, the strikers threw bricks. People not connected with either party were injured by the violence. The mayor of the town testified that some of the guards shot gas shells at some strikers near a school "and some of the school children near at the time got some of the gas."[36]

The strikers subsequently established a rest camp on an empty lot within sight of the factory. Shelter tents and a commissary wagon provided some protection against the winter cold. A few days after the camp was established, the sheriff ordered the strikers to disperse. After the workers refused to break up their camp, the guards en masse "attacked the camp, gassed it, burned the shelter tent, and arrested about 40 strikers as violators of the peace."[37] This illustration further underscores the need for effective laws to protect the rights of all parties concerned in labor disputes.

Not only do workers and the public benefit from such a legislative program, but employers also profit from such an arrangement. Many employers have fully respected the collective bargaining process. Long before the Wagner Act, a good number of companies dealt in good faith with their employees' labor organizations. Many union-recognizing employers competed with companies that resisted the attempts of their workers to bargain collectively. Such a condition resulted in a competitive disadvantage to organized firms. This was usually the case because the nonunion companies could sell products at cheaper prices. Cheaper prices resulted from the lower labor standards of the nonunion firms. In view of these considerations, it could be expected that employers who dealt in good faith with their workers' unions would have welcomed a legal environment facilitating the organization of their nonunion competitors.

Some employers derived another advantage from a legal climate requiring respect of the workers' right to self-organization and collective bargaining. Such an arrangement provided an employer with an opportunity to engage in the collective bargaining process in good faith without losing the esteem of its business associates. It is possible that many employers combated labor unions because the *general* attitude of the business group advocated this course of action. In spite of personal inclinations to the contrary, an employer may have followed this line of procedure in order to maintain standing in the group. Employers may have been concerned that should they violate the "code" of their associates, they might suffer social and economic reprisal. In a legal environment with firmly established rules, such an employer could have dealt in good faith with a labor union without fear of ostracism. Such employers would be afforded a valid basis for their actions—in the event that the law had required respect of the workers' right to self-organization and collective bargaining.

In the final analysis, legal protection of the right of workers to self-organization can be defended on the basis of the social desirability of collective bargaining. As long as the process is socially useful, the public interest is served to the degree that the right is respected. It follows therefore

CHAPTER SIX 135

that the right of workers to collective bargaining must be protected against the invasions of those who would treat this right with contempt.

🎠 SUMMARY

Government inquiry revealed that antiunion companies engaged in many tactics calculated to wipe out effective unionism. These activities were brought to light by many studies, including the celebrated findings of the La Follette Committee. Evidence revealed that spies, strikebreakers, and company unions were utilized in the attempt to destroy labor unions. Some employers attacked union leadership and set up systematic strikebreaking programs, such as the Mohawk Valley Formula, to accomplish the same objective.

Such activities stimulated long and bitter organizational strikes. These strikes would not have been necessary if there had been a recognition of the right of employees to engage in collective bargaining. This, many reportedly refused to do; the result was industrial warfare. It became apparent that legislation was necessary to curb antiunion behavior so that the right of workers to engage in collective bargaining would be protected.

🎠 DISCUSSION QUESTIONS

1. Rank the patterns of antiunion conduct reported by the La Follette Committee in the order of the effect that each might have had on worker rights to self-organization and collective bargaining. Support your decisions.
2. How important is it to attempt to eliminate or reduce organizational strikes and other related activities to lesser levels of permissible conflict?

🎠 NOTES

[1] *American Steel Foundries Company v. Tri-City Central Trades Council*, 257 U.S. 312 (1921).
[2] For example, see *Report of the U.S. Commission on Industrial Relations*, 11 vols., Washington, D.C., 1916, and *Interchurch World Movement's Study of the Steel Strike of 1919*, with its special reports on espionage and strikebreaking carried on by the United States Steel Corporation. See also books such as *The Labor Spy*, by Sidney Howard and Robert Dunn; *I Break Strikes*, by Edward Levinson; and *Spies in Steel*, by Frank Palmer.
[3] *Violations of Free Speech and Rights of Labor, Report of the Committee on Education and Labor*, pursuant to S. Res. 266, 74th Congress. This report will hereafter be cited as the La Follette Committee Report.
[4] La Follette Committee, *Report on Industrial Espionage*, Report No. 46, Part III, 75th Congress, p. 39.

[5] *Ibid.*, p. 62.

[6] *Hearings*, Part IV, pp. 1239–1240 (reference to the volumes of the hearings of the La Follette Committee will be designated throughout this chapter as *Hearings*).

[7] *Ibid.*, Part VIII, p. 3113.

[8] *Ibid.*, Part V, p. 1457.

[9] *Ibid.*, Part III, pp. 889–891.

[10] La Follette Committee, Report No. 46, *op. cit.*, p. 63.

[11] *Hearings*, Part IV, p. 1266.

[12] La Follette Committee, Report No. 46, *op. cit.*, p. 63.

[13] *Ibid.*, p. 22.

[14] *Ibid.*, p. 79.

[15] *Hearings*, Part IV, p. 1318.

[16] Pinkerton's National Detective Agency, Inc., Order 105—Business Accepting, dated April 20, 1937. Reported in La Follette Committee, Report No. 46, *op. cit.*, p. 122.

[17] La Follette Committee, *Private Police Systems*, Report No. 6, Part II, 76th Congress, 1st sess., p. 193.

[18] *Hearings*, Part XXVI, p. 11058.

[19] *Ibid.*, Part XXVI, pp. 11076–7.

[20] *Ibid.*, Part XXVI, p. 10924.

[21] *Riecke Metal Products Company*, 40 NLRB 872 (1942).

[22] *Fred A. Snow & Company*, 41 NLRB 1292 (1942).

[23] La Follette Committee, Report No. 6, *op. cit.*, p. 126.

[24] *Ibid.*, p. 128.

[25] La Follette Committee, *Strikebreaking Services*, Report No. 6, 76th Congress, 1st sess., pp. 65, 74.

[26] R. R. R. Brooks, *When Labor Organizes* (New Haven: Yale University Press, 1937), p. 146.

[27] For an authoritative and interesting account of the character and operation of company unions, see Bureau of Labor Statistics Bulletin 634, *Characteristics of Company Unions* (Washington, D.C., 1938).

[28] *Monthly Labor Review*, XXXIX (July 1934), 75; XLII (January 1936), 162.

[29] *NLRB v. Jones & Laughlin Steel Corporation*, 301 U.S. 1 (1937).

[30] Benjamin J. Taylor, *The Operation of the Taft-Hartley Act in Indiana*, Indiana Business Bulletin No. 58 (Bloomington, Indiana: Bureau of Business Research, 1967), p. 27.

[31] For an account of the Memorial Day tragedy, see La Follette Committee, *The Chicago Memorial Day Incident*, Report No. 46, Part II.

[32] La Follette Committee, Report No. 6, *op. cit.*, p. 57.

[33] *Hearings*, Part XXI, p. 9218.

[34] La Follette Committee, Report No. 6, *op. cit.*, p. 60.

[35] *Ibid.*, p. 60.

[36] *Hearings*, Part XXI, exhibit 4243, p. 9349.

[37] La Follette Committee, Report No. 6, *op. cit.*, p. 62.

CHAPTER SEVEN

PRECURSORS OF THE WAGNER ACT

THE BEGINNINGS OF LEGISLATIVE SUPPORT

The 1890s were years of transition for the American labor movement. The Knights of Labor was passing into oblivion and the young American Federation of Labor was seeking effective means of gaining social acceptance. The financial panic of 1893 brought with it difficulties in expanding unionism into new areas. It was, however, the prevailing philosophy of the courts that proved the major obstacle to union progress. In 1895, in the *Debs* case, the Supreme Court sanctioned the use of the injunction in labor disputes. This procedure was followed by the courts and enlarged upon for several years, as mentioned in previous chapters. The lower federal courts in the middle 1890s were making widespread use of the Sherman Act to constrain union activities. The executive branch of the government upon occasion intervened in labor disputes. This was the case at both the federal and state levels. For example, in 1894, President Cleveland ordered federal troops to break the Pullman strike called by the American Railway Union. Cleveland took this action despite the protests of Governor Altgeld of Illinois. By 1900, the entire union membership in the nation totaled less than 1 million.

The legislative branch of government was beginning to demonstrate more concern for the union movement. There was a marked lag between the judicial and the legislative branches of government in the development of the law of collective bargaining. The legal aspects of the labor injunction illustrate the principle. State and federal attempts to control the injunction in labor disputes antedated the recognition by the courts that such control was necessary for industrial peace and justice. A similar parallel between these two branches of government is noted with respect to positive legal protection of the right of workers to self-organization and collective bargaining. It may be worthwhile to emphasize the basic reason for such a lag. The tenure of office of the members of the judiciary is more secure than that of the legislators. In addition, many judges receive their commissions by appointment and consequently are removed from the direct control of the electorate. As a result, the legislator is more responsive to the changes in attitude of the people. It took the cataclysmic events of the 1930s plus the "court packing" threat by Roosevelt to change the structure of the Supreme Court to effect judicial approval of the social legislation enacted by Congress and the states.

The first attempts of the legislative branch of government to provide a degree of protection to workers utilizing their right to self-organization and collective bargaining took place in the 1890s. Such efforts antedated labor injunction control legislation by about a decade; they came about fifty years after *Commonwealth* v. *Hunt*, the decision that marked the beginning of judicial approval of labor unions. And, as mentioned, this legislative attempt occurred during a period of almost total judicial control of the collective bargaining process.

THE EARLY LAWS: YELLOW-DOG CONTRACTS AND DISCRIMINATION UNLAWFUL

In the 1890s, fifteen states enacted laws calculated to provide protection of the right of workers to self-organization and collective bargaining: Massachusetts, Connecticut, New York, Pennsylvania, New Jersey, Ohio, Indiana, Illinois, Wisconsin, Minnesota, Kansas, Missouri, California, Idaho, and Georgia.[1] The statutes prohibited employers from discharging employees for joining labor unions and from making the yellow-dog contract a condition of employment. The Indiana law of 1893 is characteristic of these early laws. It provided the following protection:

> It shall be unlawful for any individual, or member of any firm, agent, officer, or employee of any company or corporation to prevent employees from forming, joining and belonging to any lawful labor organization, and any such individual members, agents, officer, or employee that coerces or attempts to coerce employees by discharging or threatening to discharge from the employ of any firm, company or corporation because of their connection with such labor organization, and any officer or employer who exacts a pledge from workingmen that they will not become members of a labor

organization as a consideration of employment, shall be guilty of a misdemeanor, and upon conviction thereof in any court of competent jurisdiction shall be fined in any sum not exceeding one hundred dollars ($100), or imprisoned for not more than six (6) months, or both, at the discretion of the court.

Thus, the early laws attempted to eliminate two powerful antiunion weapons. Consideration has already been given to the yellow-dog contract. However, we must emphasize that no single antiunion procedure exceeded the effectiveness of the yellow-dog agreement. Workers could not exercise their right to self-organization and collective bargaining where employees were required to agree not to join labor unions as a condition of employment. Elimination of the effectiveness of the yellow-dog contract was a logical starting place to protect the collective bargaining process. Unlike Norris–La Guardia and some of the modern state anti-injunction statutes, the early laws outlawed the yellow-dog contract and made violators subject to fines and imprisonment if they should demand the execution of such agreements. Under Norris–La Guardia and state laws patterned after it, the method of rendering the yellow-dog contract ineffectual was merely to make the judiciary unavailable for the enforcement of such agreements. In this respect, the early laws may have been more effective than later attempts to stamp out the yellow-dog contract. However, when the National Labor Relations Board was created, it held that coercion of employees to execute such agreements constituted an unfair labor practice. Failure to comply with an order of the NLRB could result in contempt of court proceedings.[2]

Discharge of workers because of union activities is another effective weapon to forestall unionization. In modern industry, the worker's job is normally the sole means of support. Without a job, the worker and family are helpless. The fear of loss of job is a prominent factor in the discouragement of union membership. Should a few workers be discharged because of union activities, the remaining workers would possibly have little appetite for union affairs. Workers could scarcely enjoy their right to self-organization and collective bargaining if they were fearful that union activities could terminate their means of livelihood.

In 1898, Congress passed the Erdman Act. The purpose of the law was to promote interstate commerce. This objective was to be realized by setting up procedures designed to reduce labor conflict in the nation's railroads. Though the law provided for the mediation and arbitration of labor disputes, our concern at this point is with the provisions of the Erdman law that protected the right of railroad workers to self-organization and collective bargaining. The Erdman law in part resulted from the celebrated Pullman strike of 1894. Fundamentally, this strike was caused by the refusal of the Pullman Company to enter into collective bargaining negotiations with its workers. As noted, the strike eventually spread to the railroads themselves. Congress was aware that organizational strikes could again interrupt railroad traffic among the states. Such strikes could result from the demand by the railroads that workers execute yellow-dog contracts, and from the discharge of workers because of union activities. Congress reasoned that if these two antiorganizational practices could be eliminated, the necessity for organizational strikes on the railroads would be reduced. Consequently, the interstate commerce of the nation would thereby be promoted.

As a result of these considerations, the Erdman Act contained the famous Section 10. This section made it a misdemeanor for railroad employers to

> require any employee or any person seeking employment, as a condition of such employment, to enter into an agreement, either written or verbal, not to become or remain a member of any labor corporation, association, or organization; or to threaten any employee with loss of employment or unjustly to discriminate against any employee because of his membership in such labor corporation, association, or organization.

Similar to the state laws mentioned previously, the Erdman Act outlawed the yellow-dog contract. But the railroad law was more effective than the state laws, for it prohibited railroad employers from discriminating in any way against workers who exercised their right to self-organization and collective bargaining. The state laws prohibited only discrimination by discharge, but permitted other acts to discourage union activities, such as discriminating against union-minded workers with respect to promotions, layoffs, transfers, and the like. Under the Erdman Act, all forms of discrimination against union employees were outlawed.

Compared to modern legislation, the early attempts to protect the rights of workers to self-organization and collective bargaining were ineffective. They did not prohibit the formation of company-dominated unions. Nor did they outlaw methods often used to break strikes and prevent the organization of labor unions. In addition, the early laws did not require that employers recognize their employees' unions and enter into negotiations with these unions. Finally, the method of enforcement of the statutes was ineffective. Enforcement was left entirely to court proceedings. This meant that violators of the law might avoid prosecution. The modern collective bargaining statute places the responsibility for enforcement on an expert administrative agency. This feature, as will be discussed in detail in the next chapter, means the effective enforcement of such statutes.

Despite their obvious shortcomings, the early statutes were landmarks of industrial relations law. They reflected a growing awareness of the need for government action if the right of workers to self-organization and collective bargaining was to be effective. The early

CHAPTER SEVEN

laws represented a beginning in the effective implementation of the collective bargaining process.

ATTITUDE OF THE JUDICIARY

The modest beginnings of legislative support of the collective bargaining process were snuffed out by the courts. The judiciary failed to give weight to the factors producing legislative action. Many of the state laws were declared unconstitutional by state supreme courts. However, the decisive factor came at the hands of the Supreme Court of the United States. In 1908, the Court invalidated Section 10 of the Erdman Act.[3] Seven years later, the Kansas statute suffered a similar fate.[4] Observers should have expected these decisions. They were handed down in a period in which the Supreme Court was not convinced of the necessity for collective bargaining. The jurists were not impressed with the social and economic factors justifying the attempts of government to protect workers in their employment relationship. The Court's position that the Constitution was to be protected from arbitrary invasions by the legislative branch caused it to rule against legislative action calculated to raise the collective bargaining power of the nation's workers. The record of the Supreme Court in the 1890s and in particular during the first two decades of the present century reveals unmistakably that the judiciary was not convinced that collective bargaining was a needed institution in light of its definition of individual property rights. The judges were determined that the economic welfare of worker groups should not be raised either by legislative action or workers' self-help activities. In their view, economic welfare was determined by the manner in which property was utilized. They feared that interference with the use of property could stifle competition and decrease the welfare of national trade.

In 1895, the Supreme Court sustained the use of the injunction in labor disputes.[5] In 1908, it applied the Sherman Act to labor union activities.[6] This decision set the precedent for subsequent prosecution of unions under the antitrust provisions. Such prosecution, as indicated, retarded the development of the American labor union movement. In 1917, two years after the Kansas attempt to outlaw the yellow-dog contract was held unconstitutional, the Supreme Court held that the yellow-dog contract could be protected by the labor injunction.[7] In 1921, the Supreme Court interpreted the legislative intent of the Clayton Act to hold unconstitutional the efforts of state governments to regulate the labor injunction.

Not only did the Court display this attitude toward labor relations legislation, but it likewise struck down laws designed to protect workers from the inexorable operation of the economic system. Thus, in 1918 and again in 1922, the Court held unconstitutional a congressional measure to control the use of child labor in American industry.[8] In 1923, the high court refused to sustain legislation that established a minimum wage for women employed in industry.[9]

Such was the record of the Supreme Court in the period in which legislative attempts were made to protect the right of workers to collective bargaining. In view of its pattern, one scarcely could have expected the high court to sustain these legislative efforts. And the Supreme Court did not deviate from its established pattern of interpretation of protective labor relations law. Both the *Adair* and *Coppage* decisions were consistent with the overall direction of the Court.

In characteristic fashion, the Supreme Court refused to give serious weight to the economic reasons that justified Section 10 of the Erdman Act. The Court could not see how Section 10 might prevent interruptions to interstate commerce by eliminating the need for strikes that resulted from the interference of railroad employers with the right of workers to self-organization and collective bargaining. In this connection, the Court asked: "What possible legal or logical connection is there between an employee's membership in a labor organization and the carrying on of interstate commerce?" Such a statement reflects the Court's philosophy during this period. Many years elapsed before the judiciary decided that there was both a logical connection and a valid legal relationship between the promotion of interstate commerce and government protection of the right of workers to self-organization and collective bargaining.

Once the Court held that there was no positive relationship between the objectives of Section 10 and the promotion of interstate commerce, it found the section unconstitutional. The Court reached the conclusion that Section 10 deprived both railroad operators and workers of their property without due process of law. Freedom to contract is a liberty guaranteed by the Fifth Amendment to the Constitution. Congress may pass no law that deprives people of this liberty. Thus, the Court declared that "such liberty and right embraces the right to make contracts for the sale of one's own labor." From this premise the Court held that workers and employers could agree on the execution of a yellow-dog contract. This was a freedom that could not be circumscribed by the legislature. The railroad employer had the right to establish conditions of employment and the employee had the right "to become or not, as he chose, an employee of the railroad company upon the terms offered to him." In other words, the Court said that if railroad workers did not like the idea of signing a yellow-dog contract, they had the right not to accept employment under such conditions. The implication was that the employee was free to seek other employment. What the Court failed to consider was that workers might have few alternative employment possibilities. Either they worked for the railroad or they were forced to seek another job, which might be an inferior alternative. The facts of economic life might have forced employees to sign

CHAPTER SEVEN

the agreement even though they objected vigorously to such an employment agreement. At this time, the Court was more concerned with abstract and formal notions of law than with social and economic reality. Such an approach invariably resulted in harm to the interests of the nation's workers.

That portion of the Erdman Act forbidding the discharge of workers because of union activities was likewise held unconstitutional. The Court did not understand the new industrial life. The employer had the right to discharge a worker for union activities in the same way that the individual worker had the right to quit the employment of an employer who persisted in hiring nonunion workers. The Court declared that "in all such particulars the employer and the employee have equality of right, and any legislation that disturbs that equality is an arbitrary interference with the liberty of contract which no government can legally justify in a free land." In short, the Court did not understand that the employer, who possesses infinitely greater economic power than the worker, could use that power to deny workers their right to collective bargaining. It was assumed that there was already balanced power between the two groups. The worker was free to join a labor union. But that "freedom" was not realized if employers could deny workers their right to collective bargaining. If government had decided to protect this right against the arbitrary invasion of employers, it appears that the cause of freedom would have been advanced, not limited. The conduct of the employer would be limited by government only insofar as such restriction permitted the worker to enjoy the exercise of a lawfully recognized right.

In *Coppage*, in which the Supreme Court invalidated the Kansas statute, essentially the same arguments that appeared in *Adair* were offered. Constant reference was made to the *Adair* opinion to support the *Coppage* decision. The Court utilized *Adair* as a precedent to strike down the Kansas law. Thus, the Court declared in *Coppage* that "this case cannot be distinguished from *Adair* v. *United States*." Only changes in the formal approach appear in the *Coppage* decision. Since Kansas passed the statute under the authority of its police power, the Court was required to show that the statute had no relationship to the promotion of the general welfare of the people of the state. It accomplished this task by asking, "What possible relation has ... the Act to the public health, safety, morale, or general welfare?" In *Adair*, the Court held that Section 10 of the Erdman Act did not constitute a valid exercise of the power of Congress to promote interstate commerce. In *Coppage*, the Court held that the passage of a state law outlawing the yellow-dog contract and prohibiting discharge for union reasons was not "a legitimate object for the exercise of the police power." In a ruling similar to the *Adair* decision, the Court in *Coppage* held that the Kansas law deprived both employers and employees of their property and personal liberty without due process of law. In this respect, the Court ruled on the Fourteenth Amendment (the constitutional provision that limits the power of the states) and not the Fifth Amendment (the one that checks the power of the Congress).

THE HOLMES'S DISSENT

Justice Holmes dissented sharply from the viewpoint of the majority of the Court. Holmes, in *Adair*, upheld the right of Congress to fashion the public policy of the United States. He felt that there was a reasonable relationship between the promotion of interstate commerce and a law calculated to reduce the need for strikes in the railroads. Holmes felt that the Court, the judicial arm of government, should not overrule Congress, the legislative branch of government, in matters of public policy. He was even less impressed with the argument of the Court that Section 10 of the Erdman Act violated the Fifth Amendment to the Constitution. On this point, he declared that Section 10 "is, in substance, a very limited interference with the freedom of contract, no more. The section simply prohibits the more powerful party to exact certain undertakings, or to threaten dismissal or unjustly discriminate on certain grounds against those already employed." Holmes's dissent in the *Coppage* case rested on his reasoning in the *Adair* proceeding. He made the following simple statement:

> in present conditions a workman not unnaturally may believe that only by belonging to a union can he secure a contract that shall be fair to him. If that belief, whether right or wrong, may be held by a reasonable man, it seems to me that it may be enforced by law in order to establish the equality of position between the parties in which liberty of contract begins. Whether in the long run it is wise for the workingmen to enact legislation of this sort is not my concern, but I am strongly of opinion that there is nothing in the Constitution of the United States to prevent it, and that *Adair v. United States*...should be over-ruled.

This position was representative of Holmes's general attitude toward public policy. He consistently held that Congress and the states should be given wide latitude in legislative matters. The judiciary should respect the opinion of Congress and the state legislatures in matters of public policy. The Constitution should only be employed to check the legislative branch of government when a law flagrantly and unmistakably violated its terms.

🍃 EVENTS OF WORLD WAR I

By its position in *Adair* and *Coppage*, the Supreme Court denied to legislative bodies the authority to protect the right of workers to collective bargaining. The effect of these decisions meant that government could not control their bargaining relationships. In a normal peacetime economy, it was the considered opinion of the Court that judicial restraint of the collective bargaining process was necessary.

Had World War I not occurred, it is possible that legislative action in the area of collective bargaining would have been forestalled for many years. However, World War I served to focus the attention of the public on the state of the nation's labor relations policy. The need for uninterrupted production was essential. Any strike for any purpose was seen as detrimental to the interests of the nation. In order to establish a procedure to eliminate wartime strikes, President Wilson called a conference of outstanding representatives of industry and organized labor. At the conference, employers and unions gave a no-lockout and no-strike pledge, not including union-recognition strikes, which remained legal. To settle all labor-management disputes peacefully, the conference recommended the setting up of a war labor board. This proposal was accepted by President Wilson, and on April 8, 1918, the National War Labor Board (NWLB) was established. To guide the operation of the Board, the conference adopted a series of principles agreed to by labor and management representatives. Our concern here is with only one of these principles. This was the declaration by the conference representatives that the War Labor Board should protect employees in their right to self-organization and collective bargaining. The Board was to enforce the following policy: "The right of workers to organize in trade unions and to bargain collectively through chosen representatives is recognized and affirmed. This right should not be denied, abridged, or interfered with by the employers in any manner whatsoever.... Employers should not discharge workers for membership in trade unions, nor for legitimate trade union activities."[10]

By adopting this policy, it was hoped that strikes caused by employers' denial of the employees' right to self-organization and collective bargaining would be sharply reduced. It is noteworthy that organizational strikes were not outlawed. To have adopted the latter course of action would have meant the disintegration of the union movement.

The National War Labor Board enforced in good faith the right of employees to self-organization and collective bargaining. The Board ordered the reinstatement with back pay of workers who were discharged because of union activities, required employers to bargain collectively with representatives of workers' labor unions, and ordered the polling of workers in elections to determine their choices of bargaining agents.[11] Many of these policies were to be embodied in the National Labor Relations Act passed by Congress in 1935. Although the National War Labor Board had no express authority to enforce its rulings, Wilson in practice did require compliance with the Board's orders through the exercise of his war powers. For example, Wilson seized the properties of the Western Union Telegraph Company because the carrier had discharged workers who joined unions. Similarly, the Smith & Wesson Arms Company was seized when the firm refused to bargain collectively.[12]

Still another circumstance of World War I served to shape the character of future public policy in industrial relations. With the entry of the United States into World War I, the federal government took over the operation of the nation's railroads. The task of supervising the operation of the railroads was lodged in the Railroad Administration. A director-general headed the agency. Early in 1918, the director-general issued General Order No. 8, which provided that "no discrimination will be made in the employment, retention, or conditions of employment of employees because of membership or nonmembership in labor organizations." In short, General Order No. 8 reestablished the principle of Section 10 of the Erdman Act, and thereby conflicted directly with the doctrine that the Supreme Court had laid down in the *Adair* decision. No one, however, chose to question the right of the federal government to protect collective bargaining rights in the railroad industry during World War I. Of course, the government, not private individuals, operated the roads. This may have had a bearing on any eventual court proceedings involving General Order No. 8.

The Railroad Administration recognized the railway unions as lawful bargaining agents. Of course, since the final determination of the conditions of work rested with the federal government, there was no actual collective bargaining in the industry during the war. Controversy as to whether there can be free collective bargaining in an industry owned or operated by the government continues to this day. It is known that the public, the vast majority of union leaders, and the rank-and-file workers frown on strikes when a plant or industry is owned or operated by the government under conditions of war. Free collective bargaining implies that workers have the moral and legal right to strike. Nevertheless, the Railroad Administration did entertain the demands of the railway unions. In many cases, the administration granted such demands. From this point of view, the railway unions performed an active role in shaping the conditions of work on the railroads during World War I.

Federal protection of the right of workers to collective bargaining during World War I served a dual purpose. In the first place, it demonstrated that a peaceful procedure could be instituted by government to decrease the need for the organizational strike. Such a wartime experiment was a harbinger of future labor relations policy. If protection of the right to collective bargaining during wartime promoted the cause of industrial peace, it appeared equally valid that the same result could follow from such a program during peacetime. In the second place, the favorable government policy toward organized labor during World War I stimulated the growth of the union movement. In 1917, union membership in all labor organizations totaled about 3 million. At the termination of World War I, this figure was 4 million, an increase of 33 percent.

NATIONAL WAR LABOR BOARD ABOLISHED: DECLINE IN UNION MEMBERSHIP

This increase in union membership reflects the profound effect of government policy on the collective bargaining process. It indicates that a favorable legal environment stimulates union growth. After World War I ended, the National War Labor Board was abolished. This meant that once again the worker was left without government protection in collective bargaining relationships. As a result, union membership declined steadily; by 1933, membership was less than 3 million. The decline appears more serious if adjustment is made for the growth of the population and the labor force over the period 1919 to 1933. In 1920, the population of the United States was about 105 million; by 1930, the figure had increased to approximately 123 million. The labor force increased from about 40 million in 1920 to about 47 million in 1930. In the same period, there occurred a noticeable shift in the composition of the labor force. The number of people employed in agriculture declined sharply. In 1920, about 27 percent of the labor force was in agriculture, but in 1930, agriculture accounted for only 21 percent of the labor force. This meant that there was a shifting of workers to occupations more amenable to union organization. The agricultural worker for a variety of reasons was not easily organized. Yet despite the increase and change in the character of the labor force, the level of union membership was no higher in 1933 than it had been in 1917.

The Great Depression of the thirties contributed its share to thwart the progress of the union movement. Labor history does demonstrate that the strength of organized labor, in terms of numbers and bargaining power, is reduced in depression periods. Giving full weight to the depression of the thirties, the fact still remains that the chief factor preventing the growth of the union movement from World War I until the advent of the New Deal was the lack of legislative support. The union movement showed no progress, indeed actually declined in strength, during the relatively prosperous years of the twenties. In these years, the level of unemployment averaged about 5 percent of the labor force. This figure does not represent a condition conducive to a decline in union membership, given the state of technology at the time. But, in spite of the relatively high level of employment, the union movement showed no progress and, if adjustment is made for changes in the size and composition of the labor force, organized labor actually lost ground in the twenties. The average union membership during these years was about 3.5 million.

Contrast this experience with that for the years 1932–1939. By 1939, the union movement claimed about 8 million members. Organized labor made progress in the face of severe unemployment. Despite all efforts of the government to combat unemployment, the economy still suffered from serious unemployment until entry into World War II. In 1939, for example, about 17 percent of the labor force was unemployed. Obviously, better business conditions during the New Deal period as compared with the depression years of 1929–1932 had something to do with the growth of the union movement, but the most important factor is commonly held to be the positive support given by government to collective bargaining.

Some attribute this lack of progress in the prosperous years of the twenties to deficiencies in union leadership. Granted the importance of vigorous leadership to the union movement, the fact still remains that such leadership may not have arisen precisely because of the uncertainties of the environment. It is more than a coincidence that the split in the union movement occurred during a period in which the organs of government were sympathetic to organized labor. Organization of the mass-production worker by the CIO was a result of favorable government policy. It is difficult to contend that labor leaders of the twenties simply did not see the overall desirability of the organization of the mass-production worker into industrial unions. As a matter of fact, the same union leaders who were responsible for the rise of the CIO were operating in the twenties. But in the twenties, despite the high level of employment, union leaders were not in agreement on the possibility of successfully concluding huge organizing drives. They were aware that efforts to organize the unskilled who did not possess well-entrenched skills would likely result in defeat. Why undertake such a venture if they were doomed to defeat? Clearly, the court experiences of the twenties dictated against such efforts. Industry's open-shop campaign of the period presented insurmountable obstacles to organization because of the relative ease of striker replacement. Moreover, the position of the judiciary on collective bargaining profoundly affected attitudes toward organizing activities. Some employers intensified their resistance to unions to the degree permitted by the organs of government. Rather than feeling that their techniques were antisocial in character, many employers considered that they were performing a public service by destroying the collective bargaining process. The prevailing attitude toward collective bargaining was in all probability a reflection of general public sentiment.

Workers themselves were not isolated from the effects of the legal atmosphere. Some have attributed the decline in union membership in the twenties to the increasing real income of the workers. It is true that real income of workers did increase, but that should not have prevented some progress in the union movement. Workers may have refrained from union activities out of fear of loss of job because of open-shop tactics, because of the effectiveness of the labor injunction, or because of the disrepute of association with a labor union. Those who argue that the lack of progress of the union movement in the twenties resulted from increasing real income do not fully appreciate the profound effect of government on collective bargaining. Since the legal climate operated to prevent the demonstration of effective union leadership, and inasmuch as the legal environment operated to discourage the unorganized worker from union activity, the union movement was bound to lose ground. Moreover, the real-income argument cannot be supported by empirical data. No actual investigation has been made to test the thesis. Social phenomena are not to be explained solely by statistics. On the other hand, the record testifies to the imprisonment and fines imposed on workers for union activity, to the number of strikes broken as a result of the injunction, and to the antiorganizational activities of employers. Finally, the real-income explanation, if extended to its logical conclusion, would mean that there is no need for any labor union movement. From the dawn of history, the worker has experienced a constantly increasing material standard of life. Fundamentally, this progress results from the advancing state of the arts of production. Since this progress is relentless, and if the real-income argument has validity, workers should show little propensity toward union organization. That such is not the case is demonstrated by the union movements of the western democracies.

On the basis of the foregoing observations, the conclusion must be reached that the character of the law of labor relations constitutes a most vital element influencing the growth of the union movement. The condition of the business cycle, the nature of union leadership, and the attitude of employers are of only secondary importance. An analysis of the union movement from World War I through the New Deal period supports this point of view. Given a favorable legal environment, the union movement will expand in numbers and in bargaining strength. Given a restrictive legal environment, the collective bargaining process will lose ground.

🌑 *RAILROAD LEGISLATION*

In 1926, Congress passed the Railway Labor Act.[13] The chief purpose of this law was to establish a variety of procedures, including mediation and voluntary arbitration, to reduce labor conflict in the railroads. These procedures, however, rested on the assumption that workers would be represented by labor organizations. In short, Congress felt that industrial peace on the railroads could be achieved through the collective bargaining process. Accordingly, the Railway Labor Act of 1926 provided that "representatives...shall be designated by the respective parties in such manner as may be provided in their corporate organization or unincorporated association, or by other means of collective action, without interference, influence, or coercion exercised by either party over the self-organization or designation of representatives by the other." Briefly, both workers and management were to be free in the selection of their own representatives without interference. Once chosen, these representatives were to confer together to settle labor disputes. Thus, Congress passed a law calculated to protect the railroad worker's right to collective bargaining. The Railway Labor Act of 1926 provided for a greater degree of protection than had Section 10 of the Erdman Act. In the 1926 law, the railroad employers were required to negotiate with the freely selected collective bargaining representatives of their workers. This feature was not included in the Erdman Act.

Previous to the passage of the Railway Labor Act of 1926, the railroads had sponsored a number of company-dominated unions. Attention was given to the ability of these organizations to serve as true collective bargaining agencies. Since they were creatures of the company, they were not considered equipped to represent workers in collective bargaining. After the passage of the statute, the question immediately arose as to their legality. The law did not specifically proscribe company-dominated unions. On the other hand, these organizations did not appear to have received support from the new law. Under its terms, workers were given the right to choose freely their representatives for collective bargaining. A company-dominated union might not fall within this classification.

In 1930, the question of the legality of the company union merited the attention of the Supreme Court of the United States. Once again, the Court was to rule on the constitutionality of the law that protected the right of railroad workers to collective bargaining. The railroads contended that the *Adair* decision, handed down by the Court in 1908, controlled the present proceedings. The Texas & New Orleans Railroad, the railroad involved in the case, refused to recognize or bargain with the Brotherhood of Railroad Clerks, a labor union free from company influence. Instead, the railroad supported the company sponsored and dominated "Association of Clerical Employees—Southern Pacific Line." The union claimed that the railroad was violating the Railway Labor Act of 1926.

In a decision that contrasted in every respect with the *Adair* doctrine, the Supreme Court upheld the constitutionality of the Railway Labor Act of 1926.[14] It ordered the railroad to cease interfering with the right of workers to choose whichever bargaining agents they wished. In this case, the Court held that promotion of the collective bargaining process was of the "highest public interest," for such a procedure would prevent "the interruption of interstate commerce by labor disputes and strikes." In other words, the protection of the right of workers to collective bargaining promoted commerce among the states. The view was held that collective bargaining reduced the need for organizational strikes, and that the collective bargaining process itself provided the means for industrial peace.

With respect to the Railway Labor Act of 1926 violating the "due process" clause of the Constitution, the Court had this to say:

> The Railway Labor Act of 1926 does not interfere with the normal exercise of the right of the carrier to select its employees or to discharge them. The statute is not aimed at this right of the employers but at the interference with the right of employees to have representatives of their own choosing. As the carriers subject to the Act have no constitutional right to interfere with the freedom of the employees in making their selections, they cannot complain of the statute on constitutional grounds.

In effect, the Supreme Court overruled *Adair*. It did not do so in so many words. But for practical purposes, it recognized that the *Adair* decision was no longer applicable in railroad disputes. This was not the last time the Court was to reverse itself on matters of labor legislation. For example, in 1937, in the *West Coast Hotel* case,[15] the Court reversed itself on the matter of minimum-wage laws. From 1923, the Court had held such laws unconstitutional. In 1937, it ruled differently. Precedent is always a major factor in the decision-making process of the judiciary. On the other hand, factors such as changes in court personnel, political pressure, and fundamental changes in the economic and social environment at times overshadow the importance of precedent.

❦ RAILWAY LABOR ACT AMENDED IN 1934

The *Texas & New Orleans Railroad* decision stands as a landmark in the law of industrial relations. For the first time, the Supreme Court of the United States had recognized the authority of government to provide a measure of protection to the right of workers to self-organization and collective bargaining. The decision represented a clear-cut victory for those who contended that the collective bargaining process could not be carried out successfully without government encouragement. Moreover, the decision indicated the possibility of additional legislation to implement the collective bargaining process.

In 1934, Congress strengthened the provisions of the Railway Labor Act. It enacted a series of important amendments to the 1926 law. Some of the new provisions added more protection to the right of workers to self-organization and collective bargaining. Despite the policy and provisions of the 1926 law, the collective bargaining process was not functioning as Congress had intended. An investigation pointed up the following employer practices:[16]

1. Carrier officers have participated in or supervised, directly or indirectly, the formation of, and carrier managements have retained a measure of control

over constitutions, bylaws, and other governing rules of organizations of their employees.

2. Carrier officers have supervised, or taken part in prescribing, the rules governing nominations and elections or other methods of choice of the representatives, committees and officers of such organizations.

Such practices of the railroads meant that their employees were being denied the right to select unions of their own choosing. Since the railroads sponsored company-dominated unions, the collective bargaining procedures provided for in the Railway Labor Act could not operate. The law was grounded in the belief that industrial peace and interstate commerce would be promoted to the degree that the collective bargaining process was utilized. Obviously, the objective of the statute could not be realized when the carriers interfered with the selection of workers' representatives.

Aware of these circumstances and encouraged by the outcome of the *Texas & New Orleans* case, Congress passed the 1934 amendments to strengthen collective bargaining in the railroad industry. Aimed at eliminating employer influence over the selection of workers' representatives for collective bargaining, the 1934 law forthrightly declared that "no carrier shall, by interference, influence, or coercion seek in any manner to prevent the designation by its employees as their representatives of those who or which are not employees of the carrier." It clearly established the right of officers of national unions to represent employees of the carrier. This was accomplished by providing that "representatives of employees for the purpose of this Act need not be persons in the employ of the carrier...." In addition, the law provided that railroad employers were prohibited from using funds to support any employee organization or union representatives. They were also prohibited from deducting wages or collecting dues, fees, assessments, or contributions from employees transferable to labor organizations.

A National Mediation Board was established by the 1934 amendments. The Board was empowered to give meaning to the railroad employees' right to collective bargaining. It was authorized to conduct elections to determine which union the employees desired for collective bargaining purposes. A union receiving the majority of the votes was to be certified as the lawful representative. Railroad employers were required to bargain with the union obtaining certification.

As an adjunct to the law, Congress outlawed the yellow-dog contract on the railroads. This appeared superfluous, for Norris–La Guardia, passed in 1932, had already made the yellow-dog contract ineffectual. However, Congress in its zeal to establish the collective bargaining process in the railroads outlawed the yellow-dog contract to underscore its intent.

CHAPTER SEVEN

To enforce the provisions of the law, Congress provided severe penalties for violations. The law provided for fines up to $20,000, imprisonment, or both, for willful violations of the terms of the Act. It became the duty of the various district attorneys of the United States to prosecute any person who violated the terms of the law. With such severe penalties backing up the clear statement of the law, company-dominated unions, as expected, declined sharply after the passage of the 1934 amendments.[17] Thus, Congress was successful in eliminating employer interference with the right of the railroad employees to self-organization and collective bargaining. As will subsequently be noted, the Wagner Act drew heavily from the philosophy and techniques of the amended Railway Labor Act.

NATIONAL INDUSTRIAL RECOVERY ACT

In 1932, the nation was in the depths of the Great Depression. After the election of Roosevelt, the federal government resorted to a variety of measures to promote recovery. Underlying all these attempts was a common purpose: to increase the purchasing power of the people. The New Deal aimed at promoting economic recovery by bolstering the demand for goods. To this end, an extensive public works program was instituted. In keeping with the objective of increasing purchasing power, these projects were financed by government borrowing. An integral part of the scheme was the increase of workers' wages. If wages could be increased, workers would have more money to spend. The resulting increase in expenditures would stimulate employment and promote economic recovery.

The general plan of the New Deal to promote recovery was contained in the National Industrial Recovery Act (NIRA). This law provided for the regulation of production and prices by groups of business people. The theory underlying the NIRA was that such control would provide balance in the economy. Business people in the various industrial facilities of the nation formed groups for the purpose of production and price control. Once formed, the group executed a "code." About 550 such codes were adopted during the NIRA era. The codes provided for industrial self-government by business. Production and prices were not to be controlled by unregulated competition, but through regulations adopted by the parties to the codes. Since such an arrangement violated the Sherman Antitrust Act, the NIRA provided that the antitrust statutes were not to apply to parties to the codes.

Congress required that two provisions pertaining to labor be included in every code. In the first place, each code was required to establish a minimum wage for the workers it covered. This was in keeping with the desire of the New Deal to increase purchasing power. Actually, the average minimum wage established by the codes was about 40 cents per hour. In the second place, the National Industrial Recovery Act required that its Section 7 (a) be included in each and every code. Section 7 (a) provided legal protection for the right of workers to collective bargaining. One reason for 7 (a) was the desire of the New Deal to alleviate the causes of industrial relations warfare. Section 7 (a), as will be shown below, made it mandatory that employers respect the right of employees to self-organization and collective bargaining. It was designed to outlaw practices adopted to frustrate the collective bargaining process. On the other hand, the economic motive of Section 7 (a) cannot be disregarded. Legal protection of collective bargaining would mean stronger unions from the point of view of both numbers and bargaining capabilities. Such a condition might mean effective pressure by labor unions for higher wages. Thus, a strong organized labor movement could serve the basic theory of the New Deal about how to promote economic recovery: by increasing national purchasing power.

From 1933, the year in which the NIRA was passed, until 1935, the year in which the NIRA was declared unconstitutional, union membership increased from 2,973,000 to 3,890,000—almost 33 percent.[18] These figures testify to the importance of labor relations law to the growth of the union movement.

SECTION 7 (a): NATURE AND ENFORCEMENT

Section 7 (a) contained two major principles: (1) that employees shall have the right to organize and bargain collectively through representatives of their own choosing, and shall be free from the interference, restraint, or coercion of employers of labor, or their agents, in the designation of such representatives, in self-organization, or in other concerted activities for the purpose of collective bargaining or other mutual aid and protection; and (2) that no employee and no one seeking employment shall be required as a condition of employment to join any company union or to refrain from joining, organizing, or assisting a labor organization of their own choosing.

Thus, for the first time during years of peace, Congress declared that workers throughout industry were to be protected in their collective bargaining activities. In comparison with subsequent labor relations legislation, however, Section 7 (a) contained many fundamental defects. Congress did not provide for a procedure to enforce the policy expressed in the section. Section 7 (a) failed to specify the patterns of antiunion conduct that were illegal. It did not expressly declare that company-dominated unions were unlawful. It did not state that employers were required to bargain collectively with the freely chosen representatives of their employees. Nor did Section 7 (a) forbid discrimination against employees for union activities.

These fundamental defects of Section 7 (a) soon came to light. Employers did not accept the union argument that Section 7 (a) outlawed the company-dominated union. In contrast, organized labor interpreted the section to mean that only regular labor organizations were to represent employees for collective bargaining purposes. The unions interpreted the intent of Congress as sanctioning a wide expansion of the labor union movement. Since Section 7 (a) did not provide for its own enforcement or interpretation, and since employees and employers believed it to mean different things, a wave of strikes occurred during the summer of 1933. These strikes resulted from the intensity of organizational activities. To comply with Section 7 (a), company unions were formed. Organized labor, feeling that these organizations did not reflect the policy of the government, struck for recognition of their own labor unions.

THE NATIONAL LABOR BOARD

Since the wave of strikes impaired the nation's economic recovery, President Roosevelt created the National Labor Board to administer the labor policy of the NIRA. The Board was composed of three union representatives, three industry representatives, and one "impartial" person. It was established on August 5, 1933. At first the Board was successful in its attempts to regulate industrial relations. Almost immediately after its creation, it intervened in a hosiery strike in Berks County, Pennsylvania. More than 10,000 workers were involved in the strike, and every full-fashioned hosiery mill in the county was shut down. The National Labor Board settled the strike on the basis of a procedure known as the "Reading Formula." This formula provided that (1) the strike was to be called off; (2) the striking workers were to be reinstated in their jobs without prejudice or discrimination; (3) an election was to be held under the supervision of the National Labor Board to designate representatives for collective bargaining; and (4) representatives chosen in such elections were to be authorized to negotiate with employers with a view to executing agreements concerning wages, hours, and working conditions.[19] In all but eight of the forty-five mills, workers chose the Hosiery Workers Union as their collective bargaining representative. After the elections were held, a large number of mills in the area still refused to negotiate a contract with the union representatives. The National Labor Board ordered these employers to negotiate written agreements with the unions. Eventually, practically all firms executed collective bargaining agreements with the freely chosen representatives of their workers.

The success of the National Labor Board in the hosiery industry was repeated in other industries. On the basis of the Reading Formula, the

Board peacefully settled disputes involving hundreds of thousands of workers in the wool, silk, clothing, street railways, and machine shop industries.[20] The high-water mark of the Board's operations was reached in November 1933. In this month, the number of strikes subsided considerably. On November 22 and 23, the Board conducted the most extensive elections of its existence, involving some fourteen thousand workers in captive coal mines. By November, the Board had established several regional boards. This decentralization permitted the national Board to deal with major controversies and, most important, permitted its members to reflect more carefully on matters of policy. A special study of the National Labor Board states that, for a time, "it seemed that, thanks to the Board's application of 7 (a), an ideal of industrial democracy was in the process of realization in the field of industrial relations."[21] However, by the end of the year, it was apparent that the National Labor Board could not offer adequate remedies for violations of its orders. Since it could not function effectively, the Board did not serve the public interest, for unions resorted to the organizational strike to enforce Section 7 (a).

❦ COLLAPSE OF NATIONAL LABOR BOARD

A series of events operated to weaken the prestige and operating ability of the National Labor Board. The first blow was delivered by the Weirton Steel Company and the Budd Manufacturing Company. Both concerns refused to respect the principles of the Reading Formula. Determined in their positions, the corporations refused to agree to elections to determine the question of union representation. The Weirton Company refused to allow its workers to vote on whether they desired to be represented by the Amalgamated Association of Iron, Steel and Tin Workers, a regular labor union; or by a union created and sponsored by the company. Despite protests from the federal government, the Weirton Company held an election in which workers merely voted to designate representatives under the company union plan. This open conflict with the National Labor Board seriously impaired the Board's prestige.

By February 1934, mainly as a result of its futile efforts to settle the *Weirton* and *Budd* disputes on the basis of the Reading Formula, the National Labor Board was on the verge of collapse. The example had been set by *Weirton* and *Budd* for others to follow. Orders of the Board were not respected and its authority was disregarded. Because the peaceful procedures of the Board had broken down, the frequency of organizational strikes increased sharply. Workers and employers were both determined to prevail in organizational contests. Since the National Labor Board could not control the situation by holding elections, employees resorted to the strike to gain their objective.

Aware of these circumstances, President Roosevelt attempted to bolster the authority and prestige of the disintegrating National Labor Board. In February 1934, he issued two Executive Orders that increased the power of the Board.[22] These orders provided that the National Labor Board was to conduct elections to determine collective bargaining representatives of workers. If at such an election a majority of workers chose a particular labor union for representation, the employer would be required to recognize and negotiate with this union. If an employer should refuse, the National Labor Board was to refer the case to the Compliance Division of the National Recovery Administration and/or to the office of the Attorney General of the United States. These agencies were to obtain compliance with the orders of the Board.

It appeared at first that the National Labor Board might now function as an effective organization. The intent of the President was clear. He had clothed the Board with status and power. Heretofore the Board had functioned on a more or less informal basis. It developed on its own initiative the Reading Formula, other policies, and its administrative procedures. Moreover, the great defect of the Board lay in its inability to enforce its decisions. Consequently, there was reason to believe that the Executive Orders of February 1934 would correct these shortcomings. This point of view, however, failed to materialize because of the intensity of the organizational conflicts.

Immediately after the President issued the Executive Orders, the "majority principle" laid down by the orders was challenged. It was contended that this principle would deprive nonunion workers of their employment rights, for the National Labor Board held that an employer must bargain with a majority-selected labor union as the exclusive representative of all employees. Unions argued that on the other hand, collective bargaining could not be carried out effectively if employers were free to make private deals with individual workers. If such an arrangement were established, it would not be difficult to undermine a labor union. This could be done by showing favoritism to the nonunion worker. To avail themselves of such benefits, it was argued, some workers might give up their union membership. Any sizable withdrawal from the labor union would mean its collapse. Once this occurred, the employer would then be free to determine employment conditions on a unilateral basis and need no longer show concern for the nonunion worker.

General Johnson and Donald R. Richberg, high-ranking officers of the National Recovery Administration, shared the employer point of view. This proved to be a determining factor in the decline of the National Labor Board. It could not implement the majority principle and assure parties to a dispute that its views were supported by all members of the government. Actually, the National Labor Board refused to heed the viewpoint of Johnson-Richberg; however, their position served to promote confusion in National Labor Board policy.

In March 1934, the National Labor Board suffered another blow to its prestige. During this month, the nation was threatened with an industry-wide automobile strike. The automobile companies refused to recognize an automobile union that was then being organized under the sponsorship of the AFL. To prevent their workers from enjoying the benefits of true collective bargaining, the automobile manufacturers sponsored company-dominated unions. The AFL insisted on a free election to determine the bargaining desires of the automobile workers. The manufacturers refused, and the AFL threatened to close down the nation's major automobile plants.

Such a strike, of course, would have seriously retarded the recovery efforts of the New Deal. The National Labor Board, aware of the implications of a nationwide automobile strike, diligently attempted to settle the dispute on the basis of the Reading Formula. However, the Board failed to effect a settlement. President Roosevelt and Johnson of the National Recovery Administration then intervened in the dispute. This intervention made it clear to the public that the National Labor Board did not have the authority or the capability to settle important labor controversies. On March 25, 1934, President Roosevelt obtained a peaceful settlement of the dispute. The fact that White House pressure had prevented the strike added further to the impairment of the National Labor Board's status as an effective labor agency.

The National Labor Board never recovered from this blow to its prestige. Employers and unions had little respect for or faith in its procedures. Labor unrest again mounted in intensity as unions became aware of the impotence of the Board. Organized labor, convinced of National Labor Board inadequacies, undertook to enforce 7 (a) through its own economic strength. Organizational strikes occurred during the early summer of 1934 in Toledo, Minneapolis, and San Francisco; and a nationwide steel strike was threatened by the Amalgamated Association of Iron, Steel and Tin Workers.[23] The National Labor Board did not prevent the outbreak of these strikes, nor was it capable of obtaining a settlement once they occurred. Its failure in this respect was inevitable. Its prestige was irreparably damaged by presidential intervention in the automobile dispute.

Finally, on May 29, 1934, the judiciary completed the cycle of Board humiliations. A district court refused to order the Weirton Steel Company to participate in a representation election to permit workers to choose freely their representatives for collective bargaining. Both the Reading Formula and the Executive Orders of February 1934 had underscored the right of workers to make this choice. However, the district court refused to order the collective bargaining election. On the basis of such a judicial ruling, it is not difficult to see why both employers and unions lost confidence in Board procedures.

PUBLIC RESOLUTION NO. 44:
THE FIRST NATIONAL LABOR RELATIONS BOARD

Congress recognized the shortcomings of the National Labor Board. Its failure stimulated members of Congress, particularly Senator Wagner of New York, to search for more effective protective procedures. Congress was alerted to the danger of relying on an inept agency to preserve industrial peace. Strikes for organizational purposes would continue in number and intensity to the degree that Congress failed to provide for the speedy and adequate enforcement of the free selection by workers of bargaining representatives. If unions had been reluctant to strike for recognition purposes prior to 1933, Section 7 (a) had completely changed this state of affairs. Collective bargaining had become a matter of public policy. The nation's workers were determined to engage in collective bargaining with or without government protection. As a result, 45.9 percent of all strikes in 1934 occurred wholly or in part from organizational issues.[24]

Congress, fully aware of this stream of events, undertook the task of providing workers with adequate machinery to select their bargaining representatives. Senator Wagner of New York led the drive for legislation to accomplish this objective. As early as February 1934, he introduced the so-called Wagner Labor Disputes Act.[25] Later he proposed still another law, the Industrial Adjustment Act, which would have provided even broader protection for the collective bargaining process. Fundamental to Wagner's program was a streamlined method for enforcement. He would have set up a quasi-judicial agency, termed the "National Industrial Adjustment Board," empowering this agency to prevent employer antiunion practices. In addition, the agency was to have the authority to conduct elections enabling workers to select bargaining representatives. Employers would be expected to recognize and negotiate with these representatives. Orders of the Board would be enforceable in the United States circuit courts of appeals. Unlike the ill-defined authority upon which the National Labor Board operated, the Wagner agency would have derived its power from a statute of Congress. Its mandate would have been clearly defined and, to obviate the possibility of disrespect for Board orders, as was the case with the National Labor Board, the Wagner Board could have called upon the courts to enforce its decisions.

Despite the approval of the Wagner program by President Roosevelt, Congress did not enact the Wagner Labor Disputes Act or the Industrial Adjustment Bill. Congress adjourned without passing legislation to govern the nation's labor relations policy. However, the 73d Congress did not adjourn without providing for the replacement of the defunct National Labor Board. For this purpose, Congress on June 16, 1934, passed Joint Resolution No. 44. Three days later it was approved by the President.

The purpose of Joint Resolution No. 44 was to provide for the interpretation and enforcement of Section 7 (a) of the National Industrial Recovery Act. Unlike the Wagner program, which would have set up a labor board on the basis of legislation independent of NIRA, the National Labor Relations Board, created by Joint Resolution No. 44, was tied to Section 7 (a) of the NIRA. This Board expired with the decision that the National Industrial Recovery Act was unconstitutional.

The National Labor Relations Board appeared more fortified to provide adequate protection to the right of workers to self-organization and collective bargaining than the defunct National Labor Board had been. The spirit in which the NLRB had been created demonstrated the desire of Congress for vigorous legal implementation of collective bargaining. More specifically, the NLRB was empowered to conduct representation elections to permit workers to choose their collective bargaining representatives. In addition, it was authorized to investigate alleged violations of Section 7 (a).

On the other hand, this Board suffered from the defect that had proven fatal to the National Labor Board; that is, the National Labor Relations Board did not have the power to enforce its own orders. Enforcement depended on the action of the Compliance Division of the National Recovery Administration or on the Department of Justice. This proved a serious barrier to the effective operation of the agency. In addition, employer antiunion practices, supposedly prohibited by Section 7 (a), were not spelled out in Joint Resolution No. 44. This meant that the new Board, like its predecessor, had to establish its own principles. Joint Resolution No. 44 in effect placed the responsibility for establishing a national labor relations policy on the shoulders of a government agency. In any matter so important and complicated, it is essential that Congress provide guides for an agency to follow. Section 7 (a) declared in general terms that workers had the right to self-organization and collective bargaining without employer interference. But it did not spell out what constituted "employer interference." For example, as mentioned, it was not clear whether or not company-dominated unions were unlawful.

Vagueness with respect to the scope of authority of the National Labor Relations Board, and the division of responsibility for the enforcement of its decisions, constituted the two chief obstacles to effective operation of the agency. In short, Board orders were not respected. The Compliance Division of the NRA did order the removal of the "Blue Eagle" from firms which ignored Board decisions. However, this technique of enforcement proved highly unsatisfactory. Consumers did not particularly care whether a company sported the Blue Eagle, the emblem showing compliance with the overall policy of the NIRA. The Department of Justice likewise did not provide an adequate vehicle for enforcement. The Board referred thirty-three cases to the Department of Justice. Of these, the department sought only one injunction for enforcement purposes.[26] Sixteen

CHAPTER SEVEN

cases were sent back to the NLRB for additional evidence. In three other cases the department exercised its prerogative to overrule the Board and held that no suit was justified. Finally, in the remaining cases, the Department of Justice for one reason or another refused to enforce orders of the Board.

Such an enforcement program did not enhance the prestige of the Board. Employers were not greatly impressed by its orders, for it was apparent that enforcement was a remote possibility. For effective operation, an administrative agency must have the ability to enforce its decisions. Had the NLRB been authorized by Joint Resolution No. 44 to solicit the courts for enforcement orders, the record of the agency would have been more imposing. As it was, the Board held that employers violated Section 7 (a) in eighty-six instances during the first eight months of its operation, but in only thirty-four cases did employers comply with orders of the Board.

❦ PASSAGE OF THE WAGNER ACT

When the 74th Congress assembled for the first time in 1935, Senator Wagner again led a drive for labor relations legislation. He was convinced that the National Labor Relations Board established under Joint Resolution No. 44 did not provide a sound basis for adequate protection of the collective bargaining process. Wagner's bill received support from the American Federation of Labor. President Roosevelt also gave his approval to the measure.

The factor that resulted in the speedy passage of Wagner's proposal, however, was the declaration by the Supreme Court that the entire National Industrial Recovery Act was unconstitutional.[27] As noted, Joint Resolution No. 44 and the National Labor Relations Board created under its terms were rooted in the NIRA. When this law was held invalid, the NLRB had no legal basis for its actions. Since its legislative authority was swept away, the orders of the Board had no legal validity. The Supreme Court's decision in the famous *Schecter* case was handed down on May 27, 1935. After this date, all federal protection of workers' rights to self-organization and collective bargaining terminated. Section 7 (a) and the National Labor Relations Board created under Joint Resolution No. 44 became dead letters.

After the *Schecter* decision, the legislative pace quickened. Senator Wagner pushed for speedy passage of his bill, which by this time was popularly termed the "Wagner Act." House and Senate hearings on the measure were intensified. Members of these committees were well aware of the need for legislation to promote industrial peace. It was apparent that such peace could not be obtained in the absence of a law that would effectively establish the collective bargaining process in American industry. The American Federation of Labor pressed for new legislation. The campaign that the AFL conducted for the passage of the Wagner Act centered on the Section 7 (a) guarantees. Mass meetings to urge the passage of the Wagner Act were held under the sponsorship of the AFL and other labor groups. Organized labor made clear the character of its future political program. It threatened to work for the defeat of each and every senator or representative who opposed the Wagner Act. Never before did organized labor conduct such an all-out campaign to urge the passage of a particular bill.

On June 27, 1935, the Wagner Act was passed by Congress.[28] Its technical name was the National Labor Relations Act, but its popular name, and the one that will be used in this volume, was the Wagner Act. President Roosevelt approved the legislation on July 5, 1935, stating that

> this Act defines, as a part of our substantive law, the right of self-organization of employees in industry for the purpose of collective bargaining, and provides methods by which the Government can safeguard that legal right. It establishes a National Labor Relations Board to hear and determine cases in which it is charged that this legal right is abridged or denied, and to hold fair elections to ascertain who are the chosen representatives of employees. A better relationship between labor and management is the high purpose of this Act. By assuring the employees the right of collective bargaining it fosters the development of employment control on a sound and equitable basis. By providing an orderly procedure for determining who is entitled to represent the employees, it aims to remove one of the chief causes of wasteful economic strife. By preventing practices which tend to destroy the independence of labor, it seeks, for every worker within its scope, that freedom of choice and action which is justly his.[29]

With the passage of the Wagner Act, legislative approval of the collective bargaining process was reasserted. A law had been passed specifically for the purpose of protecting and encouraging the growth of the union movement. The law also set up an agency that appeared well fortified to implement the purpose of the statute. Public policy had changed considerably since the labor conspiracy cases of the early 1800s. Society now declared that collective bargaining was socially desirable. Collective bargaining was to constitute the normal procedure for the establishment of the conditions of employment within American industry. As we shall see, there were many aspects to the Wagner Act, some of them complicated and controversial, but none more important than its social approval of the collective bargaining process.

🌿 SUMMARY

For many years, the Supreme Court nullified the efforts of Congress and state legislatures to protect employees in their right to self-organization and collective bargaining. The attitude of the judiciary remained rooted in precedent even though the legislative branch of government recognized that the facts of industrial life had made legal protection of the collective bargaining process a desirable public policy. The Supreme Court had difficulties balancing the constitutional property guarantees, as it interpreted them, with laws passed by Congress. The economic doctrines of the Constitution were subject to interpretation by all three branches of government. But the high court nullified legislative attempts to implement collective bargaining because of the social and economic predilections of the judges who composed the high court. The *Adair* and *Coppage* cases revealed a philosophy not conducive to an understanding of the dynamics of the economic system. Only through speculation could one comment on the attitude of the majority of the electorate in the area of collective bargaining.

Despite such an attitude on the part of the judiciary, Congress passed legislation calculated to protect the right of the nation's railway workers to self-organization and collective bargaining. Part of this legislation was patterned after the principles established by the first National War Labor Board. The National Industrial Recovery Act, passed by Congress to implement economic recovery, attempted to extend federal protection of collective bargaining throughout all industry. This policy was set up in Section 7 (a) of the NIRA. However, this section contained basic defects, which made its effective enforcement impossible. When the Supreme Court held the NIRA unconstitutional, Section 7 (a) became a dead letter. Subsequently, Congress enacted the Wagner Act to protect employees in their right to self-organization and collective bargaining.

🍎 DISCUSSION QUESTIONS

1. What was the purpose of the Erdman Act? How did the Supreme Court deal with it? Did the law serve any useful purpose for later consideration?
2. Which labor policy experiences of World War I were later utilized in New Deal legislation?
3. How could the Railway Labor Act of 1926 be ruled on as it was in the *Texas & New Orleans Railroad* case with *Adair* as a precedent?
4. Why would legislation be enacted affecting railroads but not for industry in general?
5. The Railway Labor Act was amended in 1934. Which conditions in 1934 that had not been apparent in 1926 led Congress to make changes in the law?
6. Discuss the economic reasoning behind passage of the National Industrial Recovery Act of 1933.
7. What were the strengths and weaknesses of the National Industrial Recovery Act?
8. Discuss the Court's rationale in its *Schecter* decision. What effect did the decision have on Congress in subsequent legislation?

🎔 NOTES

[1] *Report of the Industrial Commission on Labor Legislation*, V (Washington, D.C.: U.S. Government Printing Office, 1900), p. 128.

[2] National Labor Relations Board, *Rules and Regulations and Statements of Procedure* (Washington, D.C.: U.S. Government Printing Office, 1965), p. 63.

[3] *Adair v. U.S.*, 208 U.S. 161 (1908).

[4] *Coppage v. Kansas*, 236 U.S. 1 (1915).

[5] *In re Debs*, Petitioner, 158 U.S. 564 (1895).

[6] *Loewe v. Lawlor* (Danbury Hatters case), 208 U.S. 274 (1908).

[7] *Hitchman Coal & Coke Company v. Mitchell*, 245 U.S. 229 (1917).

[8] *Hammer v. Dagenhart*, 247 U.S. 251 (1918); *Bailey v. Drexel Furniture*, 259 U.S. 20 (1922).

[9] *Adkins v. Children's Hospital*, 261 U.S. 525 (1923).

[10] National War Labor Board, *Report, April, 1918, to May, 1919*, pp. 121–122.

[11] *Ibid.*, pp. 53–156.

[12] *Ibid.*, p. x.

[13] 44 Stat. 577 (1926).

[14] *Texas & New Orleans Railroad v. Brotherhood of Railroad Clerks*, 281 U.S. 548 (1930).

[15] *West Coast Hotel v. Parrish*, 300 U.S. 391 (1937).

[16] *Statement of Federal Co-ordinator of Transportation*, December 8, 1933, pp. 5–7.

[17] Twentieth Century Fund, Inc., *Labor and Government* (New York: McGraw-Hill Book Company, 1935), p. 88.

[18] Florence Peterson, *American Labor Unions* (New York: Harper & Brothers, 1935), p. 56.

[19] National Recovery Administration, Release No. 285, dated August 11, 1933.

[20] Lewis L. Lorwin and Arthur Wubnig, *Labor Relations Boards* (Washington, D.C.: Brookings Institution, 1935), p. 100.

[21] *Ibid.*, p. 102.

[22] Executive Order No. 6580, February 1, 1934; Executive Order No. 6612-A, February 23, 1934.

[23] Lorwin and Wubnig, *op. cit.*, p. 115.

[24] *Monthly Labor Review*, XLII (1935), p. 162.

[25] S. 2926, 73d Congress, 2d sess. (1934).

[26] D. O. Bowman, *Public Control of Labor Relations* (New York: The Macmillan Company, 1942), p. 45.

[27] *Schecter Poultry Corporation v. United States*, 295 U.S. 495 (1935).

[28] 49 Stat. 449 (1935).

[29] *Public Papers and Addresses of Franklin D. Roosevelt* (New York: Random House, 1938–1950), pp. 294–295.

CHAPTER EIGHT

THE WAGNER ACT

THE SOCIOECONOMIC RATIONALE OF THE WAGNER ACT

The National Labor Relations Act, hereinafter referred to as the Wagner Act, provided a partial answer to changing problems of labor relations. It was a product of modern industrialism, rooted in the growth of big business and the corporate organization of industry. Supporters of the legislation recognized that the modern industrial environment rendered obsolete the concept of individual bargaining as the regulator of industrial relations. Social and economic change brought greater attention to the need for effective collective bargaining. Moreover, the Wagner Act recognized the incongruity of industrial autocracy in the context of political democracy. It appeared to Wagner Act supporters that the extension of the democratic process to the employment relationship was necessary and appropriate if the nation were to remain free and democratic. As Senator Wagner once put it, "Let men know the dignity of freedom and self-expression in their daily lives, and they will never bow to tyranny in any quarter of their national life."[1] The Wagner Act assumed democracy to be an indivisible process. Denial of the implementation of the process in any quarter of society would constitute a threat to free institutions.

The Wagner Act had still another express purpose. It was to act as an economic stabilizer for the nation. As mentioned, the New Deal, of which the statute was an integral part, resulted from the failure of traditional practices to provide the nation with economic prosperity. The theory of the

New Deal was that sufficient purchasing power in the hands of the people would constitute one road to a healthy economic life. According to the architects of the New Deal, the nonunion employee did not possess actual liberty of contract. Such an employment relationship meant that an employer could keep for the firm a disproportionate share of its revenues under conditions of persistent excess supply of labor. This condition could prolong the downturn stage of the business cycle, for the purchasing power to buy the commodities and services turned out by industry might not be available to unemployed consumers. Effective collective bargaining, according to New Deal policy, provided one way out of the difficulty. Through collective bargaining, wages would tend to increase, the result being the increase of effective demand for the products of American industry. One employer spokesperson supported this approach to economic stability when he declared:

> It became obvious to the management of our company that no mass production could long be carried on unless there was increased purchasing power by the great masses of people. To us this meant there must be increases in wages and shortening of hours. This became the very fixed conviction of our management. The more difficult question was as to how this should be accomplished, and we arrived at the conclusion that collective bargaining by employer and employee ... was the only means by which, under our system, any adjustment in the equitable distribution of income could be accomplished. We realized the difficulty of this method, but we felt that if this method did not accomplish the desired end, then the present capitalistic system would collapse.... There is a further and more selfish reason as to why we took the step which we did in co-operating with the organization of our plants. We felt that if the present economic system was to continue, it was inevitable that in the future there should be the organization of labor, and that real collective bargaining would eventually be made effective.[2]

🐛 POWER TO REGULATE INTERSTATE COMMERCE

Under the provisions of the Constitution, it was not sufficient for Congress to declare that the Wagner Act plan would serve the public interest by accomplishing its economic objectives. The national government is one of delegated powers.[3] This means that Congress had to find specific authority in the Constitution before it could enact a specific law. In the case of the Wagner Act, Congress, to meet the constitutional obligations, hooked the statute to the power of the federal government to regulate interstate commerce. Attention has already been directed to the large number of strikes engaged in by workers to force employers to accept the collective bargaining process. These strikes were bitterly contested. Frequently, they resulted in destruction of property, injuries, and even loss of life. Congress reasoned that such strikes, termed organizational strikes, obstructed interstate commerce by impairing the flow of raw materials and processed goods among the states, and caused diminution of employment and wages in such volume as to impair substantially the market for goods flowing from or into the channels of commerce. An organizational strike in the telephone and telegraph industry, for example, would obviously prevent the exchange of goods among the states. Entrepreneurs rely on the telephone and telegram to effectuate the sale and purchase of goods. Likewise, an organizational strike in a factory would obstruct interstate commerce. Unless goods were first produced, they could scarcely enter the channels of interstate commerce. Finally, organizational strikes meant that wages of workers and profits of companies were either decreased or temporarily nonexistent. This resulted in the reduction of the sale and purchase of goods in interstate commerce. If organizational strikes resulted in such obstruction to commerce, the obvious inference was that reduction of the frequency of such strikes would promote trade among the states. The Wagner Act aimed to eliminate the cause of such strikes by outlawing employer antiunion practices.

Congress also believed that legal protection of the right of workers to self-organization and collective bargaining would result in a diminution in the number of nonorganizational strikes. In this connection, the Wagner Act declared that "experience has proved that protection by law of the right of employees to organize and bargain collectively safeguards commerce from injury ... by encouraging practices fundamental to the friendly adjustment of industrial disputes arising out of differences as to wages, hours, or other working conditions...." By such a statement Congress meant that the collective bargaining process, once firmly established within the economy, could serve as a bridge to industrial harmony. The record of industrial relations testified to the fact that a labor union secure in its status was apt to be more responsible, more responsive to the problems of management, and more reasonable than one whose status was in a constant state of uncertainty. Studies sponsored by the National Planning Association pointing up the causes of industrial peace supported this observation.[4] Management would likewise be more prone to reach a peaceful settlement in a labor dispute when dealing with a strong and secure labor union. If management felt that a union was so weak that it could not possibly withstand a serious challenge to its existence, the company officials could purposely force a showdown. Frequently, the result was unnecessary industrial warfare. Collective bargaining, if it was to serve the cause of industrial peace, presupposed an arrangement in which the contesting parties possessed equality in bargaining power. Should one side be very weak and the other very strong, the possibilities for industrial warfare would be increased.

Beyond this reasoning, Congress could point to the history of industrial relations on the railroads to support the contention that employees had been denied the right of free collective bargaining. Despite the defects of the Railway Labor Act of 1926, the promotion of the collective bargaining process in the railroad industry by law did serve the cause of industrial peace. When Congress passed the Wagner Act, there was no conclusive evidence indicating how the 1934 amendments to the Railway Labor Act of 1926 would function. The amendments were passed on June 30, 1934, and the Wagner Act was enacted one year later. However, in that one year, marked by a great amount of industrial warfare, the railroads were not affected by the wave of strikes. Railroad workers, secure in their right to self-organization and collective bargaining, had no occasion to resort to the organizational strike.

This then was the underlying philosophy of the Wagner Act. Industrial strife was promoted to the degree that employers denied to workers their right to self-organization and collective bargaining. The legal requirements of the Constitution were met by the Wagner Act, for interstate commerce was burdened by strikes resulting from such denial. In addition, Congress placed great faith in collective bargaining as the vehicle for industrial peace. Finally, it was hoped that the effect of economic depressions could be lessened by legal protection of the collective bargaining process, for this might mean more purchasing power for the nation's workers. That is, workers could win more purchasing power if unions possessed the economic power often attributed to them.

❦ PUBLIC POLICY OF THE UNITED STATES

On the basis of such observations, Congress set forth the public policy of the United States, proclaiming:

> It is hereby declared to be the policy of the United States to eliminate the causes of certain substantial obstructions to the free flow of commerce and to mitigate and eliminate these obstructions when they have occurred by encouraging the practice and procedures of collective bargaining and by protecting the exercise by workers of full freedom of association, self-organization, and designation of representatives of their own choosing, for the purpose of determining the terms and conditions of their employment or other mutual aid or protection.

Opposition in some quarters was evident almost immediately after passage of the Act. Some employers attempted to prevent the effective operation of the law by seeking injunctions to restrain the activities of the National Labor Relations Board. Court actions were so numerous that the NLRB spent its first months of operation defending itself in court. However, it should be made clear at this point that a majority of employers

CHAPTER EIGHT

either supported the Wagner Act provisions or offered no opposition to their implementation.

An event almost unique in the field of federal law stimulated injunctive attack against the NLRB. On September 5, 1935, a few months after the passage of the Wagner Act, the National Lawyer's Committee of the American Liberty League declared that the statute was unconstitutional.[5] This pronouncement was made long before the Supreme Court had had an opportunity to review the legislation. The League pronouncement stimulated widespread violation of the Act's provisions. The National Labor Relations Board, commenting on this, declared:

> During its first months, and before the Board had opportunity even to announce its procedures, an incident occurred which was to stimulate injunction suits against the Board, and even to provide a sample brief for those wishing to attack the act. This was the publication by the National Lawyer's Committee of the American Liberty League, on September 5, 1935, of a printed assault on the constitutionality of the act. This document, widely publicized and distributed throughout the country immediately upon its issuance, did not present the argument in an impartial manner for the use of attorneys. It was not a review of the cases which might be urged for and against the statute. It was not a brief in any case in court nor was it an opinion for any client involved in any case pending. Under the circumstances it can be regarded only as a deliberate and concentrated effort by a large group of well-known lawyers to undermine public confidence in the statute, to discourage compliance with it, to assist attorneys generally in attack on the statute, and perhaps to influence the courts.[6]

Soon after the National Lawyer's Committee circulated its anti-Wagner Act tract, the injunction proceedings began. The Board reported that the process was "like a rolling snowball." In a matter of weeks, the legal attacks against the Board became uniform throughout the nation. Thus "the allegations or pleading filed by an employer in Georgia, for example, would show up in precisely the same wording in a pleading filed in Seattle."[7] Such a procedure testified to the organized nature of the attack against the Wagner Act. The pleas for injunctions were successful. In some cases, the judges did not themselves understand the provisions of the National Labor Relations Act. Some judges, the NLRB reported, had the impression that the Act provided for mediation and arbitration. Others believed it was no more than a law of conciliation. The fact was that there were absolutely no features of conciliation or arbitration in the Wagner Act. In the first few months of the life of the Board, the federal district courts issued twenty injunctions restraining the operations of the NLRB. However, some judges, aware of the fact that NLRB orders could not be enforced except upon review by the circuit court of appeals and the

Supreme Court, refused to act favorably upon employer applications for injunctions.

❦ STATE OF AFFAIRS BEFORE JONES & LAUGHLIN

The attack against the Wagner Act, spearheaded by the National Lawyer's Committee, prevented the successful operation of the law. Its administrative agency, the National Labor Relations Board, could not effectively exercise the powers granted it by Congress. Criticized and ridiculed in the daily press, hamstrung by legal proceedings, the NLRB suffered crushing blows to its prestige. Organized labor began to lose faith in the law. Its purpose and provisions were clear enough. On paper it purported to permit employees to form—free from employer influence—labor unions and to utilize their organizations as collective bargaining agencies. In practice, however, it soon became obvious that neither the law nor the NLRB could operate as a protector of collective bargaining rights. With the decrease of workers' confidence in the law, the number of organizational strikes increased. From the summer of 1935 until the spring of 1937, the period of the passage of the Wagner Act, strikes that were at least partly for recognition and organizational issues accounted for about 50 percent of all strikes.[8] Workers were impressed with the declaration by Congress that collective bargaining constituted the national policy of the United States. Their organizational efforts had their roots in the public approval of labor unions. These roots were nourished by the growing recognition of the possible effects of the collective bargaining process on the life of the nation. Citizens were engaged in a search for new answers to the financial ills plaguing the economy. Workers were no longer to be denied their right to self-organization and collective bargaining. If the NLRB could not enforce this right, the employees of the nation might resort to violence. Some regard the relatively large number of organizational strikes in the first years of the Wagner Act as demonstrating the failure of the law. Such an observation is without convincing support. The real reason for this great wave of strikes was the ineffective operation of the Wagner Act. Since the law's provisions were not widely accepted at first, employees resorted to organizational strikes to seek their objective of recognition of bargaining agents. Outward manifestations of employer resistance to collective bargaining were not checked by the NLRB in court proceedings. Thus, the organizational strike and not the NLRB, an agency largely neutralized through early court proceedings, served to implement the public policy set forth in the Wagner Act.

Only a clear-cut declaration of constitutionality of the Wagner Act by the Supreme Court could effectuate the law. If the Court validated the Act, the legal proceedings against the NLRB would cease. The agency could then devote full energies to the enforcement of the statute. Voluntary compliance to the Wagner Act, indispensable to the successful operation of any law, would increase, since lengthy and costly legal proceedings against the NLRB would prove futile. Under such conditions, the peaceful procedures of the Wagner Act would be substituted for industrial warfare. Labor leaders and workers alike could seek legal remedies for violations of the right to self-organization and collective bargaining. The need for the organizational strike would be reduced, if not virtually eliminated.

The effect of a validation of the Wagner Act by the Supreme Court appeared clear enough. What was doubtful was whether or not the high court would sustain the legislation. Would the Court hold the Wagner Act unconstitutional on the basis of the *Adair* decision? Or would the more recent *Texas & New Orleans* decision control the proceedings? Even the avid supporters of the Wagner Act recognized the strong possibilities for an adverse decision. The Railway Labor Act, sustained in the *Texas & New Orleans* decision, applied only to the railroad industry, whereas the Wagner Act covered all workers engaged in interstate commerce. It was recognized that the Supreme Court might choose to distinguish between a general statute and one very limited in scope.

The composition of the Court was a source of uncertainty to supporters of the Wagner Act. On the Court were Van Devanter, Sutherland, McReynolds, and Butler. Students of the Supreme Court were well aware of the social and economic philosophies of these men. Their philosophies were present in decisions denying the right of government to legislate for the benefit of the working population. The judges believed that the operation of the economic system provided payment to workers in accordance with their worth to their employers. They assumed that the forces of a competitive economy would protect the worker from exploitation. In short, this group believed that the type of economic system described by Adam Smith in 1776 was in operation in the 1930s. These men felt that the government should not protect the weak from the strong, but that workers should exercise their economic prerogatives to effect such protection. Thus, if workers were dissatisfied with the conditions of work determined unilaterally by the employer, they were free to quit and seek employment elsewhere. Characteristics of the contemporary economy—such as chronic unemployment, concentration of economic power, monopolistic control of product markets, formation of huge corporations, and the inherent disparity of bargaining power between the worker and the company—failed to impress these members of the Supreme Court. It was not generally recognized that Adam Smith had advocated government intervention when necessary to restore competitive conditions to an economy.

❦ SCOPE OF LAW

Still another factor worried supporters of the Wagner Act. Even granted that the statute as such would be validated, the question still remained as to how far the Court would apply the law. The specific issue was whether or not the law would apply to manufacturing. Approximately 10 million workers were employed in manufacturing in 1935. These workers constituted a highly organizable group. If the Court upheld the Wagner Act but denied its application to manufacturing, the statute would not serve to expand significantly the area of unionization and collective bargaining. On the other hand, the application of the law to manufacturing facilities would result in the protection of the right of self-organization and collective bargaining for a group which could spearhead an expansion of the union movement. In addition, if manufacturing were included within the scope of the Wagner Act, the Court would establish a precedent that would likely result in the application of the statute to industries such as mining, foresting, fishing, finance, and some sectors of wholesale and retail trade. By denying the application of the law to manufacturing, even though upholding the general constitutionality of the law, the Supreme Court could limit its terms to interstate bus lines, truck and water transportation, and telephone and telegraph systems. The workers involved in these industries constituted a mere fraction of the nation's organizable workers.

In light of judicial precedent, there was some basis to believe that the Supreme Court might hold manufacturing to be beyond the scope of the Wagner Act. In 1894, the Court had held that "commerce succeeds to manufacturing and is not a part of it."[9] In 1936, in *Carter Coal*, the Court could not see how regulating the labor relations of a coal company advanced and safeguarded interstate commerce.[10] Although the *Carter Coal* case did not involve the manufacturing industry, the 1936 decision represented a line of reasoning that indicated a limited construction of interstate commerce and caused considerable uncertainty about the future of the Act. Thus, in the *Carter* case, decided after the passage of the Wagner Act, the Court declared:

> mining brings the subject matter of commerce into existence. Commerce disposes of it. A consideration of the foregoing ... renders inescapable the conclusion that the effect of the labor provision of the [Bituminous Coal Conservation Act], including those in respect of minimum wages, wage agreements, collective bargaining, and the Labor Board and its powers, primarily falls upon production and not upon commerce; and confirms the further resulting conclusion that production is a purely local activity. It follows that none of these essential antecedents of production constitutes a transaction in or forms any part of interstate commerce.

Such language appeared almost to preclude the Court's application of the Wagner Act to manufacturing facilities.

Balanced against the foregoing, some factors served to support the view that the Wagner Act would be sustained and its terms applied to manufacturing. As noted, a great number of organizational strikes occurred after the employees of the nation became aware that the NLRB could not effectively carry out the provisions of the new labor policy. The vast majority of these strikes occurred in the nation's manufacturing facilities. Some of the strikes were unprecedented in scope, intensity, and destruction. They resulted in destruction of property, in physical injury, and in loss of life. Such developments were likely to have an effect on the Supreme Court. Moreover, the Court must have been impressed with the overwhelming reelection of Roosevelt in 1936. The result of the election, in which Roosevelt failed to receive the electoral votes of only Maine and Vermont, served to underscore the people's satisfaction with New Deal policies, in that they were willing to experiment in areas previously considered best left alone. It was reasonable to believe that the Court would consider these election results. Finally, the threat of Roosevelt to "pack" the Supreme Court must have had some influence on its members. Impressed by his astounding success at the polls, Roosevelt was reluctant to permit the Supreme Court complete freedom to evaluate New Deal policies. He was determined to satisfy the demands of the people that social legislation be implemented. Accordingly, he proposed legislation that would have minimized the influence of the conservative element of the Supreme Court. Even though Congress refused to enact the law, the attempt undoubtedly left its mark on the members of the Court. Alternatively, it was clear from the legislative history of the Act exactly what Congress intended. This had not been the case in much of the earlier legislation dealing with labor policy.

❦ *THE* JONES & LAUGHLIN *DECISION*

Such was the environment in which the Supreme Court ruled on the Wagner Act. The nation was aware of the magnitude of the forthcoming decision and, as perhaps never before, anxiously awaited the high court's decision. Labor hoped for a clear-cut decision of constitutionality, for that would mean legal protection of bargaining rights. Many employers hoped for the opposite ruling, for that would mean little government influence would affect the collective bargaining process. The issue was settled in April 1937 in the case involving the Jones & Laughlin Steel Company.[11] By the slim majority of a single vote, the Supreme Court upheld the Wagner Act and, of equal importance, validated its application to the manufacturing sector of the

American economy. On the majority were Chief Justice Hughes and Associate Justices Roberts, Stone, Cardozo, and Brandeis.

As some observers expected, the minority of the Court was composed of Sutherland, McReynolds, Van Devanter, and Butler. Once again, these men affirmed that constitutional prohibitions precluded the government from aiding and encouraging union organizations to establish collective bargaining. The minority group held that employers could utilize any antiunion tactic to defeat the collective bargaining process. The minority held that the *Texas & New Orleans* decision did not apply to a proceeding involving a manufacturing establishment. It was further avowed that the government could regulate the labor relations of the railroads, for this industry was considered a part of interstate commerce. But, it was argued, Congress had violated the Constitution by endeavoring to protect the right of workers to collective bargaining in manufacturing, for this industry was not a part of commerce. In short, whatever happened in the manufacturing industry did not directly affect trade among the states. Should a strike in manufacturing result from the discharge of workers because of union activities, or from the refusal of an employer to bargain collectively, the effect upon commerce was "far too indirect to justify congressional regulation." One may take issue with this point of view. For example, if the steel industry was shut down because of the reluctance of the owners to recognize the steelworkers' union, there would likely be a real and substantial effect upon interstate commerce. The effect would depend upon the extent of stockpiling in anticipation of the work stoppage. In addition, the lack of worker income to expend upon consumer goods would have an indirect effect on commerce. Such a strike, for whatever reason, would mean that there was no steel for shipment between the states. Production is as essential for interstate commerce as are the transportation facilities that carry the goods from one state to another. The breakdown of either production or transportation has an effect on interstate commerce. On the basis of these practical observations, the position of the minority group in the *Jones & Laughlin* decision appears untenable and unrealistic. In any event, the group held that the federal government could not lawfully regulate the labor relations of a manufacturing facility. Manufacturing, these members concluded, was not a part of interstate commerce, and consequently the Constitution prohibited federal control over the steel industry.

❦ *APPLICATION TO MANUFACTURING*

This point of view was not shared by the majority of the Court. Chief Justice Hughes, speaking for the Court, declared that strikes in manufacturing facilities, such as in a steel mill, "would have a most serious effect upon interstate commerce." The majority argued that it was proper for Congress to take action to prohibit employers from interfering with the right of workers to bargain collectively because organizational strikes might result in "catastrophic" effects on commerce. In masterful language, Hughes struck at the contention of the minority that the effect of organizational strikes in commerce would be "indirect or remote." Thus, Hughes remarked:

> We are asked to shut our eyes at the plainest facts of our national life and to deal with the question of direct and indirect effects in an intellectual vacuum. Because there may be but indirect and remote effects upon interstate commerce in connection with a host of local enterprises throughout the country, it does not follow that other industrial activities do not have such a close and intimate relation to interstate commerce as to make the presence of industrial strife a matter of the most urgent national concern. When industries organize themselves on a national scale, making their relation to interstate commerce the dominant factor in their activities, how can it be maintained that their industrial labor relations constitute a forbidden field into which Congress may not enter when it is necessary to protect interstate commerce from the paralyzing consequences of industrial war?

It was by the use of such language that the Supreme Court upheld the Wagner Act's application to manufacturing. The entire theory of the authors of the law was given judicial approval. It was accepted by the Court that not only did organizational strikes involving the railroads or other instruments of commerce burden trade between the states, but work stoppages in manufacturing, resulting from employer antiunion activities, likewise burdened interstate commerce. It was therefore deemed proper for Congress to eliminate the causes of such strikes, because such action protected and promoted interstate commerce.[12]

❦ DUE PROCESS AND CONSTITUTIONALITY OF ACT

Beyond dealing with the applicability of the Wagner Act to manufacturing, the Supreme Court directed its attention to another constitutional question. Did the statute violate the due process clause of the Fifth Amendment to the Constitution? Again the majority of the Court upheld the statute. It was held that the procedural provisions of the law adequately protected employers from the arbitrary action of the NLRB. Foremost in this connection, the Court stressed that the judiciary constituted the ultimate source of enforcement authority for the provisions of the law. As will be pointed out below, an employer aggrieved with a decision of the Board has the right to appeal to the courts. Not only was the Wagner Act upheld with respect to the procedural aspects of due process, but the Court held also that the substance of the Wagner Act did not deprive an employer of property or liberty without due process of law. On this point, the majority leaned heavily on the *Texas & New Orleans* decision. Since manufacturing was deemed to fall within the concept of interstate commerce, the railroad decision was applicable. Thus, the Court in the *Jones & Laughlin* decision reaffirmed the principle that law "cannot be considered arbitrary or capricious if it prohibits interference with the right of workers to self-organization."

It is important to stress that even if the Court had held the law applicable to manufacturing, the Wagner Act could have been declared unconstitutional on the basis of interfering arbitrarily and unreasonably with the freedom of employers to run their businesses. However, the Court refused to hold unlawful a statute that protected the right of workers to collective bargaining. Since workers were extended the right to collective bargaining by both the judiciary and legislature, it appeared reasonable and prudent that government should outlaw practices calculated to prevent self-organization and collective bargaining. Such was the conclusion of the Supreme Court.

It also stressed the law did not interfere with the right of employers to select their employees and discharge them for any reason except for union activities. The high court said "the employer may not, under cover of that right, intimidate or coerce its employees with respect to their self-organization and representation, and, on the other hand, the Board [NLRB] is not entitled to make its authority a pretext for interference with the right of discharge when the right is exercised for other reasons than such intimidation and coercion."

Thus, on April 12, 1937, the Supreme Court validated the Wagner Act. Not only were its terms consistent with the due-process clause of the Constitution, but the application of the law was to cover general industrial facilities. The *Jones & Laughlin* decision represented perhaps the most important pronouncement of the Supreme Court with respect to organized labor. At the time it was the most favorable decision that had yet been made in the interest of the nation's workers. It made possible the implementation of public policy promoting collective bargaining.

❦ SUBSTANTIVE PROVISIONS: UNFAIR LABOR PRACTICES

Section 7 of the statute declared: "employees shall have the right to self-organization, to form, join or assist labor organizations, to bargain collectively through representatives of their own choosing, and to engage in concerted activities, for the purpose of collective bargaining or other mutual aid or protection." To make this right effective, Congress outlawed employer practices that operated to deny workers the freedom to carry out the collective bargaining function. In short, Congress was not content merely to state that workers have the right to self-organization and collective bargaining. It was determined to prohibit any interference with the exercise of that right.

To accomplish the Section 7 objective, Section 8 of the Wagner Act set forth five *unfair labor practices*. These practices were declared unlawful. Subsequently, attention will be devoted to the methods by which the Wagner Act provided for remedies when employers violate the terms of Section 8. At this time, we are concerned with the nature of the unfair labor practices. It established the National Labor Relations Board to determine the circumstances when employers interfered with the right of employees to self-organization and collective bargaining.

Section 8 (a) (1). This section makes it an unfair labor practice for an employer to "interfere with, restrain, or coerce employees in the exercise of their rights under Section 7." Independent interferences with employees' rights may occur exclusive of any other violation specified by Section 8 (a). The NLRB has held that violations of Section 8 (a) (1) exist when employees are (1) threatened with the loss of their jobs or other reprisals; (2) granted wage increases timed to discourage union membership; and (3) questioned by employers about union activities under such circumstances as will tend to coerce them in the exercise of their rights under Section 7.[13] Independent violations have also been declared when the working places or homes of employees were placed under surveillance by employers to the extent that reasonable communication regarding organization was restricted. In this regard, the utilization of industrial spies constitutes a violation. An independent violation has been found when a sales manager, representing the employer, offered a more lucrative job in another city to an employee if he would drop his union activities.

Although the Wagner Act did not prevent an employer from utilizing economic power to defeat a strike by peaceful means, the NLRB has ruled that a firm interfered with the right to self-organization by hiring strikebreakers for the purpose of provoking violence or creating fear in the minds of employees. When the NLRB held that the Mohawk Valley Formula, a systematic procedure for breaking strikes, violated the Wagner Act, it stated, "Those activities were employed to defeat the strike, end the strike, rather than settling it through collective bargaining."[14] Inciting to violence against union organizers and members of labor organizations was also deemed an unfair labor practice. In one case, a company was found to have violated this subsection of the law when a forelady incited violence against a union organizer by suggesting to the employees in her section, "What do you say, girls, we give her a beating?"[15]

Some of the unfair labor practices during World War II had a distinct wartime flavor. A number of employers utilized the wartime environment to interfere, restrain, or coerce workers from exercising their right to self-organization and collective bargaining. A violation of the National Labor Relations Act was found when an employer posted notices throughout the plant suggesting that union organizers were a group of "intimidators" and threatened the "substitution of Naziism for Americanism."[16] Nor was an employer permitted to assert that a union was "backed by Germans" when the intent was to unlawfully discourage membership in the organization. A supervisor implicated his employer in an unfair labor practice by intimating that the company would not ask for occupational army service deferment for an employee if the worker persisted in union activities. Employers were not permitted to distribute "I am an American" buttons to their employees not wearing union buttons. The obvious inference that union members were not loyal Americans evidently prompted the Board's decision. Effecting the arrest of persons distributing union literature in a plant was deemed unlawful, even though the employer argued that the plant was engaged in secret war work and that the persons jailed might have been spies and saboteurs. It was noted that a labor union was organizing the plant's workers when the employer procured the arrest. Nor did the Board sustain the argument that employers could engage in unfair labor practices with impunity because the company was producing materials for the exclusive use of the government. The NLRB further ruled that an employer engaged in an unfair labor practice when it appealed to its workers' patriotism to defeat a union in a bargaining election by drawing a contrast between the hardships endured by men in the armed forces and the attempts of the employees to better their economic position through organization. On the other hand, the Board found no violation of the Wagner Act when union members were discharged because they had violated a Federal Bureau of Investigation domestic security measure. These employees were not permitted to utilize their union status as a bar to dismissal.

During the war period, the NLRB established another source of violation. Wartime wage increases were prohibited unless approved by the National War Labor Board. Consequently, one of the most effective appeals that a union could make to maintain its membership was impaired for the duration of the war. To compensate in part for this wartime condition, the NLRB ruled that an employer violated the Wagner Act if it refused to consult with the representatives of its employees' labor organization before filing a wage-increase application with the NWLB.

Over the years, of course, the NLRB and courts held that considerable employer conduct did *not* constitute a violation of this provision of the Wagner Act. For example, in 1984, a federal appeals court, upsetting a Board decision, held that an employer in a consumer-oriented business (fast foods) could lawfully ban the wearing of union buttons. In that case, the employer enforced a rule that forbade the wearing of any kind of unauthorized buttons.[17]

Section 8 (a) (2). "Domination or interference with the formation or administration of a labor organization or contribution of financial or other support to it" is a violation of Section 8 (a) (2). It has already been pointed out that a union that is the creature of an employer does not constitute a proper vehicle for the carrying out of the collective bargaining process. Congress was well aware of this fact and consequently outlawed employer domination of labor unions. The NLRB, however, was required to spell out the circumstances under which an employer dominates a labor organization. Specifically, what are the characteristics of an employer-controlled union?

The Board has found a union to be company-dominated in a case where the employer told its employees that they should establish a union and indicated the form that the labor organization should take. If an employer or its representatives actively solicits members on behalf of a labor organization, such a union is illegal. A union may be company-dominated when the employer provides the union with bulletin boards, a company automobile, and stenographic service or office space.

The Board has held that, by advancing money to employees who were unable to pay membership dues, a company contributed support to a union and the organization was ordered dissolved. Another union was held company-dominated because the employer permitted members of the organization to solicit members for the union on the employer's property during working hours and, most important, with the consent of the employer. In *Highway Trailer Company*,[18] employees were fired and threatened with discharge because of their refusal to join the organization for which the employer had expressed his preference, and consequently the NLRB ordered the organization dissolved.

Other employer practices that indicate a labor organization is the creature of the company include those instances in which the employer has suggested the form of the constitution; in which a few hand-picked employees have been urged to create the organization; and in which management has been willing and eager to sign agreements with the organization it helped to create.

An important criterion in determining whether a labor organization is company-dominated may be the extent of collective bargaining between the union and management. The NLRB said:

> If the organization did not make any effort to meet with the employer concerned, and other features of the labor organization are indicative of company-domination, the Board may conclude, on the basis of the laxity in petitioning for a meeting on the part of the labor organization, that the employee's organization is the creature of the employer.[19]

Not only is neglecting to meet with management material evidence that the labor organization is company-dominated but, even when conferences do occur, the labor organization in question may be deemed company-dominated if the negotiations "be such as to reveal the employer's domination of the organization."[20]

In a 1982 case, beyond the normal remedy directing the employer to cease and desist recognizing a company-dominated union, the NLRB also ordered the employer and union to rebate to employees all dues and initiation fees collected, plus interest.[21] What generated this unusual order was evidence demonstrating that over a three-year period, the employer had kicked back $68,000 to union officials who referred business to the employer from other contacts the union had with businesses.

To clarify this section, the Board adopted a number of principles to determine whether an organization is independent of employer domination. Thus, if members of the organization hold regular meetings on property other than the company's; if members of the union pay dues; if the union has written agreements with the company; if the organization has contacts with other workers' organizations; if the union has the right to demand arbitration of differences whereby management abandons absolute veto power; then, the NLRB found, the organization is clearly its own master and is free to submit the real wishes of its members to management.

Section 8 (a) (3). This section makes it an unfair labor practice for employers to discriminate "in regard to hire or tenure of employment on any term or condition of employment to encourage or discourage membership in a labor organization." This clause was directed against the most common and highly effective antiunion weapon—the discharge of workers who are union members or those who would promote the formation of a labor union. By adopting this provision, Congress endeavored to erase fear from the minds of union-conscious workers. Again, the Wagner Act charged the NLRB with the duty of interpreting and carrying out the terms of the provision. What constitutes discrimination? Is transferring an employee to an inferior job because of union activity discrimination within the meaning of the Act? Can union workers ever be discharged? What evidence will the Board consider material in determining whether an employer truly discriminated against workers for union activity?

The most common form of discrimination that the Board declared an unfair labor practice was discharge of an employee for union activity. When the evidence in a case proved that an employee was discharged because of union activity, the Board ordered reinstatement. In most instances, the employer denied it, and consequently the NLRB would investigate to determine whether there had really been the discrimination prohibited by the Wagner Act. When an employer denied that discharges or other forms of claimed discrimination were within the meaning of the Act, the Board took into account the entire background of the case, reviewing the totality of circumstances to determine the nature of employer action against employees.

Not only have employers usually maintained that they have not discriminated against an employee on the grounds of union activity, but in nearly all cases they have tendered some reasons to the Board for discharging an employee. The most common alleged reason given for the discharge is the employer's claim that the worker was inefficient. In determining whether the employee was inefficient or whether this was a subterfuge for dismissal for union activities, the NLRB considers the following facts: (1) length of total employment; (2) experience in the particular position from which the employee was discharged; (3) efficiency ratings by qualified persons; (4) specific acts showing efficiency or inefficiency; and (5) comparison with other employees. Other reasons advanced for discharge include decrease in productivity, insubordination, infraction of company rules, fighting, and swearing. In all instances, the NLRB determines if the reasons have "color and substance," or whether they are only a convenient pretext designed to defeat the law.

Employers discriminate against employees and thereby engage in an unfair labor practice if they refuse employment to persons because of their former or current membership in a labor organization. Moreover, discrimination can also occur in respect to other conditions of work. In one case, the Board found that a company had discriminated against employees, transferring some workers to a very difficult section of the firm as punishment for their union activities, or with the intention of making them quit. One union man would have had to move twenty to twenty-five cars of rock and dirt, and in so doing would have been forced to work for a month without pay. Another instance of discrimination occurred when an employer transferred a worker to another position in which he had no experience, with the motive of firing him for the inefficient work that would result.

The Board has also construed discrimination to include those instances in which an employer has temporarily laid off employees for union activity. Refusal to reinstate employees because of union activity also is discrimination within the meaning of the Wagner Act. Other forms of discrimination include those cases in which an employer forces an employee engaged in union activities to work the worst shifts; pays more wages to a nonunion employee than to a union employee doing equal work; violates seniority rules; and discharges a worker's spouse because the worker is a union member.

A case before the U.S. Supreme Court involved the issue of whether an employer owning several plants, Deering Milliken, had violated the discrimination provisions of the Act when it permanently closed down one of its plants for antiunion reasons.[22] The plant that was shut down was located in Darlington, South Carolina. The Darlington case was first taken before the NLRB as a result of unfair labor practices growing out of a plant shutdown after a vigorous company campaign to resist union organizational efforts. In March 1956, when the organizational campaign was initiated, the company interrogated employees and threatened to close the Darlington plant if the Textile Workers Union won the election. On September 6, 1956, the union prevailed in the Board-held election by a narrow margin. The decision was made to liquidate the plant. Employees were informed by the company that the reason for such a decision was the election result and encouragement was extended for employees to sign a petition disavowing the union. The Board found Darlington in violation of the discrimination provision of the Act. The Board ordered back pay for all employees until they obtained substantially equivalent work or were put on preferential hiring lists at the other Deering Milliken mills. Upon review, a federal court of appeals denied enforcement and argued that a company had an absolute right to close out a part or all of its business, regardless of antiunion motives.

The U.S. Supreme Court reviewed the case in 1965 and agreed partially with the court of appeals. It held that a single-plant employer could go out of business completely for whatever reason it chose. But "a discriminatory partial closing may have repercussions on what remains of the business, affording employer leverage for discouraging the free exercise of Section 7 rights among remaining employees of much the same kind as that found to exist in the 'runaway shop' and 'temporary closing' cases."[23] The Court held that "a partial closing is an unfair labor practice under Section 8 (a) (3) if motivated by a purpose to chill unionism in any of the remaining plants of the single employer and if the employer may reasonably have foreseen ... that effect."[24]

A more specific test was provided by the Court for resolving such cases. It stated:

> If the persons exercising control over a plant that is being closed for antiunion reasons (1) have an interest in another business, whether or not affiliated with or engaged in the same line of commercial activity as the closed plant, of sufficient substantiality to give promise of their reaping a benefit from the discouragement of unionization in that business; (2) act to close their plant with the purpose of producing such a result; and (3) occupy a relationship to the other business which makes it realistically foreseeable that its employees will fear that such business will also be closed down if they persist in organizational activities, we think that an unfair labor practice has been made out.[25]

The Board had ruled only on the basis of the effect the plant closing had on Darlington employees. The Court test required that a determination be made regarding the effect the closing had on the employees in other plants owned and operated by the Deering Milliken group. In June 1967, the NLRB held that there was sufficient evidence to support the charge that the shutdown of the Darlington plant was for the purpose, at least in part, of discouraging union membership in other plants owned by Deering Milliken. It also found that the closing had a "chilling" effect on the other plant employees as far as union activity was concerned.

Discrimination with regard to hire or tenure will be found only if employees in other plants are affected by the antiunion behavior of an employer. A decision will have to be made in each case, since a partial closing will not constitute a per se violation of the Act. However, it seems clear that multiplant firms cannot make antiunion decisions in one plant without intending the same result to spill over onto all the others.

In 1983, the Board applied the *Darlington* doctrine under circumstances where a single-plant employer had closed a plant permanently in retaliation for the workers filing an unfair labor practice charge.[26] Rejecting the union's argument that the employer had engaged in discrimination under the law, the NLRB held that a single-plant employer had an absolute right to close permanently and go out of business.

Strangely enough, it was not until 1983 that the issue of burden of proof was settled in discrimination cases. In 1980, the NLRB established the *Wright Line* doctrine,[27] in which it held that the General Counsel of the Board need only show by the preponderance of evidence that union activities contributed to a discharge, while the employer had the burden to prove that the discharge would have taken place even if the employee had not engaged in union activities. In the 1983 case, an employee was terminated after he attempted to organize a union. To justify discharge, the employer asserted that the employee was terminated because he had left keys in the bus to which he was assigned and had taken unauthorized coffee breaks. When a supervisor became aware of the employee's union activities, he had threatened to discharge the employee. Sustaining both the Board's reinstatement of the employee and the *Wright Line* doctrine, the U.S. Supreme Court held that the employer had not proven that the employee would have been discharged in the absence of his union activities.[28] The Court found that the employee's infraction of the plant rules was too minimal to warrant discharge.

Before concluding this section on discrimination, it may be of value to point out that an employer under the Wagner Act has the opportunity to discharge or otherwise discipline its employees for any reason except upon the grounds of union activity. It must not be forgotten that the employer retained the right to discharge an employee for other causes: disobedience, bad work, carelessness, drinking on duty, and so on. The law only forbade an employer from discriminating against a worker solely for membership or activity in a union.

Section 8 (a) (4). This section also prohibits employers from discharging or otherwise discriminating against an employee because he or she has filed charges or given testimony under the Wagner Act. Thus, Congress provided protection for workers who might bring a charge against an employer alleging violation of the terms of the law. Moreover, since the procedures of the Wagner Act require hearings and court proceedings, it was reasonable to forbid discrimination against workers who would participate in such proceedings. The Board has in the past interpreted such employer behavior as a violation of Section 8 (a) (3) as well.

Section 8 (a) (5). Finally, Section 8 (a) (5) of the Wagner Act makes it an unfair labor practice for an employer to refuse to bargain collectively with the representatives of the employees. By this provision, Congress intended to eliminate the need for the recognition strike. Since employers would be required to bargain collectively, workers would not find it necessary to strike for the recognition of the union. Moreover, this portion of Section 8 constitutes the heart of the Wagner Act, for it was enacted to promote the collective bargaining process once a bargaining unit was established. Once more, the NLRB was required to implement public policy. Specifically, what must an employer do in order to fulfill the legal obligation to bargain collectively? The answer to this problem is embedded in scores of NLRB decisions and orders. A brief analysis of them will reveal the character of employer behavior that satisfies the requirement of the law.

In the first place, if an employer refuses to meet with representatives of the employees, the employer has failed to bargain collectively and so has engaged in an unfair labor practice. Of course, the labor organization must make a proper demand to the employer requesting collective bargaining. A demand to bargain must come from the proper source of the union and must be clearly presented to the representatives of the company who usually deal with matters concerning labor relations. A casual remark is not a sufficient demand, but a request for collective bargaining by registered letter is sufficient.

In practice, employers have advanced various excuses for their refusal to meet or to bargain collectively with representatives of their employees. In various decisions, the Board has held in this respect that an employer is not relieved of the duty to bargain collectively by the outbreak of a strike; by shutting down the factory (lockout); or by asserting at one time that pension demands of the union are not proper subjects for negotiations.

A more definite action of some employers to avoid collective bargaining is evidenced in their attempts to undermine unions by engaging in other unfair labor practices. There is, of course, no duty to bargain if the union does not represent a majority of employees in the appropriate unit.

Thus, on occasion employers have attempted to evade their duty to bargain collectively by attempting to destroy the majority status of the union. The Board has ruled, however, that an employer who engages in unfair labor practices resulting in the destruction of the majority status of the labor organization is not relieved of the duty to bargain collectively with the representatives of that union.

Employers must do more than just meet with the representatives and merely go through the motions of bargaining. To satisfy the requirement of collective bargaining, an employer must bargain in "good faith."[29] In defining that term, the Board held that to bargain in good faith, an employer "must work toward a solution, satisfactory to both sides, of the various problems under discussion by presentation of counter-proposals and other affirmative conduct."[30] In another case, the Board declared that "the obligation of the Act is to produce more than a series of empty discussions, [and so] bargaining must mean more than mere negotiations. It must mean negotiations with a bona fide intent to reach an agreement if agreement is possible."[31]

The behavior of the employer at the meeting itself may indicate the desire to bargain in good faith. A conference completely dominated by the employer, with the representatives of the union mere auditors to the proceedings, has been held to constitute evidence that the employer does not desire to bargain collectively. If an employer makes no attempt to offer counterproposals during the meeting, the Board has ruled that such action indicates that the employer refuses to bargain in good faith. "The Board has considered counter-proposals so important an element of collective bargaining that it has found the failure to offer counter-proposals to be persuasive of the fact that the employer has not bargained in good faith."[32]

In a series of decisions, the NLRB has maintained that the nature of the employer's conduct after having been requested to bargain collectively is indicative of whether the employer really desired to negotiate in good faith. An employer does not intend to bargain in good faith when, after being asked to bargain collectively, it restrains and interferes with the employees' right to self-organization; when it attempts to bargain with individual employees; and when it calls a general meeting of its employees, dominates such meetings, and therein attacks the union.

The Wagner Act declared that a labor organization designated by the majority of the employees in a unit appropriate for collective bargaining shall be the exclusive representative of all employees in such unit for the purposes of collective bargaining in respect to rates of pay, wages, hours, or other conditions of work. Thus, the Board held early in its career that an employer engaged in an unfair labor practice by refusing to recognize a union as the exclusive representative of all the employees in the bargaining unit. Not only must an employer recognize a labor organization as the representative of all employees in the appropriate unit, but it must also bargain collectively with the union for all the employees in the unit, regardless of whether all are members of the union.

The Board established a rule that if an agreement between a company and a labor organization has been reached through discussion, such an agreement must be embodied in a written contract. In other words, an employer does not fulfill the obligation to bargain collectively—and thereby engages in an unfair labor practice—by refusing to render an agreement reached orally into a written trade agreement. In dealing with the matter, the NLRB declared in one case that "an assertion that collective bargaining connotes no more than discussions designed to clarify employer policy and does not include negotiations looking toward a binding agreement is contrary to any realistic view of labor relations. The protection to organization of employees afforded by the first four subdivisions of Section 8 can have meaning only when the ultimate goal is viewed as the stabilization of working conditions through genuine bargaining and [written] agreement between equals."[33] Eventually, the Supreme Court of the United States upheld this policy of the NLRB.[34]

Although the NLRB imposed upon employers the duty to bargain collectively, the law does not require that the parties must reach an agreement. Consequently, when an impasse in the negotiations between an employer and the representatives of the employees occurs, the employer is not required to continue to bargain collectively. When differences develop between parties over substantive issues and the employer has bargained in good faith, the NLRB has declared that an employer has fulfilled the collective bargaining obligations. If, however, the situation should change and new issues are introduced, the employer must resume the process of collective bargaining.

BOARD-DEVELOPED UNION RESPONSIBILITIES

During the Wagner Act years, the Board administered the unfair labor practice portion of the law in a vigorous manner. By checking employer antiunion practices, the Board gave substantial support to the growth of unions. The results of the Board's work in this direction are recorded later in this chapter. However, as unions grew stronger, the attitude of the public toward them underwent a change. A growing number of people were becoming less tolerant toward organized labor. The changing climate of opinion was in part attributable to the antisocial activities of some unions. In some cases, the growing power of unions was not matched by an increased degree of social responsibility on the part of union leadership.

This changing attitude was felt at the NLRB. Its members were aware of the growing tide of antiunion sentiment in the nation. As a result, the

Board's policies in unfair labor practice cases underwent a significant change. It began to search for ways in which the Wagner Act could impose obligations on unions even though the law did not contain any unfair labor practices for unions. There was, however, another factor making for this change in NLRB policy. Undoubtedly, the Board tried to make the statute appear more favorable to employers to forestall sweeping and fundamental changes in the Wagner Act.

There were several ways in which the NLRB utilized the Wagner Act to impose obligations on labor unions. In 1947, the NLRB handed down its decision in the celebrated *Times Publishing* case. In this case, the Board held that an employer was under no obligation to bargain with a labor organization which itself did not bargain collectively in good faith. In establishing this policy, the Board stated:

> The test of good faith in bargaining that the Act requires of an employer is not a rigid but a fluctuating one, and is dependent in part upon how a reasonable man might be expected to react to the bargaining attitude displayed by those across the table. It follows that, although the Act imposes no affirmative duty to bargain upon labor organizations, a union's refusal to bargain in good faith may remove the possibility of negotiation and thus preclude the existence of a situation in which the employer's own good faith can be tested. If it cannot be tested, its absence can hardly be found.[35]

In another case in 1947, the Board held that employees who participated in a strike, whose purpose was to compel an employer to recognize and bargain with the union of the striking employees, rather than with a certified labor organization, were not entitled to reinstatement.[36] Thus, to obtain the protection of the Wagner Act, unions and their members were not permitted to force employers to recognize one union when another organization had been certified for collective bargaining. During World War II, under another set of circumstances, the Board refused to order the reinstatement of strikers. It happened that a union called a strike to force an employer to violate the wage stabilization orders and procedures of the National War Labor Board. The employer discharged the workers, and the NLRB held that they lost their reinstatement right under the Act because the union had engaged in an illegal strike.[37]

❦ SUBSTANTIVE PROVISIONS:
THE PRINCIPLE OF MAJORITY RULE

It was necessary that Congress spell out the conditions under which employers are considered to have refused to bargain collectively with the representatives of their employees. Collective bargaining implies negotiations between representatives of management and representatives of employees. Consequently, it was indispensable for the Wagner Act to state the circumstances under which an employer was considered to have refused to bargain collectively. To resolve this problem, Congress adopted the principle of majority rule. For purposes of the Wagner Act, an employer engaged in an unfair labor practice only when it refused to bargain with a union selected by a majority of the employees for purposes of collective bargaining. If a labor organization did not possess the support of the majority, an employer was under no legal compulsion to bargain.

Still another principle of industrial democracy was embodied in the Wagner Act. Under its terms, a union selected by a majority of workers had to represent all workers in the bargaining unit, regardless of their membership status. A majority labor organization must bargain equally for members and nonmembers in respect to rates of pay, hours of work, or other conditions of employment. Moreover, if a majority of the workers in a unit vote for a union, it must represent all workers in the unit regardless of whether they voted for the union, voted against it, or failed to vote.

Some have opposed the majority-rule principle on the ground that it violates the rights of minority groups. Suppose 75 percent of the workers in a plant select a labor organization as their bargaining representative. Under the Wagner Act, the union was not only to represent this 75 percent, but also had to bargain for the remaining 25 percent. However, the fact that the labor organization chosen by the majority of workers must represent all workers does not transgress the tenets of democracy. Nothing is further from the truth. In fact, the principle of majority rule implements the democratic way of life. In political life, a Republican elected to the House of Representatives represents the Democratic members of the district as well as the Republicans. In addition, each Democratic member in the district is bound by decisions that the Republican representative might make.

Not only is the principle of majority rule consistent with democracy, but it is justified on the basis of effective collective bargaining. If nonunion workers could make their own employment agreements with their employers, the labor union would soon collapse. It would be easy for employers to favor the nonunion workers. These workers could be paid higher wages, helping to lure other workers out of the organization. If a large number of workers withdrew from the union, the labor organization would soon cease to exist. With the disintegration of a union, an employer would not need to be so considerate of the nonunion worker.

There is still another value attached to the principle of majority rule from the viewpoint of effective collective bargaining. Suppose the workers of a factory choose among five labor organizations. Assume that one union received the support of the majority of employees while the others received a scattering of the workers' support. If the minority unions were given the right to bargain for the workers who voted for them, collective bargaining could hardly be conducted successfully. Such "balkanization" of the bargaining unit would defeat the purpose of a law calculated to make collective bargaining effective. Thus, in this example, there would be five contract negotiation sessions, five grievance committees, and five different chances for the plant to shut down because of disagreement over working conditions. Management as well as workers would suffer under such a system. Membership raiding among the unions would be incessant. Production could hardly be carried out effectively in such an environment. What worth would it be to management or to workers if the company negotiated contracts successfully with four of the unions, only to have the plant shut down because the fifth union called a strike over contract terms?

Thus, it can readily be seen that the principle of majority rule satisfies the requirements of democracy and industrial harmony. Majority rule means the promotion of industrial democracy and orderly collective bargaining. Any other principle of representation would mean ineffective collective bargaining, retardation of the rate of production, and general industrial chaos.

🍃 UNFAIR LABOR PRACTICE PROCEDURE

The National Labor Relations Board was established by Congress to protect the rights prescribed by the Wagner Act. This includes the rights of employees, employers, unions, and the general public. The protection of these rights requires the remedying of unfair labor practices and the conduct of representation elections.

A director heads each regional office and has direct supervision over field examiners and attorneys. The chief function of the regional director is to issue complaints for unfair labor practices and to resolve issues involved in election cases. Field examiners investigate unfair labor practice cases and conduct elections, and on behalf of the regional director may conduct hearings involving elections. Attorneys perform the same kind of work as field examiners, but may also appear in court proceedings. One need not be an attorney to serve as a field examiner, and this position offers employment to college graduates interested in labor relations.

The NLRB hears and decides the unfair labor practice cases. It also hears and decides questions concerning representation elections referred to it by the regional offices.

The NLRB solicits neither unfair labor practices to remedy nor representation elections to conduct. Every case has its origin as a result of a charge or petition filed in one of the regional offices by some individual or organization. Specific procedures guide the administration of the statute from the regional offices through the U.S. Supreme Court.

🌿 UNFAIR LABOR PRACTICE CHARGE

An unfair labor practice charge must be filed with the regional office in the area in which the labor dispute occurred and must involve conduct defined by the law as an unfair labor practice.

After the charge is filed by an employee or union, the regional office must determine whether the Board has jurisdiction over the enterprise. The Board has established minimum standards indicating the volume of business that must be shown before it can exercise its power. These standards, expressed in terms of gross dollar volume of business or interstate transactions, differ for various categories of enterprises. Certain employers and employees are excluded from coverage under the Act. Once the jurisdictional dollar standards are met and it is determined that the employer and employees are covered by the Act, an investigation is conducted.

INVESTIGATION AND INFORMAL SETTLEMENT

An investigation is conducted by a field examiner or an attorney, who takes written statements and affidavits from available witnesses. When the investigation is completed, the case may be disposed of by withdrawal, settlement, or dismissal. If the case is not closed by one of these three methods, formal proceedings may be initiated if the regional director issues a complaint.

A charge may be withdrawn if the charging party feels that the case is without merit. Frequently, withdrawal is solicited by the regional office, but the charging party may take the initiative. A withdrawal, however, must be approved by the regional director; approval will be granted as long as it is not contrary to the purposes of the Act. The regional director will dismiss a charge when evidence of a violation of the Act is lacking. Dismissals result if the charging party refuses to withdraw the charge voluntarily. Board settlements are methods of closing cases in the regional offices by agreement of the parties, and are frequently obtained after complaints are issued.

From 1936 until 1947, the years in which the Board administered the Wagner Act, the agency managed to settle 90.6 percent of all its cases involving unfair labor practice charges on an informal basis.[38] In this period, labor unions and employees filed 43,556 charges with the NLRB, alleging employer violations of the Wagner Act. However, more than 50 percent of these cases were either dismissed by the Board or withdrawn by the filing party. Dismissal or withdrawal of cases resulted when the Board decided there was no violation of the Wagner Act. Thus, these figures disclose that, on the basis of informal procedures, the NLRB dismissed more than 50 percent of all unfair labor practice cases alleging employer violations. These figures contradict allegations that the NLRB proceeded to prosecute every employer charged with violating the law.

In about 37 percent of the unfair labor practice cases filed in 1936–1947, the Board adjusted the disputes to the satisfaction of employers, employees, and labor unions. Again, no formal proceedings were involved in such adjustments. In many cases, during an informal investigation of the case, a field examiner merely advised an employer that it was violating the law. Frequently, the employer was not aware of the unlawful conduct and, when advised of it, immediately complied with the law.

The fact that the vast majority of the cases were settled on an informal basis by the NLRB speaks well of the Board, employers, unions, and employees. If a majority of the cases filed with the Board had proceeded to formal hearings, investigations, and court proceedings, the administration of the law could not have been effective. By obtaining voluntary compliance with the law, by dismissing cases outright, and by urging labor unions to withdraw baseless charges, the NLRB was able to function successfully. Moreover, the informal settlement of cases resulted in a considerable saving of time and money for all parties involved in Wagner Act proceedings.

The record established under the Wagner Act continued under Taft-Hartley. In 1988, 31,453 unfair labor practice charges were filed. Of these, 93.5 percent were withdrawn, dismissed, or settled. Thus, the vast majority of charges continued to be disposed of without formal proceedings.[39]

FORMAL PROCEEDINGS

Formal proceedings result if the parties are unable to resolve the dispute informally, and if the regional office believes a violation of the law occurred.

The Complaint. A complaint is issued by the regional office; it is a formal charge by the government of violation of federal law. The complaint lists the provisions of the Act allegedly violated and the time and place of the hearing covering the unfair labor practice charges. The charged party must answer the complaint within ten days either by admitting, denying, or explaining the facts alleged in the complaint.

The Hearing. The hearing is the formal trial and is presided over by an administrative law judge (formerly called trial examiner), an agent of the Board. It is conducted in accordance with the rules of evidence and procedure that apply in the U.S. district courts. After the hearing, the law judge issues a decision. If a violation is found, the decision includes an appropriate remedy. Any party that disagrees with the law judge's decision may appeal to the Board within twenty days. The NLRB has full power over the decisions issued by the law judges. It may adopt the decision in whole or in part, or reverse it in whole or in part. In rare cases, the Board may direct the law judge to conduct a new hearing. As required by law, the NLRB must review each administrative law judge's decision appealed to it.

In the majority of cases, a respondent complies with the Board's decision and order. If the respondent does not comply, the Board may seek enforcement of its order through a federal court of appeals. Similarly, the party charged with a violation of the unfair labor practice provisions may also appeal the Board's decision to a U.S. court of appeals. Likewise, appeals may be made if the Board reverses a law judge's decision. If there is dissatisfaction with the circuit court decision, requests may be made for review to the U.S. Supreme Court. Once a circuit court order is finalized (by failure to seek review or denial thereof by the Supreme Court), the party charged must obey the Board order or face contempt-of-court proceedings.

Only 9.4 percent of all unfair labor practice cases filed with the Board from 1936 to 1947 involved formal proceedings. These proceedings were necessary when employers refused to comply with the law on an informal basis. They felt that their interests would best be served by not complying with informal recommendations tendered by Board officials. These employers in no sense can be censured, for it was their legal right to exhaust fully the procedures of the Wagner Act before complying with the law. The remarkable fact is that so few employers chose to bring into operation the formal procedures of the law. Undoubtedly some of those employers honestly felt that they had not violated the law even though an informal investigation may have pointed in that direction. This record continued and even improved under the Taft-Hartley Act. In 1988, only 6.5 percent of the cases involved formal proceedings.[40]

❦ THE WAGNER ACT RECORD

How the Board discharged its responsibility is a matter of public record.[41] In the Wagner Act years of 1936–1947, the NLRB reinstated 76,268 workers who had been discharged because of union activities. Moreover, the Board awarded workers $12,418,000 in back pay. Congress recognized that reinstatement of workers discharged because of union activity without awarding them pay for time lost during their period of discharge would be improper. Accordingly, the Wagner Act provided that workers discharged because of union activities would be reinstated with back pay. In addition, the NLRB disestablished 1,709 company-dominated unions; ordered

CHAPTER EIGHT   193

employers to post 8,156 notices stating that the company would henceforth comply with the Wagner Act; and on 5,070 occasions ordered employers to bargain collectively. Finally, the Board ordered 226,488 strikers reinstated in their jobs. Many of these workers had struck because of employer unfair labor practices; still others had suffered discrimination at the termination of a strike. It has been a favorite union-busting technique for employers to refuse to reinstate strike leaders in their jobs after a strike ends. These figures stand as a testimonial to a law and an agency dedicated to the promotion of collective bargaining and the union movement. This record underscores the proposition that a main source of criticism of the NLRB during its Wagner Act period resulted from the zeal of the agency to perform its duties in a positive and vigorous manner.

Though organized labor bitterly criticized Taft-Hartley when it was originally enacted in 1947 and continues to oppose certain provisions of the law, the fact remains that under the 1947 law, the NLRB still protects the rights of employees. The innovation of Taft-Hartley was not that it repealed those features of the Wagner Act that protected employees' organizational and collective bargaining rights. The major innovation of Taft-Hartley was to place restrictions on certain union activities. In other words, despite such controls, employees still enjoy the protection that they had under the Wagner Act. For example, in 1988, 4,179 employees were ordered to be reinstated in their jobs after having been unlawfully discharged, and were awarded $34.6 million in back pay.[42]

As a matter of fact, in 1979, the Board even made it easier for employees to collect back pay. Reversing a thirty-year policy, it ruled that a striker discharged discriminatorily no longer needed to request reinstatement to activate the employer's obligation for back pay.[43] Previously, unlike other unlawfully discharged employees (for example, one who was discharged for union activities), an illegally discharged striker had been compelled to request reinstatement from the employer to trigger the employer's back pay obligation. Under the current policy, all unlawfully discharged employees are treated equally. An employer's back pay obligation starts from the date of unlawful discharge and continues until the employee is offered the opportunity to return to work, whether or not the employee accepts this opportunity.

❦ REPRESENTATION PROCEDURE

Representation cases must also follow a prescribed procedure before the Board is empowered to intervene and conduct elections. Representation elections, like unfair labor practices, are initiated by the filing of a petition. The regional office is authorized to make an investigation of the petition.

The Investigation. An investigation is conducted in order to obtain information about the following: (1) whether the employer's operations meet the Board's jurisdictional standards; (2) the appropriateness of the unit of employees for purposes of collective bargaining (employees are grouped into units where similar interests exist); (3) the sufficiency of employee interest in representation by a labor organization (an election will usually be conducted by the Board if at least 30 percent of the employees indicate an interest in representation); and (4) whether the petition was filed at the proper time. An election may not be conducted if a valid election has been held during the preceding twelve-month period.

If the petition has merit and no arrangements for a consent election have been made, the parties are entitled to a hearing. The law entitles the parties to a representation hearing, which is a formal proceeding designed to obtain information to aid the regional director in deciding the adequacy of the petition. The regional director must make a decision on the appropriateness of the bargaining unit, the timeliness of the petition, the sufficiency of employee interest, and other pertinent matters. The hearing is not held if the parties enter into a consent election agreement, since the matters that must be resolved in the hearing are by such agreement voluntarily resolved by the parties.

Consent elections have the advantage of being conducted much faster than those that require formal hearings. Also, when the parties consent to an election, the work load of the regional office is reduced. Normally, the regional offices are successful in persuading the parties to accept the consent election. In 1988, of the 4,153 elections conducted, 83.7 percent were of the consent type.[44]

In hearing cases, the regional director reviews the record of the hearing and resolves eligibility, appropriateness of unit, and other requirements; then either directs an election or dismisses the petitions. The decision may be appealed to the Board.

Election Supervision. Personnel from the regional offices supervise the secret-ballot elections after elections are ordered by the regional director or consented to by the parties. Representatives of both employers and unions are entitled to observe the procedure, and to challenge any employee who applies for a ballot. Challenges must be based on "reasonable cause." When the election results depend on the challenged ballots, the regional director must conduct an investigation and make a decision on the challenged votes.

Employer or union conduct affecting an election may be subject to objections within ten days after the ballots are counted. Such objections must be investigated by the regional director and, if they are found to be justified, an election may be set aside and a new one ordered. This depends on the nature of the issues and the type of consent agreement executed by the parties. Challenges and objections might or might not be resolved on the basis of the investigation without a hearing. Depending on the circumstances, the ultimate decision on challenges or objections will be made by the regional director or the Board.

A representation petition may be withdrawn at any time—before the hearing, after the hearing, or after a second election has been ordered by the regional director or the Board. Once the election has been conducted and all the problems associated with it settled, its outcome must be certified. A certification of representatives occurs when a labor organization wins an election. Following certification of representatives, in the absence of an appeal, an employer is obligated to enter collective bargaining negotiations with the appropriate union. Should the labor organization lose, however, there is no certification of results and the employer is not required to bargain.

🥀 INDUSTRIAL DEMOCRACY

During the Wagner Act years of 1936–1947, the NLRB was called upon to determine representatives for collective bargaining in 36,969 cases.[45] Labor unions won lawful bargaining rights in 30,110 instances, and workers voted for "no union" in 6,859 cases. Slightly more than 9 million workers were eligible to vote in representation elections. Of this total, 7,677,135 workers, 84.1 percent, actually cast ballots. Votes cast for labor unions amounted to 6,145,834, and votes against unions numbered 1,531,301. These figures testify to the success of the Wagner Act in establishing an orderly manner for the selection of bargaining representatives. The law substituted the ballot box for industrial warfare. Workers in free secret-ballot elections had the opportunity to select or reject the process of collective bargaining. The Wagner Act established the principle of representative democracy in the nation's industrial life.

Indeed, in December 1976, in an election held in Millers Falls, Massachusetts, some unknown employee cast the *30-millionth* vote in the forty-two-year operation of the NLRB.[46] Speaking of this milestone, Betty Southhard Murphy, then the chair of the Board, stated:

> The statute has stood the test of time. During these four decades, the United States in large measure has achieved industrial democracy under law. The statute has been a key factor in our country's immense economic growth; it has brought an evolution of labor relations from sitdown strikes and violence to a thoughtful bargaining and productive compromise.[47]

To the union movement, however, the significance of the milestone was somewhat diminished because of the decline of union success in NLRB elections. Whereas unions had been selected as bargaining agents in about

80 percent of the polls between 1936 and 1947, their success in elections had declined to the 50 percent range in the 1970s.[48] In fiscal year 1980, unions prevailed in only 45.7 percent of the elections.[49] By 1983, union victories had edged up to 47.7 percent, a figure still far below their success rates in earlier years. There are many causes for this sharp decline in union election victories, including the structural change in the nation's labor force, particularly the growing proportion of white-collar employees and women. For a variety of reasons, unions have had difficulty in organizing these segments of the labor force in the same proportions as they have grown.

In any event, on July 5, 1985, the NLRB celebrated its 50th anniversary. In the past fifty years, it has conducted 345,000 elections involving over 32 million employees who cast ballots.[50] Clearly, national labor policy has established the principle of industrial democracy.

❦ WAGNER ACT DURING WORLD WAR II

The Wagner Act proved particularly beneficial to the nation during World War II.[51] The winning of a modern war required maximum production. The Wagner Act provided workers with a peaceful and orderly procedure to adjust their organizational controversies. Instead of resorting to the organizational strike, the nation's employees could make use of the National Labor Relations Board.

Events proved that workers and labor unions utilized the peaceful procedures of the Wagner Act in unprecedented numbers. The NLRB handled a tremendous number of cases during the war period. Three factors accounted for this. In the first place, industry greatly expanded its facilities. As a result, the level of employment reached unprecedented heights. By August 1945, the nation's labor force had reached the level of 66,650,000. This number is compared with 54,230,000 reported for 1939. Moreover, unemployment was nearly wiped out during the war years. Whereas 7,300,000 were unemployed in 1939, there were only 830,000—mostly "unemployables"—idle in August 1945. As might be expected, increased trade union activities followed the expansion of the level of employment. Whereas in 1940, union membership in all the nation's labor force was reported at 8,500,000, the figure had soared to 13,750,000 in 1944. Such augmentation of union activities constituted the second factor making for the heavy workload of the NLRB during World War II. Finally, this increase was attributable to the confidence of the nation's workers and labor unions in the Wagner Act and in the NLRB. In prewar years, the NLRB had demonstrated its power and effectiveness in protecting the right of workers to self-organization and collective bargaining. As a result, the Board entered its wartime career as an agency that had won the respect and admiration of the nation's workers.

Obviously, if unions and workers had held the NLRB in low esteem, they would not have utilized the Wagner Act as the vehicle whereby the right to self-organization and collective bargaining could be implemented.

Evidence indicating the large increase in the work of the NLRB during World War II may be briefly noted. Whereas the Board conducted only 3,386 representation elections during the years 1936–1940, in which 1,225,098 valid votes were cast, during the war years of 1941–1945, the NLRB administered 20,562 elections in which 4,889,627 workers cast valid ballots. In other words, more than 85 percent of all representation elections conducted by the Board during the first ten years of its operation were held in the war period. Workers resorted to the election procedures of the Wagner Act because, as noted, they had faith that once their unions were certified, the NLRB would guarantee that employers would recognize them as collective bargaining agencies. Actually, the NLRB issued 2,796 wartime orders requiring employers to bargain collectively with labor unions chosen by their employees. This figure is slightly in excess of the number of all such orders handed down by the NLRB during the years 1937 to 1941.

The major portion of the Board's activities during World War II involved the certification of bargaining representatives. By 1945, representation cases constituted 75.1 percent of the total of all cases, and unfair labor practice cases accounted for 24.2 percent. In comparison, in 1936, the first full year of the Board's operation, unfair labor practice cases accounted for 81 percent of the total of all cases filed with the Board, whereas representation cases accounted for only 19 percent. These figures indicate that during World War II, employers, instead of interfering with the right of employees to organize and bargain collectively, were more anxious to learn with whom they were required to bargain. The change in the comparative importance of representation cases indicated that after several years of the Wagner Act, employers and employees alike recognized the role of collective bargaining in modern industry. However, it should not be overlooked that 18,187 unfair labor practice cases were filed with the Board during the period 1941–1945. This figure was only 932 less than the number of all unfair labor practice cases filed with the NLRB in the prewar years, 1936–1940. The wartime unfair labor practice cases involved 18,108,433 employees. Consequently, in war as in peace, legal protection of the right of workers to self-organization and collective bargaining is clearly a prerequisite for industrial peace.

Another aspect of wartime labor relations should be stressed. Much of the Board's wartime work involved basic war industries. More than 50 percent of all bargaining elections conducted by the NLRB were held in the nation's crucial war industries, which included those of iron and steel, machinery, food, chemicals, wholesale trade, electrical equipment, textiles, aircraft, and shipbuilding. Approximately 50 percent of all unfair labor practices likewise involved the same nine industries.

Literally millions of the nation's war production workers resorted to the machinery of the NLRB for adjustment of their organizational disputes. War production would have been seriously retarded if employees had not had the opportunity to settle their organizational controversies through the Board's peaceful and democratic procedures. Recognizing the importance of speedy disposition of wartime representation and unfair labor practice disputes, the NLRB streamlined its regulations under which disposition of the cases was made. By granting greater authority to its regional directors and by otherwise accommodating its procedures to the exigencies of war conditions, the NLRB decreased by several months the time required to process its cases. By lawful certification of bargaining agents and through speedy elimination of unfair labor practices, the NLRB hoped to abolish completely the justification for organizational strikes.

❦ RESULTS OF THE WAGNER ACT

Organizational strike experience during World War II is one standard with which to evaluate the results of the Wagner Act. As noted, approximately 50 percent of all strikes that occurred during 1934 to 1936 resulted wholly or in part from organizational disputes.[52] These strikes involved about 43 percent of the workers who engaged in all strikes during this period. In comparison, in 1942, the first full year of U.S. involvement in World War II, organizational controversies wholly or in part caused 31.2 percent of all strikes.[53] In subsequent war years, the organizational strike was of even less comparative importance. In 1943, organizational disputes, alone or in combination with other causes, resulted in 15.7 percent of all work stoppages; in 1944, they caused 16.3 percent of all strikes; and in 1945, they wholly or in part caused 20.5 percent of all work stoppages. From the point of view of the number of workers engaged in strikes during the war years (1942–1945), work stoppages carried out for organizational purposes alone or in combination with other causes involved approximately 18.5 percent of all workers who engaged in strikes during this period. In the light of the organizational strike experience of 1934 to 1936, in the absence of the effective operation of the Wagner Act, organizational strikes would have been of greater absolute and comparative importance during World War II.

A comparison of the frequency of organizational strikes during World War I with those during World War II might further indicate the extent to which the Wagner Act was successful in decreasing such work stoppages in World War II. The Bureau of Labor Statistics has faithfully recorded throughout the years the number of strikes resulting from the refusal of employers to recognize their employees' unions. Under the terms of the Wagner Act, an employer engages in an unfair labor practice by

Chapter Eight   199

refusing to recognize a certified labor organization as the exclusive representative of the workers in the bargaining unit. Accordingly, workers during World War II had little reason to engage in strikes to gain recognition for their labor unions, since their organizations could accomplish this objective by resorting to the peaceful machinery provided by the NLRB. During World War I, when there existed no agency similar to the NLRB, it is reported that 314 strikes and lockouts were caused by employers' refusal to recognize unions in 1917, and 221 such work stoppages took place in 1918. Expressed as a ratio, recognition strikes accounted for approximately 7 percent of all 1917 strikes and lockouts, and such interruptions to production resulted in 6.5 percent of all work stoppages in 1918. On the other hand, the Bureau reports that in 1942, the first full year of World War II, only 169 recognition-caused work stoppages occurred, accounting for only 5.6 percent of all 1942 interruptions. In subsequent years, the record indicates, the recognition strike continued to be of less importance, comparative and absolute, during World War II as compared to its importance in World War I.

Even though the lack of World War I data precludes a comparison of World War I and World War II recognition strikes on a "worker-days-lost" basis, it still appears that World War II employees and unions, able to utilize the NLRB procedures, resorted to the recognition strike far less frequently than did World War I employees. The number of World War II recognition strikes would have been greater had there been no NLRB.

The record underscores the contention that the Wagner Act was a powerful force making for industrial peace during World War II. It highlights the necessity for an orderly system to provide effective and speedy protection of the right of workers to self-organization and collective bargaining. Workers and unions, aware of the remedies of the NLRB, relied more on peaceful legal procedures than on the strike to make the right to collective bargaining effective.

The success of the Wagner Act in decreasing the number of organizational strikes cannot be denied. The trend during World War II removed all doubt on the issue. However, some people contend that the Wagner Act, though decreasing the number of organizational strikes, stimulated strikes for nonorganizational issues—wages, hours, pensions, vacations, and the like. The arguments run along the following lines. Under the protection of the Wagner Act, union membership increased, the union movement expanded into new areas, and general bargaining strength of labor unions sharply increased. These circumstances increased the number of nonorganizational strikes, for under the Wagner Act, unions became a powerful force in the national economy. In other words, the Wagner Act did not promote industrial peace.

Close analysis of this argument will indicate its fundamental defects. In the first place, the Wagner Act was not passed to eliminate all types of strikes. It was enacted to reduce the number of organizational strikes. Unless we are prepared to make fundamental changes in the structure of a free enterprise system, strikes over wages, hours, and conditions of work will always characterize our national life. It is not fair to evaluate the Wagner Act on the basis of the number of all strikes arising during its operation. A valid basis for evaluating its contribution to industrial peace consists of the trend in organizational strikes.

Clearly, the Wagner Act stimulated the growth of the union movement. Union membership increased from about 4 million in 1935 to about 16 million in 1948. Under its protection, the CIO was able to organize the mass production industries on an industry-wide basis. Responding to the challenge of the CIO, the AFL likewise undertook important organizational activities. Obviously, the Wagner Act accomplished its objective of promoting collective bargaining. One may quarrel as to whether or not a large and strong labor union movement is good or bad for society. Whatever the answer to this question, the fact remains that the Wagner Act was very effective in stimulating the growth and strength of organized labor.

Other results of the Wagner Act appear equally impressive. Not only was the statute successful in reducing the number of organizational strikes and expanding the union movement, but the Wagner Act operated to increase greatly the number of effective collective bargaining agreements. In 1946, the last full year of the Wagner Act, the Bureau of Labor Statistics reported that the number of collective bargaining contracts in the nation totaled well over 50,000. These figures underscore the contention that industrial peace and not industrial warfare is the result of the collective bargaining process. By far the vast majority of labor contracts are negotiated and signed without resort to the strike. The general public is not usually aware of this fact. Strikes are more often reported than peaceful settlement of agreements. Such a focus on conflict, however, is not unique to labor-management relations.

It is noteworthy that the Wagner Act stimulated an increase in the number of collective bargaining agreements. Moreover, it should be kept in mind that these contracts, once executed, often provided the basis for peaceful industrial relations for the life of the contract. Not only did they provide a peaceful procedure for the day-to-day relationship between employees and employer, but they also served to stabilize labor relations for long periods of time. The biggest hurdle to industrial peace is the execution of the first collective bargaining agreement. In addition, during each year, many of these contracts are renegotiated in whole or in part. After the first contract is achieved, and assuming that a management and a union recognize their mutual problems and aspirations, long-run industrial peace is likely.

CHAPTER EIGHT

🕊 *SUMMARY*

The Wagner Act sought to promote collective bargaining by denying employers the opportunity to interfere with the right of workers to self-organization and collective bargaining. Through this procedure, Congress hoped to provide workers with a measure of social and economic justice, to promote a stable economic system, and to foster industrial peace. The law did not seek to promote strong unions as ends in themselves. Rather, the objectives of the Wagner Act were social in character, extending beyond the advancement of any particular economic group. Since the law effectively stopped antiunion conduct on the part of employers, the reaction of this group to the law was extremely unfavorable. Many employers attempted to nullify the law by enlisting the support of their old ally, the judiciary. However, by a majority of one, the Supreme Court of the United States in the *Jones & Laughlin* case upheld the constitutionality of the Wagner Act. The Court also assured wide coverage of the law by applying its terms to manufacturing.

The substance of the law centered on Section 7, which guaranteed the right of employees to self-organization and collective bargaining. To make this right meaningful, employers were required to bargain collectively with unions chosen by a majority of their employees and were forbidden to engage in other patterns of antiunion conduct. The National Labor Relations Board was established to enforce the Wagner Act. To sound out the collective bargaining desires of employees, the Board was required to conduct elections in appropriate bargaining units. In addition, it was empowered to prevent employer interference with the collective bargaining rights of the workers covered by the law.

Under the protection of the Wagner Act, the union movement made phenomenal progress. Union membership increased from about 4 million in 1935 to about 16 million in 1948. The effectiveness of the Wagner Act in this respect stimulated a great deal of employer hostility. However, the Wagner Act remained intact until 1947, the year of Taft-Hartley.

🕊 *DISCUSSION QUESTIONS*

1. What was the economic rationale of Congress in passing the Wagner Act?
2. What public policy statement did Congress set forth in the Wagner Act? Has it changed? Should it change?
3. How was the Wagner Act received by affected parties in the first two years of its existence?
4. What was the specific significance of the *Jones & Laughlin* decision on the Wagner Act? Were there more general applications to the ruling beyond labor relations?

5. Why did five employer unfair labor practices need to be specified in order to accomplish the objective of Section 7? How do the five unfair labor practices clarify the meaning of Section 7?
6. Discuss the significance of the original *Darlington* doctrine. How was the original position changed in the NLRB's *Contris Packing Co.* case in 1983?
7. Do you agree with the principle of majority rule established by Congress in the Wagner Act? What is that principle? How important is it for union organizational successes?
8. Set up an alleged violation of one of the unfair labor practices presented in the chapter. Then trace the procedure necessary to process the case through the procedures of the NLRB.
9. Are there identifiable trends that can be discovered from a review of the Wagner Act record in unfair labor practice cases? In representation cases?

NOTES

[1] *New York Times* Magazine Section, May 9, 1937, p. 23.

[2] Statement of H. M. Robertson, General Counsel, Brown and Williamson Tobacco Corporation, in Senate Committee on Education and Labor, *Hearing on a National Labor Relations Board*, 74th Congress, 1st sess., 1935, p. 218.

[3] U.S. Constitution, Article I, Section 8.

[4] See *Causes of Industrial Peace Under Collective Bargaining*, National Planning Association (Washington, D.C., 1948–1950).

[5] National Labor Relations Board, *First Annual Report*, 1936, p. 46.

[6] *Ibid.*, p. 47.

[7] *Ibid.*, p. 48.

[8] U.S. Department of Labor, Bureau of Labor Statistics, *Monthly Labor Review*, XLII, 162 (1936), p. 1308; XLIV, 1937, p. 1230.

[9] *United States v. Knight*, 156 U.S. 12 (1894).

[10] *Carter v. Carter Coal Co.*, 298 U.S. 238 (1936).

[11] *NLRB v. Jones & Laughlin Steel Corporation*, 301 U.S. 1 (1937).

[12] Since the *Jones & Laughlin* decision, the Supreme Court has widely construed the meaning of the interstate commerce clause for the purposes of national labor relations legislation. Decisions of the Supreme Court have empowered the NLRB to exercise jurisdiction over public utilities supplying energy to enterprises engaged in interstate commerce, *Consolidated Edison Company v. NLRB*, 305 U.S. 197 (1938); national fraternal organizations, *Polish National Alliance v. NLRB*, 322 U.S. 643 (1944); a local transportation system in an industrial city, *NLRB v. Baltimore Transit Company*, 321 U.S. 796 (1944); and a large retail department store, *NLRB v. J. L. Hudson Company*, 135 Fed. (2d) 380, certiorari denied by Supreme Court, October 11, 1943; as well as to a charitable hospital, *NLRB v. Central Dispensary and Emergency Hospital*, 324 U.S. 847 (1945). The Supreme Court has also held that a firm falls within the authority of the NLRB even if it only exports goods into interstate commerce, *Santa Cruz Fruit Packing Company v. NLRB*, 303 U.S. 453 (1938); or only

receives goods from other states, *Newport News Shipbuilding and Dry Dock Company v. Schauffler*, 303 U.S. 54 (1938). Moreover, in the *Fainblatt* case (*NLRB v. Fainblatt*), 306 U.S. 601 (1939), the Supreme Court rejected the criterion that an employer's operations must be large enough to be of great national importance in order to fall within the scope of the NLRB. It declared that the operation of the NLRB does not "depend on any particular volume of commerce affected more than that to which courts would apply the maxim *de minimis*." It should be noted here that this broad concept of interstate commerce developed by the Supreme Court for purposes of the Wagner Act applies equally to NLRB operations when it administers the Taft-Hartley law.

[13] Benjamin J. Taylor, *The Operation of the Taft-Hartley Act in Indiana* (Bloomington, Indiana: Bureau of Business Research, Indiana University, 1967), p. 3.

[14] National Labor Relations Board, *op. cit.*, p. 55.

[15] National Labor Relations Board, *Decisions and Orders of the National Labor Relations Board*, VII, 1936, p. 54.

[16] *Riecke Metal Products Company*, 40 NLRB 872 (1942).

[17] *Burger King v. NLRB*, 725 Fed. (2d) 1053 (1984).

[18] 3 NLRB 591 (1938).

[19] National Labor Relations Board, *Third Annual Report*, 1938, p. 115.

[20] 7 NLRB 877.

[21] *Jackson Engineering Co.*, 265 NLRB No. 175 (1982).

[22] *Textile Workers Union v. Darlington Mfg. Co.*, 380 U.S. 263 (1965).

[23] *Ibid.*, pp. 274–275.

[24] *Ibid.*, p. 275.

[25] *Ibid.*, pp. 275–276.

[26] *Contris Packing Co.*, 268 NLRB No. 7 (1983).

[27] *Wright Line, Inc.*, 251 NLRB 1083 (1980).

[28] *NLRB v. Transportation Management Corp.*, 426 US 393 (1983).

[29] National Labor Relations Board, *op. cit.*, p. 96.

[30] 2 NLRB 39 (1937).

[31] 3 NLRB 10 (1938).

[32] National Labor Relations Board, *op. cit.*, p. 97.

[33] 2 NLRB 39.

[34] *H.J. Heinz Company v. NLRB*, 311 U.S. 514 (1941). When Congress enacted Taft-Hartley, this principle established by the NLRB during the early years of its administration of the Wagner Act was incorporated into the legislation.

[35] *Times Publishing Company*, 72 NLRB 676 (1947).

[36] *Thompson Products, Inc.*, 72 NLRB 888 (1947).

[37] *American News Company*, 55 NLRB 1302 (1944).

[38] National Labor Relations Board, *Twelfth Annual Report*, 1947, p. 86.

[39] National Labor Relations Board, *Fifty-third Annual Report*, 1988, p. 5.

[40] *Ibid.*, p. 5.

[41] National Labor Relations Board, *Twelfth Annual Report*, 1947, pp. 83–90.

[42] National Labor Relations Board, *Fifty-third Annual Report*, 1988, p. 9.

[43] *Abilities & Goodwill*, 241 NLRB No. 5 (1979).
[44] National Labor Relations Board, *Fifty-third Annual Report*, 1988, p. 10.
[45] National Labor Relations Board, *Twelfth Annual Report*, 1947, pp. 83–90.
[46] *AFL-CIO News*, March 5, 1977.
[47] National Labor Relations Board, *Forty-first Annual Report*, 1976, p. 2.
[48] *Ibid.*, p. 17.
[49] National Labor Relations Board, *Forty-fifth Annual Report*, 1980, p. 16.
[50] National Labor Relations Board, *The Story of the NLRB 1935–1985*, p. 71.
[51] See Fred Witney, *Wartime Experiences of the National Labor Relations Board* (Urbana, Illinois: University of Illinois Press, 1949). This study discusses the operation of the Wagner Act during World War II.
[52] See U.S. Department of Labor, Bureau of Labor Statistics, *Monthly Labor Review*, XLII, 162 (1936), p. 1308; XLIV, (1937), p. 1230. Although the Wagner Act was approved by Congress on June 27, 1935, and signed by President Roosevelt on July 5, 1935, the statute was not operationally effective until the Supreme Court approved the legislation on April 12, 1937. Consequently, to ascertain the effectiveness of the Wagner Act in reducing organizational strikes, it appears appropriate to disregard 1935 and 1936, although the Act was technically in operation during these two years.
[53] U.S. Department of Labor, Bureau of Labor Statistics, *Monthly Labor Review*, LVI, (1943), p. 973.

CHAPTER NINE

GENERAL SUMMARY

ERA OF LEGAL SUPPRESSION

If one element of labor relations is a certainty, it is the changing legal climate defining the rights and obligations of workers, unions and employers. Equally certain is that the swings in the legal climate are directly related to the extent of unionism and viability of collective bargaining.

For many years the judicial system was by far the predominant force regulating the relationship between employers and unions. Starting with the dawn of unionism in the early nineteenth century until the 1930s, federal and state courts made it very difficult, if not impossible, for workers to form unions and bargain collectively. Indeed, this was the period of hostility and suppression regarding the growth of the labor movement. There was no question that federal and state courts favored the employers' side of the equation; no question that the judiciary was a willing ally of employers in opposition to unionization. First caught in the web of the conspiracy doctrine, then crippled by the labor injunction and application of antitrust legislation, unions were burdened by the court system.

Until 1842, unions under the conspiracy doctrine were illegal, and their members subject to fines and even imprisonment. They were regarded the same as criminal groups conspiring to commit murder or the violent overthrow of duly constituted government. It is a commentary of the times that courts did not distinguish between such criminal groups and the efforts of workers seeking to improve their social and economic status by collective action.

Even after *Commonwealth v. Hunt*, unions were not freed from the conspiracy doctrine. Although unions were generally regarded as per se lawful organizations, and could exist, the courts applied the conspiracy doctrine when they engaged in conduct held unlawful. When unions sought an objective, such as forcing an employer to recognize the workers' organizations, the conspiracy doctrine was applied. When unions sought an end legal in itself, but used a method declared unlawful—a strike, picketing, or boycott—unions and their members felt the sting of the doctrine.

When the conspiracy doctrine finally disappeared from the scene, it did not result from a change in the attitude of the judiciary. Indeed, it was not until Norris–LaGuardia that the federal courts were neutralized as a hostile employer-ally in labor disputes. To the contrary, the conspiracy doctrine disappeared because employers wanted a more effective legal weapon to suppress unionism and collective bargaining. This new weapon, the labor injunction, suited the employers' interest much more effectively compared with the conspiracy doctrine, what with its trials, delays, and juries sympathetic to the workers' cause.

Injunctions were issued by judges without jury trials. These injunctions were swift and certain. Judges determined the lawfulness of union objectives and methods. The judiciary delagated to itself the power to establish what unions could lawfully seek and the methodology. The injunction was the way judges implemented their social and economic philosophies on labor matters. It is not that they were dishonest or felt they were biased. Rather, coming from the same social and economic class as employers, which was suspicious of the labor movement, they invariably came down on the side of employers.

The result of the injunction manifested itself in broken strikes and unions. Generated by the judges' socioeconomic predilections, injunctions outlawed strikes for fundamental union objectives, including those for the demand for recognition, protest against refusal of employers to bargain collectively, protest against the discharge of union members, and recognition of the union shop. It did not matter that strikes, picketing, or boycotts were carried out in a peaceful manner. Peaceful union activities were outlawed despite the Constitutional guarantees of free speech and assembly. Proper injunction procedures which applied to nonlabor cases were not followed when unions were involved.

When the Supreme Court upheld the injunction to enforce yellow-dog contracts in *Hitchman Coal*, it presented employers with the ultimate union-busting weapon. To survive, workers agreed to work under yellow-dog conditions. Failing to recognize the obvious, the high court saw no difference between yellow-dog contracts and those made to purchase homes or to borrow money. Union organization in the face of yellow-dog contracts was the road to fines and imprisonment. Brandeis and Holmes could not persuade the majority that workers realistically were coerced to work under yellow-dog conditions.

Ironically, the Sherman Antitrust Act, passed to break up business monopolies, was applied more vigorously to union activities. When unions engaged in secondary boycotts as the alternative to extinction, the Supreme Court in *Danbury Hatters*, and its progeny, held such conduct in violation of antitrust legislation. Passage of the Clayton Act did not relieve unions from prosecution, as demonstrated in *Bedford Cut Stone*. The rule of reason, which permitted business to monopolize trade in several vital industries, was not applied to labor cases. In vain Brandeis complained the majority of the high court had established a double standard under the antitrust statutes—one for business and the other for unions. Brandeis's dissent in *Bedford Cut Stone* remains a classic and warrants repetition:

> If, on the undisputed facts of this case, refusal to work can be enjoined, Congress created by the Sherman Law and the Clayton Act an instrument for imposing restraints upon labor which reminds of involuntary servitude. The Sherman Law was held in *United States* v. *United States Steel Corporation*...to permit capitalists to combine in a single corporation 50 percent of the steel industry of the United States dominating the trade through its vast resources. The Sherman Law was held in *United States* v. *United Shoe Machinery Co*.....to permit capitalists to combine in another corporation practically the whole shoe-machinery industry of the country, necessarily giving it a position of dominance over shoe manufacturing in America. It would, indeed, be strange if Congress had by the same Act willed to deny to members of a small craft of workingmen the right to co-operate in simply refraining from work, when that course was the only means of self-protection against a combination of militant and powerful employers. I cannot believe that Congress did so.

While the courts blocked the progress of unions and collective bargaining, the legislative branch of government made some attempts to encourage the growth of unionism. Congress and some states passed laws calculated to prevent the employer from interfering with the right of employees to self-organization and collective bargaining. Congress limited its action to the railroad industry, though some states passed union-protection legislation that applied to general industry. Some of these laws forbade employers to discharge workers because of their membership in labor unions and outlawed the yellow-dog contract. To check abusive use of the labor injunction, Congress and some states attempted to curb the power of the judiciary.

It is noteworthy that the legislative branch of government was more favorable to organized labor than were the courts. This condition resulted from the more responsive character of the legislative branch to social change. Protected in tenure, the judiciary was more concerned with legal formalism and precedent than with social and economic realities. For many years, the legislative and judicial branches of government were in sharp conflict over the labor issue. Workers and unions of the nation stood by, hoping for a favorable outcome to the struggle so that they might realize a better socioeconomic existence. But for decades, the courts refused to confirm legislation calculated to promote unions and collective bargaining. When reviewed by the Supreme Court, it either held such legislation unconstitutional or applied the legislation in such a way as to render it meaningless.

While the judiciary hampered workers in their effort for self-organization and collective bargaining, and harassed their unions, it did not forbid employer conduct calculated to destroy unions or render them impotent. Given this freedom, employers engaged in activities which eventually were outlawed in the Wagner Act. As the La Follette Committee revealed, employers accomplished that objective by the use of industrial spies, harassed union officers, broke strikes, sponsored company-dominated unions, discharged workers for union activities, and refused to recognize unions or bargain collectively. The judiciary repeatedly used the injunction to outlaw union conduct which interfered with the right of employers to engage in business. Such union activities, the Court said, caused irreparable damage to employer property rights. The property concept included not only protection against physical violence, but the right to conduct business in a profitable manner. Judges refused to issue the injunction to forbid blatant antiunion employer conduct. They refused to recognize workers had a right to a decent standard of living by self-organization and collective bargaining. Workers' collective action did not constitute a property right to be protected against employer antiunion conduct.

Such was the state of labor relations law on the eve of the Great Depression. It is no wonder that the labor movement did not amount to much even before the advent of the depression. How could the nation's workers effectively organize and bargain collectively given the suppressive legal climate?

❦ ERA OF LEGAL ENCOURAGEMENT

The period 1929–1937 was characterized by sweeping changes in the attitude of the American people relative to the proper role of government in the area of economic activity. Stimulated by the effects of the Great Depression, the climate of opinion of the nation underwent great change. Many people came to believe that government had an important role to play if the national economy was to be restored to conditions of relatively full employment. Previously, only a small group held this view, the majority having faith in the operation of "natural" economic laws to maintain a healthy industrial environment. Indeed, prior to the Great Depression, the nation generally believed that "the government governs best that governs least." The depression changed this attitude, and great segments of the people welcomed government intervention in the economic sphere. The people saw in this approach the cure for many of the problems of the national economy. In short, the people became government-minded, supporting government efforts to restore the national economy to a state of prosperity.

This change in the climate of opinion had great implications for organized labor. If weak unions had not prevented a depression, there was reason to believe that a strong and widespread union movement might contribute to economic recovery. A strong and growing union movement depended on the action of government. It was necessary to establish a legal framework in which the collective bargaining process could function effectively. This produced the logic underlying the Norris–La Guardia and Wagner acts, the laws that set the tone of the labor policy of the New Deal. These laws were products of the Great Depression. They rested not only on the assumption that effective unionism would insure workers a greater measure of social justice, but on the idea that an effective and growing labor movement would promote economic stability. In short, a strong union movement would fit nicely into the scheme of New Deal economics; hence, the unqualified support of legislation calculated to protect the right of employees to self-organization and collective bargaining. To implement this public policy, the judiciary and employers' antiunion conduct had to be checked by law. Courts and employers had virtually made impossible a viable labor movement dedicated to improve the conditions of workers by effective collective bargaining.

Norris–La Guardia made the injunction unavailable to enforce the yellow-dog contract. No longer could judges restrain unions when they sought objectives and used methods which did not square with their social and economic philosophies. Unions could engage in activities free from the injunction. Thus, courts were neutralized in labor relations matters. Workers and their unions, however, did not obtain new rights under the law. Norris–La Guardia did not shift the power of the courts from the employer to the union side of the equation. Unions could not obtain injunctions to force employers to agree to their demands any more than injunctions could be issued to forbid unions to achieve their objectives.

Aside from eliminating judges from the labor relations arena, Norris–La Guardia established strict rules regulating courts when they still had the power to issue injunctions. Procedures customarily followed in the nonlabor cases are to be applied to labor relations disputes. No longer could courts issue temporary restraining orders without directing a prompt hearing to permit unions to tell their side of the story. Temporary injunctions would be issued only after the courts had the opportunity to review actual evidence and not to make determinations solely on the basis of lifeless and frequently contradictory and false affidavits. Unlike the pre-Norris–La Guardia period, injunctions must be written in specific terms establishing exactly who and what is to be enjoined.

Not only did the Norris–La Guardia Act free unions from the shackles of the injunction, but it relieved unions from prosecution under the antitrust statutes. By its decision in *Hutcheson*, the Supreme Court held unions did not fall under the statutes as long as they did not conspire with employers to restrain commerce. Unions would not be subject to antitrust prosecution when they sought objectives and/or engaged in action by themselves and on their own. Illegality would be found only when unions and employers jointly engaged in activities to suppress competition in interstate commerce.

Although unions were freed from the burdens of the injunction and antitrust prosecution by Norris–La Guardia, one would be dead wrong to believe they are free from all legal restraint. Taft-Hartley, passed by Congress in 1947, outlaws many union activities. As a matter of fact, under the new law, the courts have regained the power to issue injunctions against unions under certain circumstances. However, such restraint is a matter of statutory law, and not a product of the subjective social and economic predilections of the judiciary. Only to the extent that Norris–La Guardia is modified by Taft-Hartley have the courts regained the authority to issue injunctions in labor disputes. There is a vast difference in terms of public policy between an injunction issued pursuant to a law established by Congress and an injunction reflecting the socioeconomic beliefs of judges.

To make public policy a matter of reality, the Wagner Act outlawed employer antiunion conduct calculated to destroy or make unions impotent. Made illegal by the 1935 law are those antiunion practices disclosed by the La Follette Committee. Such conduct was made illegal, as it was not consistent with the public policy of encouraging unions and collective bargaining.

Section 7 of the Wagner Act established the right of employees to self-organization and to form, join, or assist labor organizations, and to bargain collectively through representatives of their own choosing. Although unions have been legal since 1842 (*Commonwealth* v. *Hunt*), the Wagner Act protects the right of workers to form unions and engage in collective bargaining. Under its provisions, no longer may employers interfere, coerce, or threaten workers in their unionization and collective bargaining rights. Company-dominated unions are illegal, and employers may not discharge or otherwise discriminate against employees who engage in union activities. When a majority of workers select a union to represent them in secret elections, employers are obligated to recognize the

CHAPTER NINE   211

organization and to bargain with it in good faith in the effort to negotiate a labor agreement.

To administer and enforce the Wagner Act, Congress established the National Labor Relations Board. Through its procedures and policies it effectively implemented the public policy of encouraging unionism and collective bargaining. The NLRB established the circumstances under which employers violate the law. To achieve the principle of industrial democracy, it conducts secret elections to determine whether workers desire to be represented by unions. Workers have the exclusive right to accept or reject unionization and collective bargaining.

To be sure, based on its track record, it was not at all certain whether the Supreme Court would hold Norris–La Guardia and the Wagner Act constitutional. Previously it had held such legislation as not compatible with the U.S. Constitution. Given the economic and political realities of the times, including Roosevelt's unprecedented victory in 1936, and his threat to pack the high court, the Supreme Court held both laws met the test of constitutionality.

With those decisions in force, the legal climate, formerly suppressive, became favorable to the growth of unionism and collective bargaining. Union membership soared, and a wave of collective bargaining contracts was negotiated. Labor relations were stabilized, and from that point of view, the nation was prepared to meet successfully the challenge to its existence in World War II.

APPENDIX A

THE NORRIS—LA GUARDIA ACT

Act of March 23, 1932, 47 Stat. 70

AN ACT

To amend the Judicial Code and to define and limit the jurisdiction of courts sitting in equity, and for other purposes.

JURISDICTION OF FEDERAL COURTS IN LABOR DISPUTES. SEC. 1. *Be it enacted by the Senate and House of Representatives of the United States of America in Congress assembled,* That no court of the United States, as herein defined, shall have jurisdiction to issue any restraining order or temporary or permanent injunction in a case involving or growing out of a labor dispute, except in a strict conformity with the provisions of this Act; nor shall any such restraining order or temporary or permanent injunction be issued contrary to the public policy declared in this Act.

DECLARATION OF PUBLIC POLICY IN LABOR CONTROVERSIES. SEC. 2. In the interpretation of this Act and in determining the jurisdiction and authority of the courts of the United States, as such jurisdiction and authority are herein defined and limited, the public policy of the United States is hereby declared as follows:

Whereas under prevailing economic conditions, developed with the aid of governmental authority for owners of property to organize in the corporate and other forms of ownership association, the individual unorganized worker is commonly helpless to exercise actual liberty of contract and to protect his freedom of labor, and thereby to obtain acceptable terms and conditions of employment, wherefore, though he should be free to decline to associate with his fellows, it is necessary that he have full freedom of association, self-organization, and designation of representatives of his own choosing, to negotiate the terms and conditions of his employment, and that he shall be free from the interference, restraint, or coercion of employers of labor, or their agents, in the designation of such representatives or in self-organization or in other concerted activities for the purpose of collective bargaining or other mutual aid or protection; therefore, the following definitions of, and limitations upon, the jurisdiction and authority of the courts of the United States are hereby enacted.

NONENFORCEABILITY OF UNDERTAKINGS IN CONFLICT WITH DECLARED POLICY—"YELLOW DOG" CONTRACTS. SEC. 3. Any undertaking or promise, such as is described in this section, or any other undertaking or promise in conflict with the public policy declared in section 2 of this Act, is hereby declared to be contrary to the public policy of the United States, shall not be enforceable in any court of the United States and shall not afford any basis for the granting of legal or equitable relief by any such court, including specifically the following:

Every undertaking or promise hereafter made, whether written or oral, express or implied, constituting or contained in any contract or agreement of hiring or employment between any individual, firm, company, association, or corporation, and any employee or prospective employee of the same, whereby

(a) Either party to such contract or agreement undertakes or promises that he will withdraw from an employment relation in the event that he joins, becomes, or remains a member of any labor organization or of any employer organization.

DENIAL OF INJUNCTIVE RELIEF IN CERTAIN CASES. SEC. 4. No court of the United States shall have jurisdiction to issue any restraining order or temporary or permanent injunction in any case involving or growing out of any labor dispute to prohibit any person or persons participating or interested in such dispute (as these terms are herein defined) from doing, whether singly or in concert any of the following acts:

(a) Ceasing or refusing to perform any work or to remain in any relation of employment;

(b) Becoming or remaining a member of any labor organization or of any employer organization, regardless of any such undertaking or promise as is described in section 3 of this act;

(c) Paying or giving to, or withholding from, any person participating or interested in such labor dispute, any strike for unemployment benefits or insurance, or other moneys or things of value;

(d) By all lawful means aiding any person participating or interested in any labor dispute who is being proceeded against in, or is prosecuting, any action or suit in any court of the United States or of any State;

(e) Giving publicity to the existence of, or the facts involved in, any labor dispute, whether by advertising, speaking, patrolling, or by any other method not involving fraud or violence;

(f) Assembling peaceably to act or organize to act in promotion of their interests in a labor dispute;

(g) Advising or notifying any person of an intention to do any of the acts heretofore specified;

(h) Agreeing with other persons to do or not to do any of the acts heretofore specified; and

(i) Advising, urging, or otherwise causing or inducing without fraud or violence the acts heretofore specified, regardless of any such undertaking or promise as is described in section 3 of this act.

DENIAL OF INJUNCTIVE RELIEF FROM CONCERTED ACTIONS. SEC. 5. No court of the United States shall have jurisdiction to issue a restraining order or temporary or permanent injunction upon the grounds that any of the persons participating or interested in a labor dispute constitute or are engaged in an unlawful combination or conspiracy because of the doing in concert of the acts enumerated in section 4 of this act.

RESPONSIBILITY FOR ACTS. SEC. 6. No officer or member of any association or organization, and no association or organization participating or interested in a labor dispute, shall be held responsible or liable in any court of the United States for the unlawful acts of individual officers, members, or agents, except upon clear proof of actual participating in, or actual authorization of, such acts, or of ratification of such acts after actual knowledge thereof.

ISSUE OF INJUNCTIONS—WHEN PERMISSIBLE. SEC. 7. No court of the United States shall have jurisdiction to issue a temporary or permanent injunction in any case involving or growing out of a labor dispute, as herein defined, except after hearing the testimony of witnesses in open court (with opportunity for cross-examination) in support of the allegations of a complaint made under oath, and testimony in opposition thereto, if offered, and except after findings of fact by the court, to the effect—

(a) That unlawful acts have been threatened or will be committed unless restrained or have been committed and will be continued unless restrained, but no injunction or temporary restraining order shall be issued on account of any threat or unlawful act excepting against the person or persons, association, or organization making the threat or committing the unlawful act or actually authorizing or ratifying the same after actual knowledge thereof:

(b) That substantial and irreparable injury to complainant's property will follow;

(c) That as to each item of relief granted greater injury will be inflicted upon complainant by the denial of relief than will be inflicted upon defendants by the granting of relief;

(d) That complainant has no adequate remedy at law; and

(e) That the public officers charged with the duty to protect complainant's property are unable or unwilling to furnish adequate protection.

Such hearing shall be held after due and personal notice thereof has been given, in such manner as the court shall direct, to all known persons against whom relief is sought, and also to the chief of those public officials of the county and city within which the unlawful acts have been threatened or committed charged with the duty to protect complainant's property: *Provided, however,* That if a complainant shall also allege that, unless a temporary restraining order shall be issued without notice, a substantial and irreparable injury to complainant's property will be unavoidable, such a temporary restraining order may be issued upon testimony under oath, sufficient, if sustained, to justify the court in issuing a temporary injunction upon a hearing after notice. Such a temporary restraining order shall be effective for no longer than five days and shall become void at the expiration of said five days. No temporary restraining order or temporary injunction shall be issued except on condition that complainant shall first file an undertaking with adequate security in an amount to be fixed by the court sufficient to recompense those enjoined for any loss, expense, or damage caused by the improvident or erroneous issuance of such order or injunction, including all reasonable costs (together with a reasonable attorney's fee) and expense of defense against the order or against the granting of any injunctive relief sought in the same proceeding and subsequently denied by the court.

The undertaking herein mentioned shall be understood to signify an agreement entered into by the complainant and the surety upon which a decree may be rendered in the same suit or proceeding against said complainant and surety, upon a hearing to assess damages of which hearing complainant and surety shall have reasonable notice, the said complainant and surety submitting themselves to the jurisdiction of the court for that purpose. But nothing herein contained shall deprive any party having a claim or cause of action under or upon such undertaking from electing to pursue his ordinary remedy by suit at law or in equity.

EFFORT TO SETTLE DISPUTES. SEC. 8. No restraining order or injunctive relief shall be granted to any complainant who has failed to comply with any obligation imposed by law which is involved in the labor dispute in question, or who has failed to make every reasonable effort to settle such dispute either by negotiation or with the aid of any available governmental machinery of mediation or voluntary arbitration.

ISSUANCE OF INJUNCTIONS BASED ON FINDINGS OF FACT. SEC. 9. No restraining order or temporary or permanent injunction shall be granted in a case involving or growing out of a labor dispute, except on the basis of findings of fact made and filed by the court in the record of the case prior to the issuance of such restraining order or injunction; and every restraining order or injunction granted in a case involving or growing out of a labor dispute shall include only a prohibition of such specific act or acts as may be expressly complained of in the bill of complaint or petition filed in such case and as shall be expressly included in said findings of fact made and filed by the court as provided herein.

APPEALS—SECURITY FOR COSTS. SEC. 10. Whenever any court of the United States shall issue or deny any temporary injunction in a case involving or growing out of a labor dispute, the court shall, upon the request of any party to the proceedings and on his filing the usual bond for costs, forthwith certify as in ordinary cases the record of the case to the circuit court of appeals for its review. Upon the filing of such record in the circuit court of appeals, the appeal shall be heard and the temporary injunctive order affirmed, modified, or set aside with the greatest possible expedition, giving the proceedings precedence over all other matters except older matters of the same character.

JURY TRIAL IN CASES OF INDIRECT CONTEMPT. SEC. 11. In all cases arising under this act in which a person shall be charged with contempt in a court of the United States (as herein defined), the accused shall enjoy the right of a speedy and public trial by an impartial jury of the State and district wherein the contempt shall have been committed: *Provided,* That this right shall not apply to contempts committed in the presence of the court or so near thereto as to interfere directly with the administration of justice or to apply to the misbehavior, misconduct, or disobedience of any officer of the court in respect to the writs, orders, or process of the court.

REMOVAL OF JUDGE IN INDIRECT CONTEMPT CASES. SEC. 12. The defendant in any proceeding for contempt of court may file with the court a demand for the retirement of the judge sitting in the proceeding, if the contempt arises from an attack upon the character or conduct of such judge and if the attack occurred elsewhere than in the presence of the court or so near thereto as to interfere directly with the administration of justice. Upon the filing of any such demand the judge shall thereupon proceed no further, but another judge shall be designated in the same manner as is provided by law. The demand shall be filed prior to the hearing in the contempt proceeding.

DEFINITIONS. SEC. 13. When used in this act, and for the purposes of this act—

(a) A case shall be held to involve or to grow out of a labor dispute when the case involves persons who are engaged in the same industry, trade, craft, or occupation; or have direct or indirect interests therein; or who are employees of the same employer; or who are members of the same or an affiliated organization of employers or employees; whether such dispute is (1) between one or more employers or associations of employers and one or more employees or associations of employees; (2) between one or more employers or associations and one or more employers or associations of employers or; (3) between one or more employees or associations of employees and one or more employees or associations of employees; or, when the case involves any conflicting or competing interests in a "labor dispute" (as hereinafter defined) of "persons anticipating or interested" therein (as hereinafter defined).

(b) A person or association shall be held to be a person participating or interested in a labor dispute if relief is sought against him or it, and if he or it is engaged in the same industry, trade, craft, or occupation in which such dispute occurs, or has a direct or indirect interest therein, or is a member, officer, or agent of any association composed in whole or in part of employers or employees engaged in such industry, trade, craft, or occupation.

(c) The term "labor dispute" includes any controversy concerning terms or conditions of employment, or concerning the association or representation of persons negotiating, fixing, maintaining, changing, or seeking to arrange terms or conditions of employment, regardless of whether or not the disputants stand in the proximate relation of employer and employee.

(d) The term "court of the United States" means any court of the United States whose jurisdiction has been or may be conferred or defined or limited by Act of Congress, including the courts of the District of Columbia.

SEPARABILITY PROVISION. SEC. 14. If any provision of this Act or the application thereof to any person or circumstance is held unconstitutional or otherwise invalid, the remaining provisions of the Act and the application of such provisions to other persons or circumstances shall not be affected thereby.

REPEAL OF CONFLICTING ACTS. SEC. 15. All Acts and parts of Acts in conflict with the provision of this Act are hereby repealed.

Appendix B

THE WAGNER ACT

Act of July 5, 1935, 49 Stat. 449

AN ACT

To diminish the causes of labor disputes burdening or obstructing interstate and foreign commerce, to create a National Labor Relations Board, and for other purposes.

Be it enacted by the Senate and House of Representatives of the United States of America in Congress assembled.

FINDINGS AND POLICY. SEC. 1. The denial by employers of the right of employees to organize and the refusal by employers to accept the procedure of collective bargaining lead to strikes and other forms of industrial strife or unrest, which have the intent or the necessary effect of burdening or obstructing commerce by (a) impairing the efficiency, safety, or operation of the instrumentalities of commerce; (b) occurring in the current of commerce; (c) materially affecting, restraining, or controlling the flow of raw materials or manufactured or processed goods from or into the channels of commerce, or the prices of such materials or goods in commerce; or (d) causing diminution of employment and wages in such volume as substantially to impair or disrupt the market for goods flowing from or into the channels of commerce.

The inequality of bargaining power between employees who do not possess full freedom of association or actual liberty of contract, and employers who are organized in the corporate or other forms of ownership association substantially burdens and affects the flow of commerce, and tends to aggravate recurrent business depressions, by depressing wage rates and the purchasing power of wage earners in industry and by preventing the stabilization of competitive wage rates and working conditions within and between industries.

Experience has proved that protection by law of the right of employees to organize and bargain collectively safeguards commerce from injury, impairment, or interruption, and promotes the flow of commerce by removing certain recognized sources of industrial strife and unrest, by encouraging practices fundamental to the friendly adjustment of industrial disputes arising out of differences as to wages, hours, or other working conditions, and by restoring equality of bargaining power between employers and employees.

It is hereby declared to be the policy of the United States to eliminate the causes of certain substantial obstructions to the free flow of commerce and to mitigate and eliminate these obstructions when they have occurred by encouraging the practice and procedure of collective bargaining and by protecting the exercise by workers of full freedom of association, self-organization, and designation of representatives of their own choosing, for the purpose of negotiating the terms and conditions of their employment or other mutual aid or protection.

DEFINITIONS. SEC. 2. When used in this Act—

(1) The term "person" includes one or more individuals, partnerships, associations, corporations, legal representatives, trustees, trustees in bankruptcy, or receivers.

(2) The term "employer" includes any person acting in the interest of an employer, directly or indirectly, but shall not include the United States, or any State or political subdivision thereof, or any person subject to the Railway Labor Act, as amended from time to time, or any labor organization (other than when acting as an employer), or anyone acting in the capacity of officer or agent of such labor organization.

(3) The term "employee" shall include any employee, and shall not be limited to the employees of a particular employer, unless the Act explicitly states otherwise, and shall include any individual whose work has ceased as a consequence of, or in connection with any current labor dispute or because of any unfair labor practice, and who has not obtained any other regular and substantially equivalent employment, but shall not include any individual employed as an agricultural laborer, or in the domestic service of any family or person at his home or any individual employed by his parent or spouse.

(4) The term "representatives" includes any individual or labor organization.

(5) The term "labor organization" means any organization of any kind, or any agency or employee representation committee or plan, in which employees participate and which exists for the purpose, in

whole or in part, of dealing with employers concerning grievances, labor disputes, wages, rates of pay, hours of employment, or conditions of work.

(6) The term "commerce" means trade, traffic, commerce, transportation, or communication among the several States, or between the District of Columbia or any Territory of the United States and any State or other Territory, or between any foreign country and any State, Territory, or the District of Columbia, or within the District of Columbia or any Territory, or between points in the same State but through any other State or any Territory or the District of Columbia or any foreign country.

(7) The term "affecting commerce" means in commerce, or burdening or obstructing commerce or the free flow of commerce, or having led or tending to lead to a labor dispute burdening or obstructing commerce or the free flow of commerce.

(8) The term "unfair labor practice" means unfair labor practice listed in section 8.

(9) The term "labor dispute" includes any controversy concerning terms, tenure, or conditions of employment, or concerning the association or representation of persons in negotiating, fixing, maintaining, changing, or seeking to arrange terms or conditions of empolyment, regardless of whether the disputants stand in the proximate relation of employer and employee.

(10) The term "National Labor Relations Board" means the National Labor Relations Board, created by section 3 of this Act.

(11) The term "old Board" means the National Labor Relations Board established by Executive Order Numbered 6763 of the President on June 29, 1934, pursuant to Public Resolution Numbered 44, approved June 19, 1934 (48 Stat. 1183), and re-established and continued by Executive Order Numbered 7074 of the President of June 15, 1935, pursuant to Title I of the National Industrial Recovery Act (48 Stat. 195) as amended and continued by Senate Joint Resolution 133 approved June 14, 1935.

🌿 *NATIONAL LABOR RELATIONS BOARD*

SEC. 3. (a) There is hereby created a board, to be known as the "National Labor Relations Board" (hereinafter referred to as the "Board"), which shall be composed of three members, who shall be appointed by the President, by and with the advice and consent of the Senate. One of the original members shall be appointed for a term of one year, one for a term of three years, and one for a term of five years, but their successors shall be appointed for terms of five years each, except that any individual chosen to fill a vacancy shall be appointed only for the unexpired term of the member whom he shall succeed. The President shall designate one member to serve as the chairman of the Board. Any member of the Board may be removed by the President, upon notice and hearing, for neglect of duty or malfeasance in office, but for no other cause.

(b) A vacancy in the Board shall not impair the right of the remaining members to exercise all the powers of the Board, and two members of the Board shall, at all times, constitute a quorum. The Board shall have an official seal which shall be judicially noticed.

(c) The Board shall at the close of each fiscal year make a report in writing to Congress and to the President stating in detail the cases it has heard, the decisions it has rendered, the names, salaries, and duties of all employees and officers in the employ or under the supervision of the Board, and an account of all moneys it has disbursed.

SEC. 4. (a) Each member of the Board shall receive a salary of $10,000 a year, shall be eligible for reappointment, and shall not engage in any other business, vocation, or employment. The Board shall appoint, without regard for the provisions of the civil-service laws but subject to the Classification Act of 1923, as amended, an executive secretary, and such attorneys, examiners, and regional directors, and shall appoint such other employees with regard to existing laws applicable to the employment and compensation of officers and employees of the United States, as it may from time to time find necessary for the proper performance of its duties and as may be from time to time appropriated for by Congress. The Board may establish or utilize such regional, local, or other agencies, and utilize such voluntary and uncompensated services, as may from time to time be needed. Attorneys appointed under this section may, at the direction of the Board, appear for and represent the Board in any case in court. Nothing in this Act shall be construed to authorize the Board to appoint individuals for the purpose of conciliation or mediation (or for statistical work), where such service may be obtained from the Department of Labor.

(b) Upon the appointment of the three original members of the Board and the designation of its chairman, the old Board shall cease to exist. All employees of the old Board shall be transferred to and become employees of the Board with salaries under the Classification Act of 1923, as amended, without acquiring by such transfer a permanent or civil-service status. All records, papers, and property of the old Board shall become records, papers, and property of the Board, and all unexpended funds and appropriations for the use and maintenance of the old Board shall become funds and appropriations available to be expended by the Board in the exercise of the powers, authority, and duties conferred on it by this Act.

(c) All of the expenses of the Board, including all necessary traveling and subsistence expenses outside the District of Columbia incurred by the members or employees of the Board under its orders, shall be allowed and paid on the presentation of itemized vouchers therefor approved by the Board or by any individual it designates for that purpose.

SEC. 5. The principal office of the Board shall be in the District of Columbia, but it may meet and exercise any or all of its powers at any other place. The Board may, by one or more of its members or by such agents or agencies as it may designate, prosecute any inquiry necessary to its functions in any part of the United States. A member who participates in such an inquiry shall not be disqualified from subsequently participating in a decision of the Board in the same case.

SEC. 6. (a) The Board shall have authority from time to time to make, amend, and rescind such rules and regulations as may be necessary to carry out the provisions of this Act. Such rules and regulations shall be effective upon publication in the manner which the Board shall prescribe.

❦ RIGHTS OF EMPLOYEES

SEC. 7. Employees shall have the right to self-organization, to form, join, or assist labor organizations, to bargain collectively through representatives of their own choosing, and to engage in concerted activities, for the purpose of collective bargaining or other mutual aid or protection.

SEC. 8. It shall be an unfair labor practice for an employer—

(1) To interfere with, restrain, or coerce employees in the exercise of the rights guaranteed in section 7.

(2) To dominate or interfere with the formation or administration of any labor organization or contribute financial or other support to it: *Provided*, That subject to rules and regulations made and published by the Board pursuant to section 6(a), an employer shall not be prohibited from permitting employees to confer with him during working hours without loss of time or pay.

(3) By discrimination in regard to hire or tenure of employment or any term or condition of employment to encourage or discourage membership in any labor organization: *Provided*, That nothing in this Act, or in the National Industrial Recovery Act (U.S.C., Supp. VII, title 15, secs. 701–712), as amended from time to time, or in any code or agreement approved or prescribed thereunder, or in any other statute of the United States, shall preclude an employer from making an agreement with a labor organization (not established, maintained, or assisted by any action defined in this Act as an unfair labor practice) to require, as a condition of employment, membership therein, if such labor organization is the representative of the employees as provided in section 9 (a), in the appropriate collective bargaining unit covered by such agreement when made.

(4) To discharge or otherwise discriminate against an employee because he has filed charges or given testimony under this Act.

(5) To refuse to bargain collectively with the representatives of his employees, subject to the provisions of section 9 (a).

REPRESENTATIVES AND ELECTIONS. SEC. 9. (a) Representatives designated or selected for the purposes of collective bargaining by the majority of the employees in a unit appropriate for such purposes, shall be the exclusive representatives of all the employees in such unit for the purposes of collective bargaining in respect to rates of pay, wages, hours of employment, or other conditions of employment: *Provided*, That any individual employee or a group of employees shall have the right at any time to present grievances to their employer.

(b) The Board shall decide in each case whether, in order to insure to employees the full benefit of their right to self-organization and to collective bargaining, and otherwise to effectuate the policies of this Act, the unit appropriate for the purposes of collective bargaining shall be the employer unit, craft unit, plant unit, or subdivision thereof.

(c) Whenever a question affecting commerce arises concerning the representation of employees, the Board may investigate such controversy and certify to the parties, in writing, the name or names of the representatives that have been designated or selected. In any such investigation, the Board shall provide for an appropriate hearing upon due notice, either in conjunction with a proceeding under section 10 or otherwise, and may take a secret ballot of employees, or utilize any other suitable method to ascertain such representatives.

(d) Whenever an order of the Board made pursuant to section 10 (c) is based in whole or in part upon facts certified following an investigation pursuant to subsection (c) of this section, and there is a petition for the enforcement or review of such order, such certification and the record of such investigation shall be included in the transcript of the entire record required to be filed under subsections 10 (e) or 10 (f), and thereupon the decree of the court enforcing, modifying, or setting aside in whole or in part the order of the Board shall be made and entered upon the pleadings, testimony, and proceedings set forth in such transcript.

PREVENTION OF UNFAIR LABOR PRACTICES. SEC. 10. The Board is empowered, as hereinafter provided, to prevent any person from engaging in any unfair labor practice (listed in section 8) affecting commerce. This power shall be exclusive, and shall not be affected by any other means of adjustment or prevention that has been or may be established by agreement, code, law, or otherwise.

(b) Whenever it is charged that any person has engaged in or is engaging in any such unfair labor practice, the Board, or any agent or agency designated by the Board for such purposes, shall have power to issue and cause to be served upon such person a complaint stating the charges in that respect, and containing a notice of hearing before the Board or a member thereof, or before a designated agent or agency, at a place therein fixed, not less than five days after the serving of said complaint. Any such complaint may be amended by the member, agent, or agency conducting the hearing or the Board in its discretion at any time prior to the issuance of an order based thereon. The person so complained of shall have the right to file an answer to the original or amended complaint and to appear in person or otherwise and give testimony at the place and time fixed in the complaint. In the discretion of the member, agent, or agency conducting the hearing or the Board, any other person may be allowed to intervene in the said proceeding and to present testimony. In any such proceeding the rules of evidence prevailing in courts of law or equity shall not be controlling.

(c) The testimony taken by such member, agent, or agency or the Board shall be reduced to writing and filed with the Board. Thereafter, in its discretion, the Board upon notice may take further testimony or hear argument. If upon all the testimony taken the Board shall be of the opinion that any person named in the complaint has engaged in or is engaging in any such unfair labor practice, then the Board shall state its findings of fact and shall issue and cause to be served on such person an order requiring such person to cease and desist from such unfair labor practice, and to take such affirmative action, including reinstatement of employees with or without back pay, as will effectuate the policies of this Act. Such order may further require such person to make reports from time to time showing the extent to which it has complied with the order. If upon all the testimony taken the Board shall be of the opinion that no person named in the complaint has engaged in or is engaging in any such unfair labor practice, then the Board shall state its findings of fact and shall issue an order dismissing the said complaint.

(d) Until a transcript of the record in a case shall have been filed in a court, as hereinafter provided, the Board may at any time, upon reasonable notice and in such manner as it shall deem proper, modify or set aside, in whole or in part, any finding or order made or issued by it.

(e) The Board shall have power to petition any circuit court of appeals of the United States (including the Court of Appeals of the District of Columbia), or if all the circuit courts of appeals to which application may be made are on vacation, any district court of the United States (including the Supreme Court of the District of Columbia), within any circuit or district, respectively, wherein the unfair labor practice in question occurred or wherein such person resides or transacts business, for the enforcement of such order and for appropriate temporary relief or restraining order, and shall certify and file in the court a transcript of the entire record in the proceeding, including the pleadings and testimony upon which such order was entered and the findings and order of the Board. Upon such filing, the court shall cause notice thereof to be served upon such person, and thereupon shall have jurisdiction of the proceeding and of the question determined therein, and shall have power to grant such temporary relief or restraining order as it deems just and proper, and to make and enter upon the pleadings, testimony, and proceedings set forth in such transcript a decree enforcing, modifying, and enforcing as so modified, or setting aside in whole or in part the order of the Board. No objection that has not been urged before the Board, its member, agent, or agency, shall be considered by the court, unless the failure or neglect to urge such objection shall be excused because of extraordinary circumstances. The findings of the Board as to the facts, if supported by evidence, shall be conclusive. If either party shall apply to the court for leave to adduce additional evidence and shall show to the satisfaction of the court that such additional evidence is material and that there were reasonable grounds for the failure to adduce such evidence in the hearing before the Board, its member, agent, or agency, the court may order such additional evidence to be taken before the Board, its member, agent, or agency, and to be made a part of the transcript. The Board may modify its findings as to the facts, or make new findings, by reason of additional evidence so taken and filed, and it shall file such modified or new findings, which, if supported by evidence shall be conclusive, and shall file its recommendations, if any, for the modification or setting aside of its original order. The jurisdiction of the court shall be exclusive and its judgment and decree shall be final, except that the same shall be subject to review by the appropriate circuit court of appeals if application was made to the district court as hereinabove provided, and by the Supreme Court of the United States and upon writ of certiorari or certification as provided in sections 239 and 240 of the Judicial Code, as amended (U.S.C., title 28, secs. 346 and 347).

(f) Any person aggrieved by a final order of the Board granting or denying in whole or in part the relief sought may obtain a review of such order in any circuit court of appeals of the United States in the circuit wherein the unfair labor practice in question was alleged to have been engaged in or wherein such person resides or transacts business, or in the Court of Appeals of the District of Columbia, by filing in such a court a written petition praying that the order of the Board be modified or set aside. A copy of such petition shall be forthwith served upon the Board, and thereupon the aggrieved party shall file in the court a transcript of the entire record in the proceeding, certified by the Board, including the pleading and testimony upon which the order complained of was entered and the findings and order of the Board. Upon such filing, the court shall proceed in the same manner as in the case of an application by the

Board under subsection (e), and shall have the same exclusive jurisdiction to grant to the Board such temporary relief or restraining order as it deems just and proper, and in like manner to make and enter a decree enforcing, modifying, and enforcing as so modified, or setting aside in whole or in part the order of the Board; and the findings of the Board as to the facts, if supported by evidence, shall in like manner be conclusive.

(g) The commencement of proceedings under subsection (e) or (f) of this section shall not, unless specifically ordered by the court, operate as a stay of the Board's order.

(h) When granting appropriate temporary relief or a restraining order, or making and entering a decree enforcing, modifying, and enforcing as so modified or setting aside in whole or in part an order of the Board, as provided in this section, the jurisdiction of courts sitting in equity, shall not be limited by the Act entitled "An Act to amend the Judicial Code and to define and limit the jurisdiction of courts sitting in equity, and for other purposes," approved March 23, 1932 (U.S.C., Supp. VII, title 29, secs. 101–115).

(i) Petitions filed under this act shall be heard expeditiously, and if possible within ten days after they have been docketed.

❦ INVESTIGATORY POWERS

SEC. 11. For the purpose of all hearings and investigations, which, in the opinion of the Board, are necessary and proper for the exercise of the powers vested in it by section 9 and section 10—

(1) The Board, or its duly authorized agents or agencies, shall at all reasonable times have access to, for the purpose of examination, and the right to copy any evidence of any person being investigated or proceeded against that relates to any matter under investigation or in question. Any member of the Board shall have power to issue subpenas requiring the attendance and testimony of witnesses and the production of any evidence that relates to any matter under investigation or in question, before the Board, its member, agent, or agency conducting the hearing or investigation. Any member of the Board, or any agent or agency designated by the Board for such purposes, may administer oaths and affirmations, examine witnesses, and receive evidence. Such attendance of witnesses and the production of such evidence may be required from any place in the United States or any Territory or possession thereof, at any designated place of hearing.

(2) In case of contumacy or refusal to obey a subpena issued to any person, any District Court of the United States or the United States courts of any Territory or possession, or the Supreme Court of the District of Columbia, within the jurisdiction of which the inquiry is carried on or within the jurisdiction of which said person guilty of contumacy or refusal to obey is found or resides or transacts business,

upon application by the Board shall have jurisdiction to issue to such person an order requiring such person to appear before the Board, its member, agent, or agency, there to produce evidence if so ordered, or there to give testimony touching the matter under investigation or in question; and any failure to obey such order of the court may be punished by said court as a contempt thereof.

(3) No person shall be excused from attending and testifying or from producing books, records, correspondence, documents, or other evidence in obedience to the subpena of the Board, on the ground that the testimony or evidence required of him may tend to incriminate him or subject him to a penalty or forfeiture; but no individual shall be prosecuted or subjected to any penalty or forfeiture for or on account of any transaction, matter, or thing concerning which he is compelled, after having claimed his privilege against self-incrimination, to testify or produce evidence, except that such individual so testifying shall not be exempt from prosecution and punishment for perjury committed in so testifying.

(4) Complaints, orders, and other process and papers of the Board, its member, agent, or agency, may be served either personally or by registered mail or by telegraph or by leaving a copy thereof at the principal office or place of business of the person required to be served. The verified return by the individual so serving the same setting forth the manner of such service shall be proof of the same, and the return post office receipt or telegraph receipt therefor when registered and mailed or telegraphed as aforesaid shall be proof of service of the same. Witnesses summoned before the Board, its member, agent, or agency, shall be paid the same fees and mileage that are paid witnesses in the courts of the United States, and witnesses whose depositions are taken and the persons taking the same shall severally be entitled to the same fees as are paid for like services in the courts of the United States.

(5) All process of any court to which application may be made under this Act may be served in the judicial district wherein the defendant or other person required to be served resides or may be found.

(6) The several departments and agencies of the Government, when directed by the President, shall furnish the Board, upon its request, all records, papers, and information in their possession relating to any matter before the Board.

SEC. 12. Any person who shall willfully resist, prevent, impede, or interfere with any member of the Board or any of its agents or agencies in the performance of duties pursuant to this act shall be punished by a fine of not more than $5,000 or by imprisonment for not more than one year, or both.

❦ LIMITATIONS

SEC. 13. Nothing in this Act shall be construed so as to interfere with or impede or diminish in any way the right to strike.

SEC. 14. Wherever the application of the provisions of section 7(a) of the National Industrial Recovery Act [U.S.C., Supp. VII, title 15, sec. 707 (a)], as amended from time to time, or of section 77B, paragraphs (l) and (m) of the Act approved June 7, 1934, entitled "An Act to amend an Act entitled 'An Act to establish a uniform system of bankruptcy throughout the United States' approved July 1, 1898, and Acts amendatory thereof and supplementary thereto" 48 Stat. 922, pars. (l) and (m), as amended from time to time, or of Public Resolution Numbered 44, approved June 19, 1934 (48 Stat. 1183), conflicts with the application of the provisions of this Act, this Act shall prevail: *Provided*, That in any situation where the provisions of this Act cannot be validly enforced, the provisions of such other Acts shall remain in full force and effect.

SEC. 15. If any provision of this Act, or the application of such provision to any person or circumstance, shall be held invalid, the remainder of this Act, or the application of such provision to persons or circumstances other than those as to which it is held invalid, shall not be affected thereby.

SEC. 16. This Act may be cited as the "National Labor Relations Act."

Approved, July 5, 1935.

BIBLIOGRAPHY

BOOKS

BARNES, JAMES A., *Wealth of the American People.* Englewood Cliffs, N.J.: Prentice-Hall, Inc., 1949.

BENT, SILAS, *Justice Oliver Wendell Holmes.* New York: Vanguard Press, 1932.

BERMAN, EDWARD, *Labor and the Sherman Act.* New York: Harper & Bros., 1930.

BOWMAN, D. O., *Public Control of Labor Relations.* New York: The Macmillan Company, 1942.

BROOKS, R. R. R., *Unions of Their Own Choosing.* New Haven: Yale University Press, 1937.

BROOKS, R. R. R., *When Labor Organizes.* New Haven: Yale University Press, 1937.

CHRISTENSON, CARROLL L., AND RICHARD A. MYREN, *Wage Policy Under the Walsh-Healey Public Contracts Act: A Critical Review.* Bloomington, IN: Indiana University Press, 1966.

COCHRAN, THOMAS C., AND WILLIAM MILLER, *The Age of Enterprise.* New York: The Macmillan Company, 1943.

COMMONS, JOHN R., AND ASSOCIATES, *History of Labour in the United States.* New York: The Macmillan Company, 1926.

COMMONS, JOHN R., AND EUGENE A. GILMORE, *A Documentary History of American Industrial Society.* Cleveland: The Arthur H. Clark Company, 1910.

FRANKFURTER, FELIX, AND NATHAN GREENE, *The Labor Injunction.* New York: The Macmillan Company, 1930.

FREY, J. P., *The Labor Injunction.* Cincinnati: Equity Publishing Company, 1927.

GREGORY, CHARLES O., *Labor and the Law*. New York: W. W. Norton & Company, 1946.
HANDLER, MILTON, *Cases and Materials on Trade Regulations*. Chicago: The Foundation Press, 1937.
HOWARD, SIDNEY, AND ROBERT DUNN, *The Labor Spy*. New York: The Republic Publishing Company, 1921.
Interchurch World Movement's Study of the Steel Strike of 1919. Published 1919.
LANDIS, JAMES M., AND MARCUS MANOFF, *Cases on Labor Law*. Chicago: The Foundation Press, 1942.
LEVINSON, EDWARD, *I Break Strikes: The Technique of Pearl L. Bergoff*. New York: R. M. McBrike and Company, 1935.
LORWIN, LEWIS L., AND ARTHUR WUBNIG, *Labor Relations Boards*. Washington, D.C.: Brookings Institution, 1935.
MASON, A. T., *Brandeis: A Free Man's Life*. New York: The Viking Press, 1946.
MASON, A. T., *Organized Labor and the Law*. Durham, N.C.: Duke University Press, 1925.
MILLER, GLENN W., *American Labor and the Government*. Englewood Cliffs, N.J.: Prentice-Hall, Inc., 1948.
MILLIS, HARRY A., AND ROYAL E. MONTGOMERY, *Organized Labor*. New York: McGraw-Hill Book Company, 1945.
NATIONAL PLANNING ASSOCIATION, CAUSES OF INDUSTRIAL PEACE UNDER COLLECTIVE BARGAINING. Washington, D.C.: 1948–1950.
PALMER, FRANK, *Spies in Steel: An Exposé of Industrial Warfare*. Denver, CO: The Labor Press, 1928.
PERLMAN, SELIG, *A History of Trade Unionism in the United States*. New York: The Macmillan Company, 1929.
PETERSON, FLORENCE, *American Labor Unions*. New York: Harper & Bros., 1935.
POWDERLY, T. V., *The Path I Trod*. New York: Columbia University Press, 1940.
Public Papers and Addresses of Franklin D. Roosevelt 1938–1950. New York: Random House, (1938–1950).
SCOTT, JOHN, AND EDWIN S. ROCKEFELLER, *Antitrust and Trade Regulation Today*. Washington, D.C.: The Bureau of National Affairs, Inc., 1967.
SEIDMAN, JOEL, *The Yellow-Dog Contract*. Baltimore: Johns Hopkins Press, 1932.
SLESINGER, REUBEN E., *National Economic Policy: The Presidential Reports*. Princeton, N.J.: D. Van Nostrand Company, Inc., 1968.
TAYLOR, BENJAMIN J., *Arizona Labor Relations Law*. Occasional Paper No. 2. Tempe: Arizona State University, Bureau of Business and Economic Research, College of Business Administration, 1967.
TAYLOR, BENJAMIN J., *The Operation of the Taft-Hartley Act in Indiana*. Indiana Business Bulletin No. 58, Bloomington, IN: Bureau of Business Research, 1967.
TWENTIETH CENTURY FUND, INC., *Labor and Government*. New York: McGraw-Hill Book Company, 1935.
WITNEY, FRED, *Wartime Experiences of the National Labor Relations Board*. Urbana, IL: University of Illinois Press, 1949.

WITTE, EDWIN E., *The Government in Labor Disputes*. New York: McGraw-Hill Book Company, 1932.
WRIGHT, CHESTER W., *Economic History of the United States*. New York: McGraw-Hill Book Company, 1949.

❦ ARTICLES

BRISSENDEN, P. F., AND C. O. SWAYZEE, "The Use of Injunctions in the New York Needle Trades," *Political Science Quarterly*, v. 44, 1929.
JONES, DALLAS L., "The Enigma of the Clayton Act," *Industrial and Labor Relations Review*, v. 10, No. 2, January 1957.
MCNATT, E. B., "Labor Again Menaced by the Sherman Act," *The Southern Economic Journal*, v. 6, No. 2, October 1939.
WATKINS, MYRON W., "Trusts," *Encyclopedia of Social Sciences*, v. 15, 1930.
WITTE, E. E., "Early American Labor Cases," *Yale Law Journal*, v. 35, 1926.

❦ GOVERNMENT DOCUMENTS AND PUBLICATIONS

BUREAU OF LABOR STATISTICS, *Characteristics of Company Unions*, Bulletin No. 634. Washington, D.C.: Government Printing Office, 1938.
LA FOLLETTE COMMITTEE, *Hearings*, 1936.
LA FOLLETTE COMMITTEE, *Private Police Systems*, Report No. 6, Part II.
LA FOLLETTE COMMITTEE, *Report on Industrial Espionage*, Report No. 46, Part III.
LA FOLLETTE COMMITTEE, *Strikebreaking Services*, Report No. 6.
LA FOLLETTE COMMITTEE, *The Chicago Memorial Day Incident*, Report No. 46, Part II.
LA FOLLETTE COMMITTEE, *Violations of Free Speech and Rights of Labor*, Report.
NATIONAL LABOR RELATIONS BOARD, *Annual Reports* (various). Washington, D.C.: Government Printing Office.
NATIONAL LABOR RELATIONS BOARD, *Decisions and Orders of the National Labor Relations Board*, v. VII. Washington, D.C.: Government Printing Office, 1936.
NATIONAL LABOR RELATIONS BOARD, *Rules and Regulations and Statements of Procedure*. Washington, D.C.: Government Printing Office, 1965.
NATIONAL LABOR RELATIONS BOARD, *The Story of the NLRB 1935–1985*. Washington, D.C.: Government Printing Office, 1985.
NATIONAL WAR LABOR BOARD, *Report, April 1918 to May 1919*.
Report of the Industrial Commission on Labor Legislation. Washington, D.C.: Government Printing Office, 1900.
Report of the U.S. Commission on Industrial Relations. 11 vols. Washington, D.C.: Government Printing Office, 1916.
U.S. CONGRESS, *Hearings on a National Labor Relations Board*, 74th Cong., 1st sess., 1935.

U.S. DEPARTMENT OF LABOR, *Growth of Labor Law in the United States*. Washington, D.C.: Government Printing Office, 1967.

U.S. DEPARTMENT OF LABOR, *Monthly Labor Review* (various).

❦ NEWSPAPERS

AFL-CIO News
New York Times

INDEX

Adair decision, 142, 143, 144, 150-51, 171
Administrative law judge, 191-92
Affidavits, 27
AFL-CIO, 8
Agent provocateur, industrial spy as, 121-22
Allen-Bradley, impact of, 106-8, 113
Altgeld, John Peter, 137
Amalgamated Association of Iron, Steel and Tin Workers, 156, 158
American Federationist (AFL), 43
American Federation of Labor (AFL), 40, 41, 137, 200
   Gompers decision and, 43-44
   involvement in politics, 43
   legislative campaign against labor injunction, 67-70
   rise of, 12
   support of Wagner Act, 161-62
American Liberty League, National Lawyer's Committee of, 169-70
American Railway Union, 20, 137
American Steel Foundries case, 71-72, 81
American Sugar Refining Company, 48
American Tobacco decision, 48, 49
Antitrust statutes, unions under, 35-64, 207, 210
   Bedford Stone decision, 58-62, 70, 99, 207
   Danbury Hatters doctrine, 40-43, 46, 50, 51, 207
   Gompers decision, 43-44, 50
   Norris-La Guardia, antitrust prosecution under, 99-117
      additional applications of antitrust violations, 108-13
      Apex doctrine and nullification of *Coronado* decision, 104-8
      consequences of Supreme Court action, 113-15
      judicial reaction to, 101-4
      labor protection and, 99
   rule-of-reason doctrine, 48-58, 61, 207
      application to business, 48-50
      application to labor organizations, 50-52
      Coronado doctrine and, 53-58
   See also Clayton Act (1914); Sherman Antitrust Act (1890)
Antiunion conduct, employer. *See* Employer antiunion conduct
Apex doctrine, 104-8
Appeals after NLRB hearing, 192
Arbitration, voluntary, 98n13, 149
Area of industrial freedom, 79-82
Arizona labor injunction law, 68-69, 70
   Truax case and, 72-76
Arts, Great Depression reflected in, 67
Attorney General, U.S., 157
Automobile industry, threatened strike of 1934, 158

Bache-Denman Coal Company, 53-57
Back pay, reinstatement with, 192, 193
Back-to-work movements, strikebreaking by, 127
Bedford Cut Stone Company v. Journeymen Stone Cutters Association, 58-62, 70, 99, 207
Big business, dominance of, 36
Bituminous Coal Operators Association, 111

233

Blanket injunction, 23-24, 87
Blue Eagle (emblem), 160
Bond, posting of, 28, 85
Boycott, use of
   Danbury Hatters doctrine and, 41
   Gompers decision on, 43-44
   secondary, 42, 51, 52, 60-61, 100-101, 102
Brandeis, Louis Dembitz, 174
   double standard and, 48, 60-62
   Hitchman decision, minority opinion on, 30, 31, 207
   on Section 20 of Clayton Act, 101
   Senn decision and, 91-92
   Truax decision, dissenting opinion on, 74-76
Breads, Gerald, 124
Brotherhood of Railroad Clerks, 150
Bucks Stove and Range Company, 43
Budd Manufacturing Company, 156
Burden of proof in discrimination cases, 182-83
Bureau of Labor Statistics, 198, 200
Burns Detective Agency, 53, 122
Business
   big, dominance of, 36
   identification of Great Depression with, 66
   rule of reason applied to, 48-50
Butchers Union, AFL, 92-94
Butler, Pierce, 171, 174

California, labor injunction controls in, 68
Cardozo, Benjamin Nathan, 174
Carnegie Steel Corporation, 12
Carter Coal decision, 172-73
Certification of representatives, 195, 197
Character of union leaders, attacks against, 126
Charge, unfair labor practices, 190-92
   protection of workers filing, 184
Child labor, 2, 3, 142
Civil liberties, blanket injunctions and, 24
Clarke, John Hessin, 30
Classical school of economics, 5
Clayton Act (1914), 44-47, 50, 99, 207
   injunction sections of, 68, 69-70, 71
   picketing under, 81
   Section 6 of, 44-46, 52
   Section 20, 69, 71, 72, 96n3, 99, 100-101, 103-4
"Clear proof" standard of Norris-La Guardia, 111-13
Cleveland, Grover, 137
Codes, NIRA, 153-54
Cohen, Sam "Chowderhead," 128
Collective bargaining, 7
   company unions and, 129-30
   effective, majority-rule principle and, 188-89
   in good faith, 87-88, 134, 185, 187
   legal climate surrounding (1806-1932), 65-67, 205-8
   need for public protection of right to, 131-35
   Norris-La Guardia and promotion of, 77-78, 87-88
   philosophical justification for, 9
   social desirability of, 134-35
   See also Legislative support of collective bargaining; Wagner Act (National Labor Relations Act, 1935)
Collusion, 110, 111
Combinations, business, 36, 48-50

Common law, 6, 8
Commons, John R., 2
Commonwealth v. *Hunt*, 8-11, 118, 206, 210
   declaration of lawfulness of unions in, 9-10
   significance of, 10-11
   state of affairs before, 8-9
Company unions, 59, 150, 158
   amendment to Railway Labor Act and, 152, 153
   as antiunion conduct, 129-31
   characteristics of, 179-80
   Section 7(a) of NIRA and, 154, 155
   as unfair labor practice under Wagner Act, 179-80
Competition
   in early twentieth century, 35-36
   industrial, 2-3
   between organized and unorganized firms, 40, 51, 134
   public policy and encouragement of, 35
Complaint, 191
Compliance Division of National Recovery Administration, 157, 160
Congress, public policy and, 144. *See also specific legislation*
Congress of Industrial Organization (CIO), 4, 148, 200
Connell case, 113, 114
Consent elections, 194
Conspiracy, defined, 4
Conspiracy doctrine applied to unions, 3-8, 10, 11, 205-6
   case against unions, 5-6
   characteristics of conspiracy trials, 6-7, 12
   defense of unions, 7-8
   English law as precedent in, 5-8
   Norris-La Guardia and, "anti-conspiracy" clause of, 82
   shift to labor injunction from, 11-12
Constitution, U.S.
   Fifth Amendment to, 142, 144, 175-76
   Fourteenth Amendment to, 73, 97n7, 144
Contempt of court, innovations in Norris-La Guardia for, 88-89
Contract, yellow-dog. *See* Yellow-dog contract
Coolidge, Calvin, 35
Coppage decision, 142, 143-44
Coronado Coal Mine, 53-57
Coronado doctrine, 53-58
   nullification by *Apex* doctrine, 104-8
Corporation Auxiliary Company, 122
Corporations, growth of huge and powerful, 36
"Court packing" threat of Roosevelt, 138, 173
Courts
   equity, 17, 23, 75, 78, 79
   trial, 17
   See also Judiciary; Supreme Court, U.S.

Damages, deciding on injunctive relief by balancing, 86
Damage suits against unions, 56
Danbury Hatters doctrine, 40-43, 46, 50, 51, 207
Darlington doctrine, 182-83
Darwinism, economic, 67
Debs, Eugene V., 20
Debs case (*In re Debs*), 19-20, 22, 39, 137

INDEX

Deering Milliken, discriminatory plant shutdown at, 182-83
Demand to bargain, 184
Democracy, industrial, 211
  majority-rule principle and, 187-89
  Wagner Act and, 165, 195-96
Democratic party, labor endorsement of, 43, 44
Department of Justice, 160
Depression
  of 1837, 8
  Great Depression, 66-67, 147-48, 153, 208-9
  after Napoleonic Wars, 8
Detective agencies, private, 122-23, 133
Discharge of worker
  reasons for lawful, 183-84
  for union activities
    most common alleged reasons given for discharge, 181
    outlawing, 138, 139-41
    Supreme Court attitude toward, 143
    as unfair labor practice, 180-84
Discrimination
  early legislation against, 139-40
  as unfair labor practice, 180-84
Dismissal of NLRB cases, 190-91
Double standard, development under Sherman Act of, 48-58, 207
  Bedford Stone decision and completion of, 58-62
  Brandeis and, 48, 60-62
  Coronado doctrine and continued, 53-58
Douglas, William Orville, 109, 110, 111, 112, 114-15
Doyle, Charles, 124
Due process of law, 73, 75, 97n7, 142, 151, 175-76
Duplex Printing Press Company, 50-51
Duplex Printing Press v. *Deering*, 51, 52, 60, 70, 72, 99, 100, 101

Economics, classical school of, 5
Economic strikes, 132
Economy
  development of, in 1800s, 1-2
  of 1930s, 66-67
  Wagner Act for stability in, 165-66
  See also Great Depression
Education, depression of 1930s and cuts in, 66-67
Elections, representation, 193-96, 197
Employee representation plans. *See* Company unions
Employer antiunion conduct, 118-36, 210-11
  La Follette Committee investigation of, 119-20, 121, 122, 124, 127, 128, 133, 208, 210-11
  need for public control of, 131-35
  patterns of, 120-31, 133-34
    attack on union leadership, 121, 123-26
    company unions, 129-31
    industrial espionage, 120-23, 133, 176
    strikebreaking tactics, 126-29, 177
  problem of, 118-20
  Wagner Act outlawing, 167
  unfair labor practices under, 176-86
Employers' associations, 4
Employment during World War II, 196. *See also* Economy
Encouragement, era of legal, 208-11
England
  laws against labor unions in, 5-8

property concept in, for injunction purposes, 21, 33n9
Equal protection clause of Constitution, 76
Equity court, 17, 23, 75, 78, 79
  regulation of. *See* Norris-La Guardia Act (1932)
Erdman Act (1898), 139-44, 150
  Section 10 of, 140-44
  Supreme Court attitude toward, 141, 142-43
Espionage, industrial, 120-23, 133, 176
Evidence
  in injunction proceedings, quality of, 27-28
  preponderance of, 112
Executive Orders of February 1934, 157, 158

Factory system, 1-3
Factory workers, early, 3-4
Fainblatt case, 203n12
Farmer, Guy, 114
Favorito, Vincent, 123-24
Federation of labor unions, first, 8
Field examiners, 189, 190, 191
Fifth Amendment to Constitution, 142, 144, 175-76
Financial panic of 1893, 137
Fourteenth Amendment to Constitution, 73, 97n7, 144
Frankfurter, Felix, 25, 27, 103-4
Freedom, area of industrial, 79-82

General Order No. 8, 146
Goldberg, Arthur Joseph, 114
Gompers, Samuel, 43, 45, 46
Gompers decision, 43-44, 50
Good faith bargaining, 87-88, 134, 185, 187
Gould, Jay, 12
Government, Great Depression and change in attitudes toward, 208-9
Great America Service Trades Council, AFL-CIO, 83
Great Depression, 66-67
  change in climate of opinion after, 208-9
  progress of union movement and, 147-48
  promotion of economic recovery after, 153-58
Great Northern Railway, 48
Greene, Nathan, 25, 27

Hamilton, Alexander, 3, 9
Hearing(s)
  before issuance of temporary injunctions, 19, 85-86
  after issuance of temporary restraining order, 18, 26, 84-85
  NLRB, 191-92
  representation, 194
Highway Trailer Company decision, 179
Hiring, discrimination in, 183
Hitchman Coal decision, 28-32, 71, 83, 206-7
Holding companies, 49
Holmes, Oliver Wendell, 30, 41, 74-76, 144, 207
Homestead strike of 1892, 12
"Hooking," "hookers," 122
Hoover, Herbert, 77
Hosiery Workers Union, 155
Hughes, Charles Evans, 174-75
Hutcheson decision, 101, 102-4, 110, 210

Impasse in negotiations, 186
Income, progress in union movement and real, 148-49
Independent local labor organization, 130-31
Industrial Adjustment Act (not passed), 159
Industrial democracy, 211
  majority-rule principle and, 187-89
  Wagner Act and, 165, 195-96
Industrial espionage, 120-23, 133, 176
Industrial freedom, area of, 79-82
Industrial peace, causes of, 167-68
Informal settlement, 190-91
Injunction(s)
  abuses of, 22-28
  blanket, 23-24
  labor. *See* Labor injunction
  nature of, 16-17
  permanent, 19, 57, 85-87
  temporary, 19, 28, 85-87, 210
In re Debs (Debs case), 19-20, 22, 39, 137
International Association of Machinists, 50-51, 52, 102
International Brotherhood of Electrical Workers (AFL), 107
International Cut Stone & Quarryers Association, 59
Interstate commerce
  Erdman Act to promote, 139-40, 142
  meaning of, since *Jones & Laughlin* decision, 202*n*12
  In re Debs and, 39
  strikes in manufacturing as burden to, 175
  Wagner Act and regulation of, 166-68
Intimidation of union leaders, 123-26
Investigation
  for representation elections, 194-95
  of unfair labor practice charge, 190-92

Jackson, 9
Jefferson, Thomas, 9
Jewel Tea case, 108-9, 114
Johnson, Hugh Samuel, 157, 158
Joint Resolution No. 44, 159-61
Jones & Laughlin decision, 173-76
  state of affairs before, 170-71
Jones & Laughlin Steel Company, 173
Journeymen Stone Cutters Association, 59-60
Judges
  administrative, 191-92
  in conspiracy trials, 7
  in injunction cases, 17, 88-89, 206
  as legislators, 22-23
Judiciary
  conspiracy doctrine applied by, 3-8, 10, 11, 12, 205-6
  in era of legal suppression, 65-67, 205-8
  legislative support of collective bargaining and attitude of, 137-38, 141-44, 208
  Norris-La Guardia Act and
    court's power circumscribed by, 78-79, 209
    judicial construction of, 89-94
    judicial reaction to, 101-4
  power to make industrial relations law, 79
  See also Labor injunction; Supreme Court, U.S.
Juries, 7, 12, 17, 88

Kansas, labor injunction controls in, 68-69
  Coppage and *Adair* decisions striking down, 143-44

Knights of Labor, 11-12, 137

Labor class, creation of distinct, 2
Labor dispute
  concept under Norris-La Guardia, 82-83, 100-101, 102
  Lauf doctrine and interpretation of, 93
Labor injunction, 15-34, 206-7, 210
  abuses of, 22-28
    blanket injunction, 23-24, 87
    judges as legislators, 22-23
    quality of evidence in proceedings, 27-28
    status quo in labor disputes, 24-25
    time lags in proceedings, 25-27
  Clayton Act and, 47
  concept of "property" in cases of, 21-22, 33*n*9, 86-87, 208
  constitutionality of, confirmation of, 19-21
  controversy over use of, 15-16
  Debs case and, 19-20
  legal aspects of, 137-38
  to restrain activities of NLRB, 168-70
  shift from conspiracy doctrine to, 11-12
  Supreme Court and, 28-32, 70-71, 141
  violations of, 88-89
  yellow-dog contract and, 28-32, 70-71
Labor Injunction, The (Frankfurter & Greene), 33*n*12
Labor injunction control legislation, 65-98
  changing economic and political scene and, 65-67
  early, 70-74
    Court attitudes and, 70-71
    as unconstitutional, 72-74
  early regulation, 67-70
  picketing, limits on, 71-72, 81
  Truax decision and, 72-76, 91
  See also Norris-La Guardia Act (1932)
Labor movement. *See* Union movement
Labor unions. *See* Union(s)
La Follette, Robert, 119
La Follette Committee, 119-20, 121, 122, 124, 127, 128, 133, 208, 210-11
Landrum-Griffin Act (1959), 20
Lauf doctrine, 92-94
Leadership, employer antiunion conduct against union, 121, 123-26
Leather Workers case, 58
Legal action, freedom of union to support persons in, 81
Legal climate
  era of encouragement, 208-11
  era of suppression, 65-67, 205-8
Legislation. *See* Labor injunction control legislation; Legislative support of collective bargaining; *specific legislation*
Legislative support of collective bargaining, 137-64, 207-8
  attitude of judiciary toward, 137-38, 141-44, 208
  beginnings of, 137-38
  early laws, 138-41
  Joint Resolution No. 44, 159-61
  National Industrial Recovery Act (NIRA), 153-58, 160, 161
    National Labor Board, 155-58
    Section 7(a), 154-55, 160

INDEX

Legislative support of collective bargaining *(cont.)*
   National War Labor Board, 145-49
   railroad legislation, 149-53, 167-68, 171
   World War I events and, 144-47
   See also Wagner Act (National Labor Relations Act, 1935)
Legislators, judges as, 22-23
Liberty, emphasis in 1800s on, 9
Literature, Great Depression reflected in, 67
"Little Steel" strike of 1937, 123-24
Loewe & Company, 40-42
Loewe v. Lawlor. See Danbury Hatters doctrine

McNatt, E.B., 105
McReynolds, James Clark, 171, 174
Majority rule, principle of, 157, 187-89
Majority status of labor organization, unfair labor practices resulting in destruction of, 185
Management, company unions and, 129-31
Manayunk, Pennsylvania, strike of 1828 in, 2
Manufacturing
   application of Wagner Act to, 172-75
   rapid rise of, after 1800, 1-2
   strikes in, 174-75
Marketing hours, limitations placed on, 108-9
Massachusetts, labor injunction controls in, 68
Mass-production workers, organization of, 148
Mediation, 149
Meetings, freedom of unions to hold peaceful, 81-82
Membership, union
   decline in 1920s of, 147-49
   effect of government policy on, 146-47, 148
   Great Depression and, 147-48
   industrial espionage to obtain lists of, 120-21
   NIRA and growth of, 154
   Wagner Act and, 200
   during World War II, 196
Memorial Day strike (1937, Chicago), 133
Milk Wagon Drivers Union decision, 101-2
Minimum wages, 142, 151, 153-54
Minority groups, majority-rule principle and, 188
Mohawk Valley Formula, 129, 177
Molders & Foundry Workers Union of North America, 29, 43
Monopolies, 39, 48-49, 107-8
Montana, labor injunction controls in, 68
Multiemployer bargaining, 114-15
Munitions, buildup in plant of, 127, 133
Murphy, Betty Southhard, 195

Napoleonic Wars, industrial depression after, 8
National Association of Manufacturers, 43, 129
National Association of Window Glass Manufacturers, 51-52
National Association of Window Glass Workers, 52
National Coal Wage Agreement of 1950, 109-13
National Corporation Service, 122
National Guard, 128
National Industrial Recovery Act (NIRA), 153-58, 160, 161
   National Labor Board, 155-58
      collapse of, 156-58
      "Reading Formula" applied by, 155-56
   Section 7(a), 154-55, 160

National Labor Relations Act. *See* Wagner Act (National Labor Relations Act, 1935)
National Labor Relations Board (NLRB), 16, 21, 83, 113, 120, 139, 170, 211
   first, 159-61
   formal proceedings, 191-92
   injunctions to restrain activities of, 168-70
   number of elections held by, 195-96
   representation procedure before, 193-95
   scope of, 202n12
   settlements of cases, 190-91
   unfair labor practice procedure, 189
   unfair labor practices established by, 176-86
   union responsibilities developed by, 186-87
   use of, during World War II, 196-98
National Lawyer's Committee of American Liberty League, 169-70
National Mediation Board, 152
National Planning Association, 167
National Recovery Administration, Compliance Division of, 157, 160
National Tea Company, 108
National Trades' Union, 8
National War Labor Board (NWLB), 145-49
New Deal, 147, 148, 153, 158, 165-66, 173, 209
New Jersey Supreme Court, 11
Norris-La Guardia Act (1932), 16, 22, 76-95, 131, 139, 152, 206, 209-10, 212-17
   "anti-conspiracy" clause of, 82
   antitrust prosecution under, 99-117
      additional applications of antitrust violations, 108-13
      Apex doctrine and nullification of *Coronado* decision, 104-8
      consequences of Supreme Court action, 113-15
      judicial reaction to, 101-4
      labor protection, 99
   area of industrial freedom under, 79-82
   "clear proof" standard, 111-13
   impact of, 94-95
   judicial construction of, 89-94
      Lauf doctrine and wide application of, 92-94
      Tile-laying industry case (*Senn* decision), 90-92
   labor dispute concept under, 82-83, 100-101, 102
   labor injunctions, procedural limitations on, 84-89
   limitations of, 118
   purpose of, 78-79, 209
   underlying theory of, 77-78
   yellow-dog contract under, 83-84
Northern Pacific Railway, 48
Northern Securities Company decision, 48

Officials, employer antiunion conduct against union, 121, 123-26
Oklahoma, labor injunction control in, 68
Organizational strikes, 40-41, 51, 140, 145, 159, 173
   collapse of National Labor Board and, 156, 158
   effect of, 175
   need for public control of antiunion conduct and, 131-33
   tactics for breaking, 126-29
   violence and, 133-34

Organizational strikes *(cont.)*
  Wagner Act and, 166-67, 170, 198-200
  during World War II vs. World War I, 198-99
Otis Steel Company, 124

Panic of 1893, financial, 137
Penalties, Sherman Act, 37-38
Pennington case, 109-11, 113-14
Perlman, Selig, 8
Permanent injunction, 19, 57, 85-87
Philadelphia conspiracy case (1806), 7
Philosophical justification for collective bargaining, 9
Picketing
  Lauf doctrine and, 92-94
  one "missionary" per entrance limitation, 71-72, 81
  right to picket, 80-81
  secondary boycott, 100-101
  Wisconsin anti-injunction law and protection of, 90-92
Pinkerton Detective Agency, 12, 122-23
Pitney, Mahlon, 30
Plant shutdown, discrimination using, 182-83
Police officers, protection of employer property by local, 86-87
Political action, 42-43, 44
Pools, 35
"Preponderance of the evidence" rule, 112
Price agreements, 35
Prices, NIRA and regulation of, 153-54
Private detective agencies, 122-23, 133
Private plant police, strikebreaking tactics of, 127
Production, NIRA and regulation of, 153-54
Professional strikebreakers, use of, 127, 128, 133
Prohibition era, 16
Property
  concept of, in labor injunction cases, 21-22, 33n9, 86-87, 208
  Truax case and definition of, 73
Property rights, 16
Public opinion, effect of labor injunction on, 24-25
Public policy
  Congress and, 144
  Wagner Act and, 162, 168-70
Pullman Car Company, 20, 139-40
Pullman strike of 1894, 39, 137, 139-40

Railroad Administration, 146
Railroad industry, 48
  strikes in, 20, 38-39, 137, 139-40
  World War I and federal operation of, 146
Railroad legislation, 149-53, 167-68
  Erdman Act (1898), 139-44, 150
  Railway Labor Act (1926), 149-51, 168, 171
    amendment of 1934 to, 151-53
Ramsey v. *Mineworkers*, 111
Rand, James H., Jr., 129
Rank and file, company union representation of, 130
Reading Formula, 155-56, 157, 158
Real income, progress in union movement and, 148-49
Recognition strike. *See* Organizational strikes

Regulation of labor injunction, early, 67-70. *See also* Labor injunction control legislation
Reinstatement of strikers, 187
  with back pay, 192, 193
Remedy at law, 86
Representation elections, 193-96, 197
Representatives for collective bargaining, workers', 152
  certification of, 195, 197
  employer's legal obligation to bargain with, 184-86
Responsibilities, union, 186-87
Restraint of trade, "reasonable" vs. "unreasonable," 48-50
Richberg, Donald R., 157
Rights
  property, 16
  workers', 80-81, 118-19, 134
    See also Collective bargaining; Legislative support of collective bargaining
Roberts, Owen Josephus, 103, 174
Roosevelt, F.D., 153, 155, 157, 158, 159, 161, 211
  "court packing" threat of, 138, 173
Rough shadowing, 125-26
Rule-of-reason doctrine, 48-58, 61, 207
  application to business, 48-50
  application to labor organizations, 50-52
  Coronado doctrine and, 53-58

Schecter case, 161
Secondary boycott, 42, 51, 52, 60-61, 100-101, 102
Senn decision, 90-92
Settlement, informal, 190-91
Shadowing, rough, 125-26
Shaw, Lemuel, 9-10, 11
Sherman Antitrust Act (1890), 47, 99
  application to unions, 36-39, 65-66, 207
  double standard constructed under, 48-58, 207
  earliest convictions under, 38-39
  enforcement provision under, 103
  penalties, 37-38
  In re Debs, 19-20, 22, 39, 137
  strikes as subject to jurisdiction of, 57-58, 61
  See also Antitrust statutes, unions under
Shoemaker employers' associations, 4
Shoemakers' unions, 4-5, 6
Sit-down strike, 105
Small employers, industry elimination of, 109-13
Smith, Adam, 171
Smith & Wesson Arms Company, 146
Social responsibility of unions, 186-87
Soft Coal Wage Agreement (1950), 1958 Protective Age Clause Amendment to, 112
Specialization of function, 2
Spies, industrial, 120-23, 133, 176
Standard of proof requirement of Norris-La Guardia, 111-13
Standard Oil decision, 48, 49
State control of labor injunction, 68-69, 70
Status quo in labor disputes, injunctions to maintain, 24-25
Stone, Harlan Fiske, 174
Strike(s)
  Apex doctrine and legality of, 106
  Coronado doctrine and legality of, 56-57

Index

Strike(s) *(cont.)*
  early, 2, 4
  economic, 132
  freedom of unions to encourage all workers to, 81
  Homestead (1892), 12
  judges interpretation of lawfulness of, 23
  labor injunction effect on, 24-25
  in late 1800s, 12
  "Little Steel," of 1937, 123-24
  Manayunk, Pennsylvania (1828), 2
  in manufacturing facilities, 174-75
  Memorial Day (1937, Chicago), 133
  organizational, 40-41, 51, 140, 145, 159, 173
    collapse of National Labor Board and, 156, 158
    effect of, 175
    need for public control of antiunion conduct and, 131-33
    tactics for breaking, 126-29
    violence and, 133-34
    Wagner Act and, 166-67, 170, 198-200
    during World War II vs. World War I, 198-99
  railroad, 20, 38-39
    Pullman (1894), 39, 137, 139-40
  "Reading Formula" procedure of settling, 155-56, 157, 158
  reinstatement of strikers, 187, 192, 193
  right to strike, 80
  rough shadowing during preparation for, 125-26
  sit-down, 105
  as subject to Sherman Act jurisdiction, 57-58, 61
  during summer of 1933, 155
  sympathetic, 38
  violence during, 53-54, 133-34
  World War I and avoidance of, 145
Strikebreaking tactics, 126-29, 177
Strike-relief funds, 80
Sundry Civil Appropriation Bill, 45
Suppression, era of legal, 65-67, 205-8
Supreme Court, U.S., 40, 66, 202n12
  Allen-Bradley case, impact of, 106-8, 113
  American Steel Foundries case, 71-72, 81
  blanket injunctions upheld by, 23
  composition of, in 1930s, 171
  Connell case, 113, 114
  consequences of recent antitrust rulings, 113-15
  "court packing" threat of Roosevelt, 138, 173
  Danbury Hatters case, 40-43, 46, 50, 51, 207
  Debs case, 19-20, 22, 39, 137
  Gompers decision, 43-44, 50
  Hitchman Coal decision, 28-32, 71, 83, 206-7
  Hutcheson decision, 101, 102-4, 110, 210
  Jewel Tea case, 108-9, 114
  labor injunction and, 28-32, 70-71, 141
  Leather Workers case, 58
  legislative support of collective bargaining and attitude of, 141-44, 208
  need for validation of Wagner Act by, 170-71
  NIRA declared unconstitutional by, 161
  Norris-La Guardia and
    construction of, 89-94
    reaction to, 101-4
  Pennington case, 109-11, 113-14
  rule-of-reason doctrine applied by, 48-58, 61, 207
  Truax case, 72-76, 91
  on yellow-dog contract, 28-32, 70-71, 142-43, 206-7

Surveillance of union leaders, 125-26
Sutherland, George, 171, 174
Sympathetic strike, 38

Taft, William Howard, 71-72, 73, 119
Taft-Hartley Act (1947), 16, 20, 42, 88, 191, 192, 193, 210
Temporary injunction, 19, 28, 85-87, 210
Temporary restraining order, 18, 24, 28, 209-10
  Clayton Act on, 69-70
  frequent use of, 25-26
  under Norris-La Guardia, 84-85
Tennessee Valley Authority (TVA), 110
Tenure, discrimination in, 183
Testimony under Wagner Act, protection of workers giving, 184
Texas & New Orleans Railroad, 150
Texas & New Orleans Railroad decision, 151, 152, 171, 174, 176
Textile industry, wages in early, 2
Textile Workers Union, 182
Tile Layers Union, 90-92
Time lags in injunction proceedings, 25-27
Times Publishing case, 187
Trade associations, 35, 50
Trial court, 17
Truax v. *Corrigan*, 72-76, 91
Trusts, 35, 36, 39

Unemployment during World War II, 196. *See also* Economy; Great Depression
Unfair labor practices, 176-86
  charge, 184, 190-92
  procedure, 189
  World War II cases of, 197
  See also Employer antiunion conduct
Union(s)
  antiunion conduct against. *See* Employer antiunion conduct
  Commonwealth v. *Hunt* and, 8-11, 118, 206, 210
    declaration of lawfulness of unions in, 9-10
    significance of, 10-11
    state of affairs before, 8-9
  company, 59, 129-31, 150, 152-55, 158, 179-80
  conspiracy doctrine applied to, 3-8, 10, 11, 205-6
    case against unions, 5-6
    characteristics of conspiracy trials, 6-7, 12
    defense of unions, 7-8
    English law as precedent in, 5-8
    Norris-La Guardia and, "anti-conspiracy" clause of, 82
    shift to labor injunction from, 11-12
  damage suits against, 56
  first federation of, 8
  injunction applied to. *See* Labor injunction
  leadership of, employer antiunion conduct against, 121, 123-26
  NLRB-developed responsibilities for, 186-87
  rule of reason applied to, 50-52
  See also Membership, union
Union movement
  decline in 1920s of, 147-49
  in era of legal encouragement, 208-11
  in era of legal suppression, 65-67, 205-8

Union movement *(cont.)*
  growth of
    government policy during World War I and, 146-47
    NIRA and, 154
    Wagner Act and, 200
  political action and, 42-43, 44
  socioeconomic content of early, 1-3
  union success in NLRB elections, decline in, 195-96
Union-recognition strikes. *See* Organizational strikes
"Union town," 86
United Automobile Workers, 121, 122
United Brotherhood of Carpenters and Joiners of America, 102
United Hatters of North America, 40-42
United Leather Workers Union, 57-58
United Mine Workers (UMW), 30-31, 53-57, 109-13, 114
  Welfare and Retirement Fund, 109, 110
United Shoe Machinery Company, 49-50
United States Steel Corporation, 49
United States v. *United Shoe Machinery Co.*, 207
United States v. *United States Steel Corporation*, 207

Van Devanter, Willis, 171, 174
Violence in labor disputes
  Apex doctrine and, 104-6
  impact of Norris-La Guardia on, 94
  incitement of
    industrial spy's role in, 121-22
    by professional strikebreakers, 128
    as unfair labor practice, 177
  organized labor's economic weapons as distinct from, 94-95
  strikes and, 53-54, 133-34
  against union leaders, 123-26
Voluntary arbitration, 98n13, 149

Wages
  case against union control of, 5, 6
  in early textile industry, 2
  minimum, 142, 151, 153-54
Wage settlements, standardized, 109-13, 114
Wagner, Robert Ferdinand, 161, 165
Wagner Act (National Labor Relations Act, 1935), 113, 115, 122, 145, 165-204, 208, 209, 210-11, 218-28
  application to manufacturing, 172-75
  due process and constitutionality of, 175-76
  industrial democracy and, 165, 195-96
  Jones & Laughlin decision and, 173-76
  state of affairs before, 170-71
  organizational strikes and, 166-67, 170, 198-200
  passage of, 161-62
  power to regulate interstate commerce, 166-68
  precursors of, 137-64
    attitude of judiciary, 137-38, 141-44, 208
    early laws, 138-41

Joint Resolution No. 44, 159-61
National Industrial Recovery Act, 153-58, 160, 161
railroad legislation, 149-53, 167-68, 171
World War I events, 144-47
as public policy of U.S., 162, 168-70
record of, 192-93
representation procedure, 193-95
results of, 198-200
scope of, 172-73
socioeconomic rationale of, 165-66
substantive provisions of, 176-89
  Board-developed union responsibilities, 186-87
  majority rule, principle of, 187-89
  unfair labor practices under, 176-86
underlying philosophy of, 168
unfair labor practice charge, 184, 190-92
unfair labor practice procedure, 189
during World War II, 196-99
Wagner Labor Disputes Act (not passed), 159
Walsh-Healey Act, 110
Weirton Steel Company, 156, 158
West Coast Hotel case, 151
Western Union Telegraph Company, 145
White, Byron R., 110
Wilson, Woodrow, 44, 45-46, 145-46
Wisconsin anti-injunction law, Supreme Court's construction of, 89-92
Withdrawal of NLRB cases, 190-91
Witte, E.E., 11, 20, 25
Women, working, 2, 3, 142
Work conditions
  discrimination using, 181
  in early factories, 2-3
Workers
  effect of labor injunction on, 25
  rights, 80-81, 118-19, 134. *See also* Collective bargaining; Legislative support of collective bargaining
  yellow-dog contract and, 29-30
World War I
  legislative support of collective bargaining and, 144-47
  organizational strikes during, 198-99
World War II
  attacks against union leadership character during, 126
  unfair labor practices during, 178
  union membership during, 196
  Wagner Act during, 196-99
Wright Line doctrine, 182
Written trade agreement, 186

Yellow-dog contract, 28-32, 53, 65, 141, 152, 206-7, 209
  early state laws against, 138-41
  labor injunction and, 28-32, 70-71
  Norris-La Guardia Act and passing of, 83-84
  Supreme Court on, 70-71, 142-43